# THE INDIGO BOOK

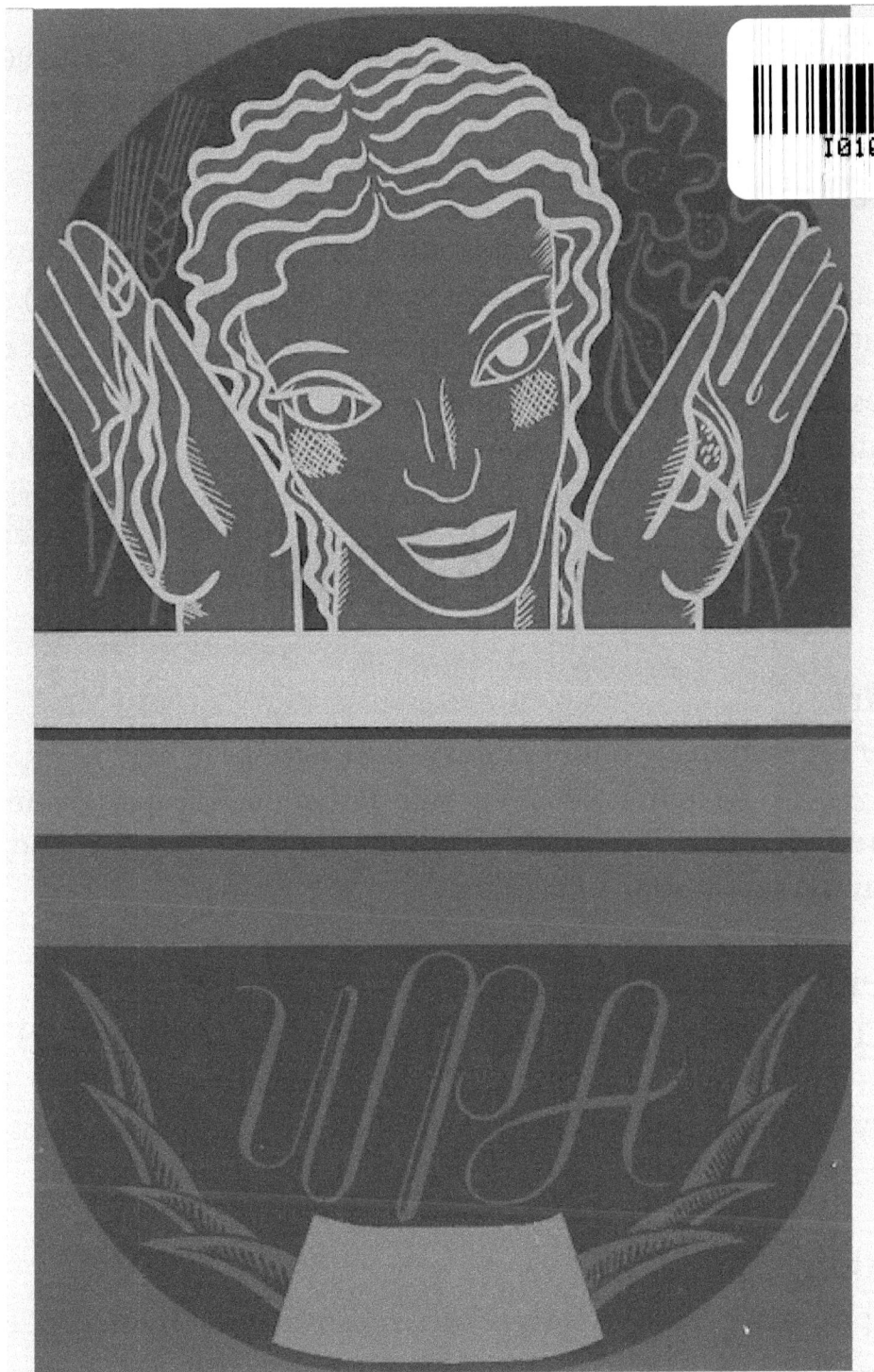

I0104764

An Open and Compatible Implementation of
A Uniform System of Citation

# Manifest

ISBN 978-1-892628-02-2

## Status

This document is in beta release and was last modified on May 2, 2016. Errors and omissions may be sent to carl@media.org or @carlmalamud.

## Publisher and License

## Cover Art

The cover art is courtesy of the Library of Congress Digital File LC-DIG-ppmsca-38347. The item is a WPA poster design on blue background created as part of the Federal Art Project between 1936 and 1941. There are no known restrictions on publication of this item.

## Statement of Nonaffiliation

**NOT AUTHORIZED BY NOR IN ANY WAY AFFILIATED WITH:** The Columbia Law Review Association, Inc., The Harvard Law Review Association, the University of Pennsylvania Law Review, The Yale Law Journal Company, Inc., or The Bluebook® A Uniform System of Citation®.

## Attribution

Cite as: Sprigman et al., *The Indigo Book: A Manual of Legal Citation*, Public Resource (2016).

## Formats

This document is available in HTML and PDF formats.

# Table of Contents

Manifest

    Status

    Publisher and License

    Cover Art

    Statement of Nonaffiliation

    Attribution

Foreword

Introduction

A. BACKGROUND RULES

    R1. Two Types of Legal Documents

    R2. Typeface Standards

    R3. In-Text Citations

    R4. Signals

    R5. Capitalization Rules

    R6. Signals for Supporting Authority

    R7. Signals for Comparison

    R8. Signals for Contradictory Authority

    R9. Signals for Background Material

    R10. Order of Authorities Within Each Signal / Strength of Authority

B. CASES

    R11. Full citation

    R12. Court & Year

    R13. Weight of Authority and Explanatory Parenthetical

    R14. History of the Case

    R15. Short Form Citation for Cases

C. STATUTES, RULES, REGULATIONS, AND OTHER LEGISLATIVE & ADMINISTRATIVE MATERIALS

    R16. Federal Statutes

    R17. State Statutes

    R18. Rules of Procedure and Evidence, Restatements, and Uniform Acts

R19. Administrative Rules and Regulations

R20. Federal Taxation Materials

R21. Legislative Materials

R22. Short Form Citation of Legislative and Administrative Materials

R23. Sources and Authorities: Constitutions

D. COURT & LITIGATION DOCUMENTS

R24. Citing Court or Litigation Documents from Your Case

R25. Citing Court or Litigation Documents from Another Case

R26. Short Form Citation for Court Documents

R27. Capitalization Within the Text of Court Documents and Legal Memoranda

E. BOOKS & NON-PERIODICALS

R28. Full Citation for Books & Non-Periodicals

R29. Short Form Citation for Books & Non-Periodicals

F. JOURNALS, MAGAZINES, & NEWSPAPER ARTICLES

R30. Full Citation for Journals, Magazines & Newspaper Articles

R31. Short Form Citation for Journals, Magazines & Newspaper Articles

G. INTERNET SOURCES

R32. General Principles for Internet Sources

R33. Basic Formula for Internet Sources

R34. Short Form Citations for Internet Sources

H. EXPLANATORY PARENTHETICALS

R35. General Principles for Explanatory Parentheticals

R36. Order of parentheticals

I. QUOTATIONS

R37. General Principles for Quotations

R38. Alterations of Quotations

R39. Omissions in Quotations

R40. Special Rules for Block Quotations

J. TABLES

T1. Federal Judicial and Legislative Materials

T2. Federal Administrative and Legislative Materials

T3. U.S. States and Other Jurisdictions

T4. Required Abbreviations for Services

    T4.1. Service Publisher Names

    T4.2. Service Abbreviations

T5. Required Abbreviations for Legislative Documents

T6. Required Abbreviations for Treaty Sources

T7. Required Abbreviations for Arbitral Reporters

T8. Required Abbreviations for Intergovernmental Organizations

    T8.1. United Nations and League of Nations

    T8.2. Europe

    T8.3. Inter-American and International Tribunal

    T8.4. Other Intergovernmental Organizations

T9. Required Abbreviations for Court Names

T10. Required Abbreviations for Titles of Judges and Officials

T11. Required Abbreviations for Case Names In Citations

T12. Required Abbreviations for Geographical Terms

    T12.1 U.S. States, Cities and Territories

    T12.2 Australian States and Canadian Provinces and Territories

    T12.3 Countries and Regions

T13. Required Abbreviations for Document Subdivisions

T14. Required Abbreviations for Explanatory Phrases

T15. Required Abbreviations for Institutions

T16. Required Abbreviations for Publishing Terms

T17. Required Abbreviations for Month Names

T18. Required Abbreviations for Common Words Used In Periodical Names

T19. Table of Citation Guides

T20. Tables of Correspondence

K. CODICIL

L. ACKNOWLEDGMENTS

# Foreword

In 2011, Frank Bennett, a law professor at Nagoya University in Japan, wrote to me about open source software he was developing that he now maintains under the name of Juris-M. Professor Bennett's work is an extended variant of an amazingly useful tool called Zotero that is created by developers around the world who want to support scholars in their efforts to "organize, cite, and share research sources." Frank added features to Zotero that support legal writing.

Professor Bennett was two years into work on his project when he contacted the Harvard Law Review Association concerning the use, in electronic form, of common abbreviations for U.S. sources as specified in *The Bluebook*. He was repeatedly rebuffed with stern "keep off the grass" warnings. I examined those abbreviations, and they are clearly facts that could only be expressed in one way. Not only are these abbreviations devoid of creativity, they are required by many legal jurisdictions in the United States before one can plead a case of law before judges. So, I posted those abbreviations on my web site, and promptly received my own "keep off the grass" missive from an outside law firm hired by the Harvard Law Review.

It is important to understand, when we are talking about *The Bluebook, A Uniform System of Citation*, that we are talking about two different things. There is a product, a spiral-bound booklet that sells for $38.50, which is accompanied by a rudimentary web site available to purchasers of the product.

Underlying that product, however, is something much more basic and fundamental, a uniform system of citation. Unpaid volunteers from a dozen law schools, under the stewardship of four nonprofit student-run law reviews, have labored mightily to reach a consensus standard for the citation of legal materials. This open consensus standard was developed, with no compensation to the authors, for the greater benefit of the legal system of the United States. By clearly and precisely referring to primary legal materials, we are able to communicate our legal reasoning to others, including pleading a case in the courts, advocating changes in legal policy in our legislatures or law reviews, or simply communicating the law to our fellow citizens so that we may be better informed.

We do not begrudge the Harvard Law Review Association one penny of the revenue from the sale of their spiral-bound book dressed in blue. However, we must not confuse the book with the system. There can be no proprietary claim over knowledge and facts, and there is no intellectual property right in the system and method of our legal machinery. The infrastructure of our legal system is a public utility, and belongs to all of us.

As Harvard professor Lawrence Lessig has famously stated, "code is law." The system of citation is code, an algorithm consisting of rules and a set of enumerations of text strings and their proper abbreviations. This is code about law.

In thinking of *The Bluebook*, I have been reminded of Big Blue, the IBM corporation. IBM made a fortune selling Genuine IBM personal computers, but this did not prevent others from making clones that were able to exercise the instructions in the underlying chipset. When technology changed the nature of the computer industry, IBM did not spend its days trying to defend an outdated mode of operation and instead moved up the food chain. The company has grown and prospered because of the computing revolution and the Internet instead of trying to preserve an outdated position of economic power that could not last.

Likewise, I wish the Harvard Law Review Association and their three companion law reviews the best in continuing to sell their Genuine Blue spiral-bound book and any associated on-line services. However, that cannot mean prohibiting an open source developer from using common abbreviations, and it certainly does not imply any ownership or control over how, in our democracy, we communicate the law with our fellow citizens. I hope you will enjoy *The Indigo Book: A Manual of Legal Citation* and that you will join me in extending my congratulations to Professor Sprigman and his students on the excellent job they have performed in re-coding those rules.

Carl Malamud
Public.Resource.Org

# Introduction

Welcome to *The Indigo Book*—a free, Creative Commons-dedicated implementation of *The Bluebook*'s Uniform System of Citation. *The Indigo Book* was compiled by a team of students at the New York University School of Law, working under the direction of Professor Christopher Jon Sprigman.

*The Indigo Book* isn't the same as *The Bluebook*, but it does implement the same Uniform System of Citation that *The Bluebook* does. The scope of *The Indigo Book*'s coverage is roughly equivalent to *The Bluebook*'s "Bluepages"—that is, *The Indigo Book* covers legal citation for U.S. legal materials, as well as books, periodicals, and Internet and other electronic resources. In addition, *The Indigo Book* offers citation guidance that is deeper than *The Bluebook*'s Bluepages—for example, *The Indigo Book* has citation guidance for bills, and for legislative history, that the Bluepages lack. For the materials that it covers, anyone using *The Indigo Book* will produce briefs, memoranda, law review articles, and other legal documents with citations that are compatible with the Uniform System of Citation.

Note that *The Indigo Book*'s scope does not extend to (now virtually unused) loose-leaf reporters, nor to foreign legal materials or the publications of international organizations like the United Nations. Most American lawyers cite these materials only rarely, and providing citation rules for the enormous number of international jurisdictions is part of what makes *The Bluebook* as unwieldy as it has become.

*The Indigo Book* offers a couple of important advantages to users, compared with *The Bluebook*. Unlike *The Bluebook*, *The Indigo Book* is free. Free in two different ways that are equally important. First, *The Indigo Book* is given to you free of charge. Considering that the Uniform System of Citation has become a basic piece of infrastructure for the American system of justice, it is vital that pro se litigants, prisoners, and others seeking justice but who lack resources are given effective access to the system lawyers use to cite to the law. That interest in access and basic fairness is part of what motivated *The Indigo Book*'s creation.

Second, and perhaps even more importantly, *The Indigo Book* is free of the restrictions of copyright. You are free to copy and distribute this work, and—most importantly—to improve on it. This is important, because we want people with a stake in our legal citation system to help make that system simpler and better. To achieve these goals, we are releasing *The Indigo Book* under a Creative Commons

"CC0" public domain dedication that allows you to use it, copy it, distribute it, and—we hope—improve it.

So, what sorts of improvement do we hope for? This original edition of *The Indigo Book* is compatible with the current, 20th edition of *The Bluebook*. We will admit, however, that our decision to make *The Indigo Book* compatible with *The Bluebook*'s Uniform System of Citation was mostly self-interested and strategic—we want people to adopt *The Indigo Book*, and the best way to achieve that goal, we reasoned, was to give people a citation guide that they could use to produce documents that look as if they used *The Bluebook*.

We think this is the right path, at least initially, but please understand that our decision to make *The Indigo Book* Bluebook-compatible doesn't stop *you* from doing otherwise. There are ways to improve *The Indigo Book* that involve breaking free of *The Bluebook*. Indeed, in some ways the recent editions of *The Bluebook* have adopted an unhelpfully over-prescriptive approach to citation that has resulted in needless complexity. It wasn't always that way. Back in 1959, the 10th edition of *The Bluebook* declared that "[t]he primary purpose of a citation is to facilitate finding and identifying the authority cited. The rules set forth in this booklet should not be considered invariable. Whenever clarity will be served, the citation form should be altered without hesitation; whenever a citation would not amplify the identification of the authority referred to, no citation should be given."

That sounds right to us. Can we get back to a more sensible, flexible system of legal citation? *The Indigo Book* takes the first step by restating the Uniform System of Citation for U.S. legal materials, and for books, periodicals, and Internet and other electronic resources. The next step is up to you. Take *The Indigo Book*, use it, enjoy it, improve it—maybe you international lawyers out there will add coverage of foreign and international law? Then, consistent with the spirit of our project—give your improvements to the world.

Professor Christopher Jon Sprigman
New York University School of Law

# A. BACKGROUND RULES

## R1. Two Types of Legal Documents

There are two basic varieties of legal documents. The Uniform System of Citation imposes somewhat different citation rules for each.

R1.1.  Standard Legal Documents (SLDs). These are the documents lawyers file in courts, agencies, or other places where practicing lawyers do what they do (e.g., briefs and motions). They also include the documents lawyers write to one another or to the public (e.g., legal letters and legal memoranda). We will refer to these as standard legal documents.

R1.2.  Academic Legal Documents (ALDs). These are articles for publication in law reviews. We will refer to them as "law review articles."

---

INDIGO INKLING

For reasons that make very little sense, the Uniform System of Citation treats law review articles and standard legal documents differently. If we were designing the system from scratch, we'd scrap this distinction. But for the moment, we're stuck with it. In *The Indigo Book*, we'll state the rules for standard legal documents. When we need to refer to law review articles specifically, we'll do that.

---

## R2. Typeface Standards

R2.1.  Only the following items should be italicized:

- Case names—both full and short case names, and procedural phrases (e.g., *In re* and *ex parte*) preceding the case names (but note the special guidance for law review articles in Rule 11.2.3);

- Book titles

- Article titles

- Legislative materials' titles

- Introductory signals (e.g., *see*, *cf.* and *accord*)

- Explanatory phrases that introduce subsequent case history (e.g., *aff'd* or *cert. denied*)

- Cross references, (e.g., *infra*, *supra* and *id.*)

- Words and phrases that introduce related authority (e.g., *reprinted in* and *available in*)

R2.2.   The following words should be *italicized* when used in the text of standard legal documents:

- Publication titles (e.g., *The Onion*)

- Words that are italicized in the original quotation; and

- All words that would be italicized in the text (e.g., foreign words that are not commonly used in English language documents).

---

INDIGO INKLING

The typewriter was invented around the 1860s. The first edition of *The Bluebook* is from 1926. Typewriters of that era did not support italics or boldface. If you wanted to emphasize text, your sole option was to underline. Throughout *The Indigo Book*, you'll see us italicizing text rather than underlining, because that's how we do it in the 21st Century. *The Bluebook* 20th Ed. still gives you the option to do either, but you know where we stand.

---

## R3. In-Text Citations

R3.1.   For standard legal documents, in-text citations are rendered either as (i) a complete sentence that supports a claim in the immediately preceding sentence of text, or, (ii) when the citation relates to a particular part of a sentence, as a clause within the sentence, immediately following the claim it supports.

- Only use footnotes for standard legal documents when allowed by a court's local rules.

- In contrast to standard legal documents, law review articles rely on footnotes for citations.

R3.2.   Citations Following Sentences

- Most citations in standard legal documents follow complete text sentences. It is common to have several citations following a sentence, with each citation separated by a semicolon (known as a "string citation").

- It is also common to employ more than one introductory signal, with citations introduced by different signals arranged as separate sentences. (For the order in which introductory signals are arranged, see Rule 4.2, below.) Use this citation method to cite to sources and authorities that relate to the sentence as a whole.

- **Example:** Even if the meaning of the statute were not plain, the FCC's construction of the 1996 Act is reasonable and therefore entitled to deference. *See Chevron U.S.A., Inc. v. Nat. Res. Def. Council, Inc.*, 467 U.S. 837 (1984); *see also Nat'l Cable & Telecomms. Ass'n. v. Brand X Internet Svcs.*, 545 U.S. 967, 1000 (2005) (holding that *Chevron* mandates that courts defer to the FCC's reasonable interpretation of its authority under the statutes that the agency administers, even where a current FCC interpretation is inconsistent with past practice); *Home Care Ass'n. of Am. v. Weil*, 799 F.3d 1084 (D.C. Cir. 2015) (finding the Department of Labor's reasonable interpretation of a provision of the Fair Labor Standards Act was entitled to deference under *Chevron*, even where it contravened previous reasonable interpretation of same provision).

R3.3.   Citations Within Sentences

- Some citations in standard legal documents are placed within sentences. Use within-sentence citations to cite sources and authorities that relate to *only a section* of the sentence. Separate within-sentence citations from the text with commas. The citation clauses directly follow the claim which they support. Do not model them after normal sentences unless:

  - the clause opens with a source that would be capitalized anyway—this is the only case where the clause should begin with a capital letter; or

  - it is the sentence's final clause—this is the only case where the clause should end with a period.

- **Example:** Knowingly throwing undersized groupers overboard to avoid federal agents investigating a violation of federal conservation regulations is not destruction of evidence within the meaning of the Sarbanes–Oxley Act of 2002, *see Yates v. United States*, 135 S. Ct. 1074 (2015), even though the Eleventh Circuit fishily held just the opposite, *United States v. Yates*, 733 F.3d 1059 (11th Cir. 2013).

---

INDIGO INKLING

Scholars have criticized this elaborate system of string citations, requiring the writer to determine not only the degrees of authoritativeness of relied-upon works but also to disclose their precise relevance, including (perplexingly) sources contrary to the writer's argument. One might ask why the legal profession chose for itself such an odd and onerous citation system. One commentator describes the system as derived from an "anxiety of authoritativeness." Michael Bacchus, *Strung Out: Legal Citation*, The Bluebook, *and the Anxiety of Authority*, 151 U Pa. L Rev. 245 (2002).

---

# R4. Signals

R4.1.   A signal illustrates the relationship between the author's assertion and the source cited for that assertion. The signal begins the citation sentence or clause.

R4.2.   There are four basic categories of signals:

| Category | Signals |
|---|---|
| Signals for Supporting Authority | (1) [No signal] |
| | (2) E.g., |
| | (3) Accord |
| | (4) See |
| | (5) See Also |
| | (6) Cf. |
| Signals for Comparison | (7) Compare `<citation to source(s), separated with "and" if multiple>` with `<citation to source(s), separated with "and" if multiple>` |
| Signals for Contradictory Authority | (8) Contra |
| | (9) But see |
| | (10) But cf. |
| Signals for Background Material | (11) See generally |

R4.3.   When more than one authority is used in the same citation, they should be ordered first according to hierarchy of introductory signals (see table above), and then within each signal by strength of authority using a semicolon in between each one (see Rule 10 below: **Order of Authorities Within Each Signal / Strength of Authority**).

---

INDIGO INKLING

For citation sentences, signals in the same category are listed within a single citation sentence, each one marked off by semicolons; signals in separate categories, however, should be listed in separate citation sentences.

- **Example:** "Legal professionals love to hate string citations, and critics have no shortage of reasons to view them with contempt." Mark Cooney, *Stringing Readers Along*, Mich. B.J. 44 (Dec. 2006); *see also* Gerald Lebovits, *Write the Cites Right—Part II*, 76 N.Y. St. B.J. 64 (Dec. 2004); Mark P. Painter, *30 Tips to Improve Readability in Briefs and Legal Documents Or, How to Write for Judges, not Like Judges*, 31 Mont. Law 6 (Apr. 2006). *But cf. The Bluebook: A Uniform System of Citation* (Columbia Law Review Ass'n et al. eds., 20th ed. 2015) (creating and maintaining a complicated system of citation signals which may encourage this kind of behavior). *See generally* Richard A. Posner, *Against Footnotes*, 38 Ct. Rev. 24 (2001).

---

INDIGO INKLING

For citation clauses, all signals (irrespective of category) are listed within a single citation clause and separated by semicolons.

- **Example:** Justice Scalia once noted that "the Constitution sometimes insulates the criminality of a few in order to protect the privacy of us all," *Arizona v. Hicks*, 480 U.S. 321, 329 (1987); *see also Maryland v. King*, 133 S. Ct. 1958, 1989 (2013) (Scalia, J., dissenting) ("Solving unsolved crimes is a noble objective, but it occupies a lower place in the American pantheon of noble objectives than the protection of our people from suspicionless law-enforcement searches."), and later applied that principle to limit police use of thermal imaging technology, *see Kyllo v. United States*, 389 U.S. 27 (2001); *cf. United States v. Jones*, 132 S. Ct. 945 (2012) (invalidating use of a GPS tracking device for long-term surveillance).

---

## R5. Capitalization Rules

R5.1.   The signal is capitalized at the beginning of a citation sentence.

  ◦ **Example:** Unbelievable as it may be, the Supreme Court has weighed in on the issue of whether a tomato is a fruit or vegetable. *See Nix v. Heden*, 149 U.S. 304 (1893).

R5.2.   The signal is left in lowercase at the beginning of a citation clause.

◦ **Example:** Even seemingly trivial issues, *see, e.g., Nix v. Heden*, 149 U.S. 304 (1893) (addressing the question of whether tomatoes are fruits or vegetables), can sometimes merit input from the Supreme Court.

## R6. Signals for Supporting Authority

R6.1.　`<no signal>`: A citation does not need a signal if--

◦ The source makes the same assertion; or

▪ **Example:** To impose the death penalty on an individual who is criminally insane is unconstitutional. *Ford v. Wainwright*, 477 U.S. 399, 410 (1986).

◦ The assertion is a direct quotation from the source; or

▪ **Example:** States are prohibited "from inflicting the penalty of death upon a prisoner who is insane." *Ford v. Wainwright*, 477 U.S. 399, 410 (1986).

◦ The source is referred to in the assertion.

▪ **Example:** In cases like *Roper*, *Atkins*, and *Ford*, the Supreme Court has established certain classes of individuals upon which the death penalty may not be imposed. *Roper v. Simmons*, 543 U.S. 551, 575 (2005); *Atkins v. Virginia*, 536 U.S. 304, 321 (2002); *Ford v. Wainwright*, 477 U.S. 399, 410 (1986).

R6.2.　*E.g.,*

◦ Use "*e.g.,*" if the cited source is one of multiple sources to make the same assertion. The citation may include however many sources the author finds to be helpful. Note that the comma in the signal "*e.g.,*" should NOT be italicized.

▪ **Example:** In a criminal case, the state bears the burden of proving the defendant's guilt "beyond a reasonable doubt." *E.g., State v. Purrier*, 336 P.3d 574, 576 (Or. Ct. App. 2014).

▪ **Example:** Prior to the Supreme Court's decision in *Riley v. California*, 134 S. Ct. 2473 (2014), several circuits had generally allowed the police to conduct warrantless searches of cell phones of individuals under arrest. *E.g., U.S. v. Murphy*, 552 F.3d 405, 411 (4th Cir. 2009); *U.S. v. Finley*, 477 F.3d 250, 260 (5th Cir. 2007).

◦ "*E.g.,*" may also be used following any other signal, in which case an italicized comma should separate the two signals. Note: The comma in the signal "*e.g.,*" should NOT be italicized.

- **Example:** Several states have enacted legislation requiring witnesses to report certain crimes to authorities. *See, e.g.,* Colo. Rev. Stat. Ann. § 18-8-115 (West 2014); Mass. Gen. Laws Ann. ch. 268, § 40 (West 2014); Ohio Rev. Code Ann. § 2921.22 (West 2014).

- **Example:** Most states have not enacted legislation requiring witnesses to report crimes to authorities. *But see, e.g.,* Colo. Rev. Stat. Ann. § 18-8-115 (West 2014); Mass. Gen. Laws Ann. ch. 268, § 40 (West 2014); Ohio Rev. Code Ann. § 2921.22 (West 2014).

R6.3.  *Accord*

- *Accord* is used when more than one source substantiates a proposition, but the text quotes just one of them. Use *accord* as the introductory signal for the non-quoted sources. Also, *accord* may be used as the introductory signal for indicating that the law of one jurisdiction is consistent with the law of another.

- **Example:** Justin Bieber might be one of the most "widely despised figures in pop music [who] still maintains a formidable fan base." Keith Girard, *Justin Bieber Seeks to Make Amends, Jump-Start Career on Ellen*, TheImproper Magazine (Jan. 25, 2015), http://www.theimproper.com/118310/justin-bieber-seeks-amends-jumpstart-career-ellen-watch/; *accord* Chrissy Makkas, *Justin Bieber Fronts V Magazine's Music Issue (Forum Buzz)*, The Fashion Spot (Jan. 11, 2012), http://www.thefashionspot.com/buzz-news/forum-buzz/171203-justin-bieber-fronts-v-magazines-music-issue-forum-buzz/ ("Justin Bieber is a polarizing figure . . . .").

R6.4.  *See*

- *See* is used when an authority does not directly state but clearly supports the proposition. *See* is used instead of `<no signal>` when an inferential step is required to connect the proposition to the authority cited.

- **Example:** The defendant in a criminal case cannot be forced to testify against himself or herself. *See* U.S. Const. amend. V.

R6.5.  *See also*

- *See also* is used for additional sources that support a proposition. Use *see also* when authority that states or clearly supports the proposition has already been cited or discussed. The use of a parenthetical is recommended when using *see also*.

- **Example:** Slow and steady wins the race. *See* Don Daily, *The Classic Treasury of Aesop's Fables* 43-46 (1999); *see also The Shawshank Redemption* (Castle Rock Entertainment 1994) (prisoner tunnels out of a prison by removing a few stones per day).

R6.6.  *Cf.*

◦ *Cf.* is used for supporting authority that is analogous to your proposition, or which is related but which requires some interpretive work to connect to your proposition. Always use a parenthetical with *cf.* to explain the logical connection required for the argument.

▪ **Example:** In the legal realm, there is a need for an easy-to-use, standard set of citation rules. *Cf. The Bluebook: A Uniform System of Citation* (Columbia Law Review Ass'n et al. eds., 20th ed. 2015) (demonstrating, by virtue of 20 editions, the need for such a system, but producing a system that is overly complex).

# R7. Signals for Comparison

R7.1.  *Compare* `<citation to source or authority>`, *with* `<citation to source or authority>`

◦ *Compare . . .* is used when the relationship of multiple authorities will demonstrate or offer support for the proposition. It is highly recommended that each authority in the comparison be explained with a parenthetical in order to make the relationship and argument clear to the reader. Each portion of the *compare . . .* signal may contain multiple sources; separate these sources using commas and italicized "*and*" as follows.

▪ **Example:** The 20th Century saw sweeping changes in the definition and scope of the Due Process Clause. *Compare Lochner v. New York*, 198 U.S. 45 (1905) (showing the Supreme Court's historical interpretation of the Due Process Clause as solely protecting an individual's right to contract), *with McDonald v. Chicago*, 561 U.S. 742 (2010) (incorporating the Second Amendment using the Due Process Clause), *BMW of North America, Inc. v. Gore*, 517 U.S. 559 (1996) (utilizing the Due Process Clause to reduce punitive damages), *and Dolan v. City of Tigard*, 512 U.S. 374 (1994) (limiting the zoning and ordinance powers of local governments under the Due Process Clause).

# R8. Signals for Contradictory Authority

R8.1.  *Contra*

◦ *Contra* is used when a cited authority directly conflicts with the proposition it follows. *Contra* is the opposite signal to `<no signal>`.

- **Example:** *The Bluebook* is an example of absolute efficiency in the formulation and expression of the rules of legal citation. *Contra* Richard A. Posner, *The Bluebook Blues*, 120 Yale L.J. 950 (2011).

R8.2. *But see*

○ *But see* is used for authority that, while not directly contradicting the main proposition, nonetheless clearly opposes it. *But see* is the opposite signal to *see*.

- **Example:** I have the right to falsely shout "Fire!" in a crowded theater. *But see Schenck v. United States*, 249 U.S. 47 (1919).

R8.3. *But cf.*

○ *But cf.* is used to indicate that an authority supports a proposition that is similar to the opposite of the author's main proposition. *But cf.* is the opposite signal to *cf.* Always use a parenthetical with *but cf.* to explain the logical connection required for the argument. This is the weakest signal for contrary authority.

- **Example:** Restaurant commercials sell a vision of dinner as a cornerstone daily meal. *But cf. 5 Things to Know About McDonalds All Day Breakfast*, TIME, (Oct. 6, 2015), http://time.com/money/4062667/mcdonalds-all-day-breakfast/.

## R9. Signals for Background Material

R9.1. *See generally*

○ *See generally* is used for useful background material. It is recommended that you use a parenthetical with *see generally* in order to explain the authority's relevance to the proposition.

- **Example:** Some commentators have argued that the Supreme Court does more than "call balls and strikes," and that politics may even be involved in some decisionmaking. *See generally* Jeffrey Toobin, *The Nine: Inside the Secret World of the Supreme Court* (2007) (arguing that the work of the Supreme Court often involves the Justices imposing values and even political preferences).

# R10. Order of Authorities Within Each Signal / Strength of Authority

INDIGO INKLING
Follow the order below for citing authorities within a signal. However, there is one exception: if an authority is more helpful than others cited within a signal, it should be cited first.

R10.1. Constitutions. Order constitutions from the same jurisdiction from most recent to oldest.

1. Federal

2. State (alphabetize according to state)

3. Foreign (alphabetize according to jurisdiction)

4. Foundational Documents of International Groups (United Nations, the League of Nations, and the European Union, in that order)

R10.2. Statutes

R10.2.1. Federal:

1. Statutes in U.S.C., U.S.C.A., or U.S.C.S. (in ascending order by U.S.C. Title)

2. Current statutes that are not in U.S.C., U.S.C.A., or U.S.C.S. (from most recently enacted to oldest)

3. Rules of Evidence and Procedure

4. Repealed Statutes (from most recently enacted to oldest)

R10.2.2. State (alphabetize according to state):

1. Statutes currently codified (in ascending order within the codification)

2. Statutes currently in force but not currently codified (from most recently enacted to oldest)

3. Rules of Evidence and Procedure

4. Repealed Statutes (from most recently enacted to oldest)

R10.2.3. Foreign (alphabetize according to jurisdiction):

1. Codes or Statutes currently codified (in ascending order in the codification)

2. Statutes currently in force but not currently codified (from most recently enacted to oldest)

3. Repealed Statutes (from most recently enacted to oldest)

R10.3. Treaties and Other International Agreements (other than those above) are cited from most recently ratified/signed to oldest.

R10.4. Cases. Order cases from the same court from most recent to oldest, without regard to prior or subsequent history. There's no difference between Federal Circuit Court of Appeals or Federal District Courts.

R10.4.1.  Federal:

1. Supreme Court

2. Court of Appeals, Emergency Court of Appeals, and Temporary Emergency Court of Appeals

3. Court of Claims, Court of Customs, and Patent Appeals and Bankruptcy Appellate Panels

4. District Courts, Judicial Panel on Multidistrict Litigation, and Court of International Trade (formerly the Customs Court)

5. District Bankruptcy Courts and Railroad Reorganization Court

6. Court of Federal Claims (formerly the Trial Division for the Court of Claims), Court of Appeals for the Armed Services (formerly the Court of Military Appeals), and Tax Court (formerly the Board of Tax Appeals)

7. Administrative Agencies (alphabetize according to agency)

R10.4.2.  State:

1. Courts (alphabetize according to state, then by hierarchy in descending order)

2. Agencies (alphabetize according to state, then by agency)

R10.4.3.  Foreign:

1. Courts (alphabetize according to jurisdiction, then by hierarchy in descending order)

2. Agencies (alphabetize according to jurisdiction, then by agency)

R10.4.4.  International:

1. International Court of Justice, Permanent Court of International Justice

2. Other International Tribunals and Arbitral Panels (in alphabetical order)

R10.5. Legislative Materials (always cite federal materials first)

    1. Bills and Resolutions (most recent to oldest)

    2. Committee Hearings (most recent to oldest)

    3. Reports, Documents, and Committee Prints (most recent to oldest)

    4. Floor Debates (most recent to oldest)

R10.6. Administrative and Executive Materials

    R10.6.1. Federal:

        1. Executive Orders

        2. Current Treasury Regulations, Proposed Treasury Regulations

        3. All Other Regulations currently in force (numerically by C.F.R. title in ascending order)

        4. Proposed Rules not yet in force (numerically by future C.F.R. titles, if any, in ascending order; otherwise from most recently proposed to oldest)

        5. All Materials repealed (from most recently promulgated to oldest)

    R10.6.2. State:

        1. State (alphabetize according to state), currently in force, then repealed

    R10.6.3. Foreign:

        1. Foreign (alphabetize according to jurisdiction), currently in force, then repealed

R10.7. Resolutions, Decisions, and Regulations of Intergovernmental Organizations

    1. United Nations and League of Nations (from most recent to oldest by issuing body, listing General Assembly first, then Security Council, then other organs alphabetically)

    2. Other Organizations (in alphabetical order by name)

R10.8. Records, Briefs, and Petitions are cited in the same order as discussed in Rule 10.4. Briefs from the same case and court are ordered: (i) plaintiff/petitioner; (ii) defendant/respondent; (iii) amicus curiae (alphabetize according to amicus party)

R10.9. Secondary Materials

1. Uniform Codes, Model Codes, and Restatements, in that order (from most recent to oldest within each category)

2. Books, Pamphlets, and Shorter Works in a collection of single author's works (in alphabetical order by author's last name; when there is no author, by the title's first word)

3. Journal Pieces (excluding magazines, newspapers, and student-written materials), including Forthcoming Works and Shorter Works in a collection of various authors' works (in alphabetical order by first author's last name)

4. Book Reviews not written by students (alphabetize according to reviewer's last name)

5. Student-Written Law Review Pieces including Book Reviews (in alphabetical order by author's last name; if there is no author, by the title's first word; if there is no title, alphabetically by the periodical's abbreviation)

6. Annotations (from most recently published to oldest)

7. Magazine and Newspaper Articles (in alphabetical order by author's last name; if there is no author, by the title's first word)

8. Working Papers (in alphabetical order by author's last name; if there is no author, by the title's first word)

9. Unpublished Materials not forthcoming (in alphabetical order by author's last name; if there is no author, by the title's first word)

10. Electronic Sources, including Internet Sources (in alphabetical order by author's last name; if there is no author, by the title's first word)

R10.10. Cross-references to the author's own text or footnotes.

# B. CASES

> INDIGO INKLING
> Although *The Bluebook* encourages citations to Lexis or Westlaw when appropriate, note that many of the states have adopted public domain or media neutral citation of cases, as shown in Table T3. *The Indigo Book* encourages the use of public domain or media neutral citations. When giving a public domain citation, also include a parallel citation to the appropriate regional reporter if possible.

## R11. Full citation

R11.1.  Elements of a full citation. When providing a full citation to a case, you should generally include the following:

1.  case name;

2.  volume number, reporter, first page;

3.  pincite (the exact page number you are referring to, if necessary);

4.  court, year (see special instructions below for pending and unreported cases);

5.  explanatory parenthetical (if necessary);

6.  prior or subsequent history of the case (if any).

**Examples:**

○ *Leonard v. Pepsico, Inc.*, 88 F. Supp. 2d 116, 127 (S.D.N.Y. 1999) ("Plaintiff's understanding of the commercial as an offer must also be rejected because the Court finds that no objective person could reasonably have concluded that the commercial actually offered consumers a Harrier Jet."), *aff'd*, 210 F.3d 88 (2d Cir. 2000).

○ *Toolson v. N.Y. Yankees, Inc.*, 346 U.S. 356 (1953) (per curiam) (affirming baseball's exemption from the scope of federal antitrust laws).

R11.2.  Case Name. Case names are often lengthy. Therefore when citing to a case, do not always include the case name in full.

R11.2.1.  When referring to a case with an individual's name in the case name, use the person's full family name (i.e., their last name). Delete first name and initials, except when the full name of the person is in a language that lists the surname first, or when referring to the name of a business or where the court has abbreviated the party's surname.

**Example:** *Van Leeuwen v. Souto de Moura*

**Example:** *James T. Kirk & Assocs. v. Luke S.*

**Correct:** *Smith v. Jones*
**Incorrect:** *Jonathan H. Smith v. Allison T. Jones*

**Correct:** *Xu Lanting v. Wong*
**Incorrect:** *Xu Lanting v. James Wong*

R11.2.2. Only include the last name of the first listed party of the plaintiffs and the first listed party of the defendants.

R11.2.3. Italicize everything in the case name, but don't italicize the comma at the end of the case name. Exception for law review articles: *do not* italicize case names in law review full citations, but *do* italicize case names in law review article short form citations and procedural phrases such as "*In re.*"

R11.2.4. Delete "et al.", nicknames, and aliases.

**Correct:** *Jackson v. Leviston*
**Incorrect:** *Curtis James Jackson III, p/k/a 50 Cent v. Lastonia Leviston*

R11.2.5. Replace procedural phrases, and omit all besides the first procedural phrase.

1. When you see "on the relation of," "on behalf of," and similar expressions, replace with "*ex rel.*"

    **Correct:** *Affleck ex rel. Damon v. Kimmel*
    **Incorrect:** *Ben Affleck, on behalf of Matt Damon v. Jimmy Kimmel, et al.*

2. When you see "in the matter of," "petition of," and similar expressions, replace with "*In re*", except do not use "*In re*", or any procedural phrases besides "*ex rel.*" when the case name contains the name of an adversary.

    **Correct:** *In re Nat'l Football League Players' Concussion Injury Litig.*
    **Incorrect:** *In the Matter of Nat'l Football League Players' Concussion Injury Litig.*

**Correct:** *Estate of Jones v. Smith*
**Incorrect:** *In re Estate of Jones v. Smith*

R11.2.6. Abbreviate words in case names according to Table T11. If the resulting abbreviation is not ambiguous, words of eight or more letters may be abbreviated to save substantial space. Also omit terms such as "L.L.C." and "Inc." that indicate the party is a business when that fact is made clear because the party name includes a word such as "Co." or "Ins."

**Correct:** *Cont'l Paper Bag Co. v. E. Paper Bag Co.*
**Incorrect:** *Continental Paper Bag Company v. Eastern Paper Bag Co.*

**Exception:** do not abbreviate if the citation appears in a textual sentence as explained in Rule 11.2.19, below

R11.2.7. Abbreviate countries, states, and other geographical places according to Table T12.

**Correct:** *Church of Scientology of Cal. v. Blackman*
**Incorrect:** *Church of Scientology of California v. Blackman*

**Exception:** if the geographical place is one of the parties in the case, do not abbreviate it

**Correct:** *South Dakota v. Fifteen Impounded Cats*
**Incorrect:** *S.D. v. Fifteen Impounded Cats*

**Exception:** do not abbreviate if the geographical place is part of a citation that appears in a textual sentence as explained in Rule 11.2.19, below

R11.2.8. Spell out "United States" when it is a named party.

**Correct:** *United States v. Ninety Five Barrels, More or Less*
**Incorrect:** *U.S. v. Ninety Five Barrels, More or Less*

R11.2.9. Omit "People of," "State of," and "Commonwealth of," unless citing a court located in that state, in which case retain only "People," "State," or "Commonwealth."

**Correct:** *Lessig v. Colorado*, 17 U.S. 107 (1998).
**Incorrect:** *Lessig v. State of Colorado*, 17 U.S. 107 (1998).

**Correct:** *Lessig v. State,* 109 P.3d 224 (Colo. 1997).
**Incorrect:** *Lessig v. State of Colorado,* 109 P.3d 224 (Colo. 1997).

R11.2.10. Omit phrases such as "Town of" and "City of" if the expression does not comprise the first part of the name of a party.

**Correct:** *James v. Village of Jamestown*
**Incorrect:** *James v. Jamestown*

**Correct:** *James v. King of Jamestown*
**Incorrect:** *James v. King of the Village of Jamestown*

R11.2.11. Do not include a prepositional phrase indicating location, unless the resulting party name would have only one word, or the phrase is part of a business' full name.

**Correct:** *Stevenson v. Board of Trade*
**Incorrect:** *Stevenson v. Board of Trade of Colorado*

**Correct:** *ACLU of N.D. v. Jones*
**Incorrect:** *ACLU v. Jones*

**Correct:** *Dam Things from Denmark v. Russ Berrie & Co.*
**Incorrect:** *Dam Things v. Russ Berrie & Co.*

R11.2.12. Include geographical designations introduced by a preposition, but omit those that follow a comma. Use "United States" instead of "United States of America," but otherwise omit designations of national or larger geographical areas.

**Correct:** *Cal. Bd. of Commerce v. City of Sacramento*
**Incorrect:** *Cal. Bd. of Commerce v. City of Sacramento, California*

R11.2.13. Delete "the" as the first word of a party's name, unless the party is "*The Queen*" or the "*The King,*" or when referring to the established popular name in a citation or citation clause.

**Example:** *The Railroad Comm'n Cases*

**Correct:** *Int'l Soc'y for Krishna Consciousness of Cal., Inc. v. City of Los Angeles*
**Incorrect:** *Int'l Soc'y for Krishna Consciousness of Cal., Inc. v. The City of Los Angeles*

**Exception:** retain "the" if it is part of the name of the object of an *in rem* action.

**Correct:** *In re the Snug Harbor*
**Incorrect:** *In re Snug Harbor*

R11.2.14. The Commissioner of Internal Revenue should be cited as "Commissioner" (abbreviated as "Comm'r" in citations).
**Correct:** *Plainfield-Union Water Co. v. Comm'r*
**Incorrect:** *Plainfield-Union Water Co. v. Commissioner of Internal Revenue*

R11.2.15. For cases with multiple dispositions, include an italicized identifier if useful. In future citations of that case, the identifier can replace the full case name.

**Example:** *Liriano v. Hobart Corp.* (*Liriano II*), 92 N.Y.2d 232 (1998).

*Liriano v. Hobart Corp.* (*Liraino III*), 170 F.3d 264, 266 (2d Cir. 1999) (citing *Liriano II*, 92 N.Y.2d at 236–37).

R11.2.16. If a mandamus action is known by the name of the judge against whom the writ is sought, that name can be indicated in an italicized parenthetical.

**Example:** *Jones v. United States District Court (Smith)*, 89 U.S. 233 (2011).

R11.2.17. If a case is known both by the reported name and a distinct short form name, always include the reported name in a full citation. The short name may be included in italics in a parenthetical.

**Example:** *Indus. Union Dep't, AFL-CIO v. Am. Petroleum Inst. (The Benzene Case)*, 448 U.S. 607, 645 (1980).

R11.2.18. Abbreviate any commonly recognized organizations, such as the SEC and the ACLU.

**Correct:** *Red Lion Broad. Co. v. FCC*, 395 U.S. 367 (1969).
**Incorrect:** *Red Lion Broad. Co. v. Federal Communications Commission*, 395 U.S. 367 (1969).

R11.2.19.

If you're including the case name within a sentence (instead of a citation sentence or clause or a footnote) do NOT abbreviate words listed in the tables referenced in Rule 11.2.6 and Rule 11.2.7 above.

**Correct:** According to *Texas Department of Community Affairs v. Burdine*, once the plaintiff has established a *prima facie* case, there is a rebuttable presumption of unlawful discrimination. 450 U.S. 248, 254 (1981).

**Incorrect:** According to *Texas Dep't of Cmty. Affairs v. Burdine*, once the plaintiff has established a *prima facie* case, there is a rebuttable presumption of unlawful discrimination. 450 U.S. 248, 254 (1981).

**Exception:** Shorten well-known acronyms and the following eight words: "&," "Ass'n," "Bros.," "Co.," "Corp.," "Inc.," "Ltd.," and "No."

**Correct:** In *McDonnell Douglas Corp. v. Green*, the Supreme Court held that in a disparate treatment case, the plaintiff bears the initial burden of establishing a *prima facie* case of employment discrimination. 411 U.S. 792 (1973).

**Incorrect:** In *McDonnell Douglas Corporation v. Green*, the Supreme Court held that in a disparate treatment case, the plaintiff bears the initial burden of establishing a *prima facie* case of employment discrimination. 411 U.S. 792 (1973).

---

INDIGO INKLING

There are multiple ways to incorporate a case citation in the text of an article, brief, or other written work. In the previous example (reproduced below), the case name is stated in the text and the rest of the citation is included as a separate sentence. There is no strict rule here, so choose whichever method will be clearer to the reader.

In *McDonnell Douglas Corp. v. Green*, the Supreme Court held that in a disparate treatment case, the plaintiff bears the initial burden of establishing a *prima facie* case of employment discrimination. 411 U.S. 792 (1973)

Alternatively, one can include the entire citation in-text as follows:

In *McDonnell Douglas Corp. v. Green*, 411 U.S. 792 (1973), the Supreme Court held that in a disparate treatment case, the plaintiff bears the initial burden of establishing a *prima facie* case of employment discrimination.

R11.3. Volume Number, Reporter, First page. The citation should include: volume number of the reporter, abbreviated name of the reporter (listed by jurisdiction in accordance with Table T1), first page of the case.

- **Example:** *Terrible v. Terrible*, 534 P.2d 919 (Nev. 1975) (denying ex-husband's petition to split up property he and ex-wife owned as tenants in common).

This is how you decode case citations. The left column shows what your citation should look like. The right column shows what the citation means for someone looking for the case.

| Citation | Reporter |
| --- | --- |
| *Demosthenes v. Baal*, 495 U.S. 731 (1990). | Vol. 495, p. 731 of United States Reports |
| *United States v. $124,570 U.S. Currency*, 873 F.2d 1240 (9th Cir. 1989). | Vol. 873, p. 1240 of Federal Reporter, Second Series |
| *Gucci America, Inc. v. Guess?, Inc.*, 831 F. Supp. 2d 723 (S.D.N.Y. 2011). | Vol. 831, p. 723 of Federal Supplement, Second Series |
| *Hamburger v. Fry*, 338 P.2d 1088 (Okla. 1958). | Vol. 338, p. 1088 of Pacific Reporter, Second Series |
| *Camp v. Superman*, 119 Vt. 62 (1955). | Vol. 119, p. 62 of Vermont Reports |

R11.4. Pincite. To direct the reader to the specific page you are referring to, you must include a **pincite** after you list the first page where the case is found in the reporter. If the pincite is the first page of the opinion, be sure to still include it by just repeating the number.

- **Example:** *Mattel, Inc. v. MCA Records, Inc.*, 296 F.3d 894, 908 (9th Cir. 2002) ("The parties are advised to chill.")

- **Example:** *Brown v. State*, 216 S.E.2d 356, 356 (Ga. Ct. App. 1975) ("The D. A. was ready. His case was red-hot. Defendant was present, His witness was not.").

R11.5. Pincite referencing multiple pages or a page range:

1. Multiple pages: *Gordon v. Secretary of State of New Jersey*, 460 F. Supp. 1026, 1026, 1028 (D.N.J. 1978) (dismissing a complaint charging that plaintiff, by reason of his illegal incarceration in jail, had been deprived of the office of the President of the United States).

2. Page range: *Helton v. State*, 311 So. 2d 381, 382–84 (Fla. Dist. Ct. App. 1975) (reciting the prosecutor's closing arguments in a parody of "*'Twas the Night Before Christmas*").

3. *Passim.* If your proposition appears in many locations in the opinion, or if you are referring to a general idea that pervades a source, feel free to append the word *"passim"* instead of a pincite.

    ◦ **Example:** Anyone alive in the eighteenth century would have known that the problem of determining a ship's longitude at sea was one of the most prominent scientific quests of the day. Dava Sobel, *Longitude: The True Story of a Lone Genius Who Solved the Greatest Scientific Problem of His Time passim* (1995).

---

INDIGO INKLING

For page ranges consisting of page numbers 100 or greater, you need only provide the last two digits of the second number in the page range, providing that the preceding digits are identical between the two numbers (e.g., 284–89; 4158–72). Otherwise, include both numbers in their entirety (e.g., 199–231).

---

• **Example:** *Selmon v. Hasbro Bradley, Inc.*, 669 F. Supp. 1267, 1272-73 (S.D.N.Y. 1987) (comparing a "Leo-Lamo" (a hybrid lion/lamb animal character) to a "Bumblelion" (a hybrid bumblebee/lion toy animal) in the context of a copyright infringement claim).

---

INDIGO INKLING

Learn to differentiate between hyphens, en dashes, and em dashes. These three marks all comprise short, horizontal lines that with the help of glasses and/or a magnifying glass, you will see have microscopically varying lengths.

• **Hyphens** (shortest in length) are used for: phrasal adjectives (e.g., "laser-sharp focus," "larger-than-life character," and compound words (e.g., "daughter-in-law," "over-the-counter").

• **En dashes** (longer than hyphens, shorter than em dashes) are used for: ranges of values (e.g., page ranges) and contrasting or connected pairs of words (e.g., Sarbanes–Oxley Act).

• **Em dashes** (longest in length) are used for: inserting a break in a thought; isolating a concluding phrase; setting on a parenthetical explanation or amplification; and signaling a collection of ideas (e.g., When her new Volkswagen was finally delivered—nearly three months after it was ordered and following the revelation of VW's massive scheme of emissions control fraud—Alice decided she didn't want it).

---

R11.6. Citing a footnote. To cite a footnote, provide a page number followed immediately with a footnote number, using "n." to show footnote number. There is no space between "n." and the footnote number:

- **Example:** *Davis v. City of New York*, 902 F. Supp. 2d 405, 412 n.22 (S.D.N.Y. 2012) (describing how Jay-Z "showcased his knowledge of these Fourth Amendment rights" in his song *99 Problems*).

## R12. Court & Year

R12.1. Citations should include both the deciding court and the year of decision in parentheses.

R12.2. See Table T1 for how to abbreviate the names of all U.S. federal and state courts.

See the chart below for common examples:

| Court | Rule | Example |
|---|---|---|
| United States Supreme Court | Use U.S. if the opinion is published in the United States Reports. If not, use S. Ct.<br><br>***When citing to a Supreme Court decision, just cite the year and omit the court's name. | *Two Pesos, Inc. v. Taco Cabana, Inc.*, 505 U.S. 763 (1992).<br><br>*Brown v. Entm't Merchs. Ass'n*, 131 S. Ct. 2729, 2738 (2011) (noting that Justice Alito has done "considerable independent research" on violent video games for his dissent). |
| Federal Courts of Appeals | Either F., F.2d, or F.3d, depending on the decision. | *Batman v. Commissioner*, 189 F.2d 107 (5th Cir. 1951).<br><br>*Nance v. United States*, 299 F.2d 122, 124 (D.C. Cir. 1962) ("How do you know it was me, when I had a handkerchief over my face?"). |
| Federal District Courts | Either F. Supp. or F. Supp. 2d depending on the decision. | *Frigaliment Importing Co. v. B.N.S. International Sales Corp.*, 190 F. Supp. 116, 117 (S.D.N.Y. 1960) ("The issue is, what is chicken?").<br><br>*Cartier v. Aaron Faber Inc.*, 512 F. Supp. 2d 165 (S.D.N.Y. 2007). |
| State High Courts | Cite to the regional reporter for the region in which the court sits, if the opinion appears there. If not, cite to the state's official reporter, as listed in Table T1.<br><br>Note: If citing an official reporter that publishes only decisions of the state's highest court (e.g., "Cal." for the California Supreme Court's reporter), do not include the court's name in parentheses. | *Terrible v. Terrible*, 534 P.2d 919 (Nev. 1975).<br><br>*State v. One 1970 2-Door Sedan Rambler*, 136 N.W. 59 (Neb. 1974). |

| Court | Rule | Example |
|---|---|---|
| Other State Courts | Cite to the regional reporter for the region in which the court sits, if the opinion appears there. If not, cite to the state's official reporter in Table T1.<br><br>Note: Do **NOT** include the department or district of intermediate state courts. | *Brown v. Swindell*, 198 So. 2d 432, 434 (La. Ct. App. 1967) (holding plaintiff could not recover damages for emotional distress allegedly due to embarrassment of owning a three-legged dog).<br><br>*State v. Stroud*, 30 Wash. App. 392 (1981). |

---

INDIGO INKLING

See Table T12.1 for the correct abbreviation for each state—even though some may not be consistent (e.g., New York is N.Y., whereas Michigan is Mich.). Also, be mindful of spacing.

---

R12.3.   Parallel Citation in State Court Documents

   R12.3.1.   When submitting documents to state courts, follow the local rules for citations in Table T3.

   R12.3.2.   State courts' local rules often require a parallel citation: i.e., a citation to both the official state reporter *and* the unofficial regional and/or state-specific reporter, the latter following the former.

   R12.3.3.   Two important notes:

   - Use one pincite per reporter citation.

   - When the official reporter title makes the state or court name apparent, then don't include it again in parentheses.

   - **Example:** *Harden v. Playboy Enterprises, Inc.*, 261 Ill. App. 3d 443, 633 N.E.2d 764 (1993).

R12.4.   Special Note on Pending and Unreported Cases: Some cases or opinions are not assigned to reporters. They generally can be found in one of the following three sources:

   R12.4.1.   **LEXIS and Westlaw cases:** Citations to these electronic databases are similar to regular citations, except that they (a) replace the case code with a docket number *and* a database code supplied by LEXIS or Westlaw, and (b) include the full date of the decision in the following parenthetical, not just the year.

   Citations to these electronic databases should be formatted as follows: <Case Name>, <case docket number>, <database

```
identifier and electronic report number>, at *<star page
number> <(court, full date)>.
```

- **Example:** *Yates v. United States*, No. 13–7451, 2015 U.S. LEXIS 1503, at *40 (Feb. 25, 2015) (Citing Dr. Seuss, Justice Kagan explained, "[a] fish is, of course, a discrete thing that possesses physical form.").

- **Example:** *State v. Green*, No. 2012AP1475–CR, 2013 WL 5811261, at *7 (Wis. Ct. App. Oct. 30, 2013) (rejecting Green's argument that there was a reversible error due to bailiff's distribution of leftover Halloween candy to the jury).

R12.4.2. Slip opinions: A slip opinion is a published decision by a court that has not yet been included in a reporter. If there is a slip opinion for an unreported case, but it's not in LEXIS or Westlaw, include the docket number, the court, and the full date of the most recent major disposition of the case:

- **Example:** *Beastie Boys v. Monster Energy Co.*, No. 12 Civ. 6065 (S.D.N.Y. Dec. 4, 2014).

R12.4.3. Opinions only available online, but not in an electronic database: Some cases, particularly ones that are pending, may be accessed only through a court's website. If so, include the URL.

- **Example:** *Macy's Inc. v. Martha Stewart Living Omnimedia, Inc.*, No. 1728, slip op. at 1 (N.Y. App. Div. Feb. 26, 2015), http://www.nycourts.gov/reporter/3dseries/2015/2015_01728.htm.

R12.4.4. Different courts and publishers use different acronyms to identify civil and criminal docket numbers (e.g., CIV-A, Civ. A., Civ., No., etc.). Cite to the case docket number exactly as it appears. If a case has more than one docket number, these acronyms do not need to be included after the first reference:

- **Example:** *In re Salomon Inc. Sec. Litig.*, Nos. 91 Civ. 5442 (RPP), 91 Civ. 5471, 1992 WL 150762 (S.D.N.Y. Nov. 13, 1992).

## R13. Weight of Authority and Explanatory Parenthetical

R13.1. To highlight information regarding the weight of the cited authority (e.g., for concurring and dissenting opinions), insert an additional parenthetical after the date parenthetical. Remember to separate the parentheticals with a space.

**Examples:**

- *United States v. Leggett*, 23 F.3d 409 (6th Cir. 1994) (unpublished table decision).

- *Ward v. Rock Against Racism*, 491 U.S. 781 (1989) (Marshall, J., dissenting).

- *Harris v. State*, 887 S.W.2d 514 (Ark. 1994) (per curiam).

- *Dep't of Revenue v. James B. Beam Distilling Co.*, 377 U.S. 341, 349 (1964) (7–2 decision) (Black, J., dissenting) (disagreeing with Justice Goldberg as to the relative merits of bourbon and scotch).

R13.2. To explain the proposition for which the case stands, insert an explanatory parenthetical.

**Examples:**

- *Stambovsky v. Ackley*, 572 N.Y.S.2d 672, 674 (App. Div. 1991) ("[A]s a matter of law, the house is haunted.").

- *People v. Foranyic*, 74 Cal. Rptr. 2d 804, 807 (Ct. App. 1998) (police have probable cause to detain someone they see riding a bike at 3 a.m., carrying an axe).

## R14. History of the Case

R14.1. When citing a case, include the prior or subsequent history of the case, subject to several exceptions. Refer to Table T14 for how to abbreviate explanatory phrases when introducing case history. Italicize the explanatory phrase.

---

INDIGO INKLING

The United States is a common law system, where court decisions play an important role in defining what the law is. Simply put, there's good case law and bad case law. To figure out the difference, we have to look at the case's prior and subsequent history, because our view of what is good law may evolve as a case moves through the appeals process.

---

R14.2. Always use the following explanatory phrases when applicable and italicize them:

- *aff'd*

- *aff'g*

- *cert. denied* (but drop this explanatory phrase when the Supreme Court's certiorari denial is more than two years in the past)

- *cert. granted*

- *rev'd*

- *rev'd on other grounds*

**Examples:**

- *Energy & Env't Legal Inst. v. Epel*, 43 F. Supp. 3d 1171 (D. Colo. 2014), *aff'd*, 793 F.3d 1169 (10th Cir.), *cert. denied*, 136 S. Ct. 595 (2015).

- *In re Verizon Internet Servs., Inc.*, 257 F. Supp. 2d 244 (D.D.C. 2003), *rev'd on other grounds, Recording Indus. Ass'n of Am., Inc. v. Verizon Internet Servs., Inc.*, 351 F.3d 1229 (D.C. Cir. 2003).

---

INDIGO INKLING

Note that in the above examples, the relevant explanatory phrases precede the subsequent history. Explanatory parenthetical information about the preceding case should be included before any subsequent history.

---

R14.3. When the case has a different name in the subsequent history, provide the new case name after the italicized phrase "*sub nom.*" ("under the name of").

**Example:** *Lerman v. Comm'r*, 939 F.2d 44 (3d Cir. 1991), *rev'd sub nom. Horn v. Comm'r*, 968 F.2d 1229 (D.C. Cir. 1992).

**Exception:** Do **not** provide the new case name if either the parties' names are merely reversed or if the subsequent history is simply a denial of certiorari or rehearing:

**Correct:** *United States v. Schmuck*, 840 F.2d 384 (7th Cir. 1988), *aff'd*, 489 U.S. 705 (1989).

**Incorrect:** *United States v. Schmuck*, 840 F.2d 384 (7th Cir. 1988), *aff'd, Schmuck v. United States*, 489 U.S. 705 (1989).

## R15. Short Form Citation for Cases

R15.1. In Text

    R15.1.1. The first time a case is mentioned in the text, include a full citation as shown here:

- **Example:** In *Fenton v. Quaboag Country Club*, the court held that the house owners were entitled to an abatement of the trespasses by flying golf balls. 233 N.E.2d 216, 219 (Mass. 1968).

- **Example:** In *Fenton v. Quaboag Country Club*, 233 N.E.2d 216, 219 (Mass. 1968), the court held that the house owners were entitled to an abatement of the trespasses by flying golf balls.

R15.1.2.  For subsequent cites in text, refer to one party's name (or an unambiguous reference to the case name), as well as a short form citation in the form of `<volume> <Name of Reporter>` at `<pincite>`, as shown here:

- **Example:** The court in *Fenton* also held that there was error in the award of damages based on loss of fair market value of property due to the flying balls. 233 N.E.2d at 219.

## R15.2.  In Citations

R15.2.1.  If the reference is unambiguous and the full citation is easily accessible elsewhere, then you may use a short form citation.

R15.2.2.  For cases, a short form citation usually includes: `<The First Party of the Case Name>, <volume number> <Reporter>` at `<pincite>`.

- **Example:** *Malletier v. Dooney & Bourke, Inc.*, 500 F. Supp. 2d 276, 279 (S.D.N.Y. 2007) becomes *Malletier*, 500 F. Supp. 2d at 281.

R15.2.3.  Don't use the first party of the case name if that party either is a geographical or governmental unit or a party name that is used for multiple cases. Otherwise, it may confuse the reader.

- **Example:** *United States v. Carmel*, 548 F.3d 571 (7th Cir. 2008) becomes *Carmel*, 548 F.3d at 573.

- **Example:** *Gonzalez v. Raich*, 545 U.S. 1 (2005) becomes *Raich*, 545 U.S. at 8.

R15.2.4.  Shorten a long party name . . . but only if the reference remains clear.

- **Example:** *A Book Named "John Cleveland's Memoirs of a Woman of Pleasure" v. Attorney Gen. of Com. of Mass.*, 383 U.S. 413, 418 (1966) can become *Memoirs*, 383 U.S. at 418.

INDIGO INKLING

In the absence of a clear rule on this matter, a "preceding five" norm has developed wherein one may continue to use a short form citation as long as the full citation appears in one of the previous five footnotes.

There has been some variation in the application of this rule; for example, some practitioners will continue to use the short form throughout an entire article or brief unless they need to use "*id.*" repeatedly, in which event they follow the "preceding five" rule to avoid potential ambiguity. However, none of these conventions are absolute.

R15.3. Using *Id.*

R15.3.1. If you are citing to the same case referenced in the immediately preceding citation, use *id.* as the short form citation.

R15.3.2. *Id.* should be used only if the preceding citation cites to one source.

- **Correct:** In examining the third factor—the proximity of the parties' products in the marketplace—courts assess whether the parties occupy "distinct merchandising markets." *Hormel Foods Corp. v. Jim Henson Prods., Inc.*, 73 F.3d 497, 504 (2d Cir. 1996); *Naked Cowboy v. CBS*, 844 F. Supp. 2d 510, 517-18 (S.D.N.Y. 2012). For example, would an unsophisticated viewer confuse the source of the long-running daytime television series with another party's street performances or his souvenirs? *Naked Cowboy*, 844 F. Supp. 2d at 517-18.

- **Incorrect:** In examining the third factor—the proximity of the parties' products in the marketplace—courts assess whether the parties occupy "distinct merchandising markets." *Hormel Foods Corp. v. Jim Henson Prods., Inc.*, 73 F.3d 497, 504 (2d Cir. 1996); *Naked Cowboy v. CBS*, 844 F. Supp. 2d 510, 517-18 (S.D.N.Y. 2012). For example, would an unsophisticated viewer confuse the source of the long-running daytime television series with another party's street performances or his souvenirs? *Id.*

R15.3.3. If you are referring to the immediately preceding case, but to a different page, use *id.* at `<pincite>`.

- **Example:** In addition to suing all the federal judges in the Southern District of Georgia, the plaintiff also requested the government to fund a sex change for him. *Washington v. Alaimo*, 934 F. Supp. 1395, 1398 (S.D. Ga. 1996). Accordingly, the court ordered plaintiff to show cause why he should not be sanctioned for "filing a motion for improper purposes," such as those hinted at in the title of the pleading, "Motion to Kiss My Ass." *Id.* at 1401.

R15.3.4.  *Id.* can be used for all types of authorities—not only for cases.

- **Example:** After conducting research on the use of Yiddish words in law, the authors found that the word "chutzpah" had appeared in 101 cases since 1980. Alex Kozinski & Eugene Volokh, *Lawsuit Shmawsuit*, 103 Yale L.J. 463, 463 (1993). Their search for the use of "schmuck" was impeded "by the fact that many people are actually named Schmuck." *Id.* at 464–65.

- **Example:** The Supreme Court has consistently proven hostile to any statute that could be interpreted as imposing prior restraint on publications. *See, e.g., Near v. Minnesota ex rel. Olson*, 283 U.S. 697 (1931) (holding that a statute that enabled the state to close down newspapers on grounds they contributed to public nuisance violated the Fourteenth Amendment). The conspicuous absence of prior restraint laws in our nation's history are indicative of a consistent belief they violate constitutional rights. *Id.* at 718.

---

INDIGO INKLING

If there is an explanatory parenthetical or phrase in the preceding citation, it is not incorporated with the use of *id.*

---

## C. STATUTES, RULES, REGULATIONS, AND OTHER LEGISLATIVE & ADMINISTRATIVE MATERIALS

### R16. Federal Statutes

---

INDIGO INKLING

Don't italicize anything in a statute citation. The symbol "§" means "section," and "§§" is the plural form. The section symbol(s) are always followed by a space.

---

R16.1.  Basic citation form

R16.1.1.  A full citation to a federal statute includes three things: (1) the official name of the statute; (2) the published source where the act may be found; and (3) indication of either (i) the source publication date or (ii) the year the statute was passed.

R16.1.2. U.S. Code: For citations to the U.S. Code (the preferred citation): `<Name of Statute [optional]>, <title> U.S.C. § <section number> <(year published)>`.

1.  The U.S.C. is codified once every six years. Therefore, citations to the U.S.C. should be to the appropriate codifying year (*e.g.*, 2000, 2006, 2012). Cite the most recent edition that includes the version of the statute being cited.

2.  Supplements: If you are citing to a statute that may have been amended after the most recent official codification, be sure to consult the supplements, which are published each year between codifications and are cumulative.

    **Examples:**

    - Federal Food, Drug, and Cosmetic Act, 21 U.S.C. § 387 (2012).

    - Lanham (Trademark) Act, 15 U.S.C. §§ 1051-1141n (2012).

    - Communications Act of 1934, 47 U.S.C. § 223 (2012 & Supp. I 2013).

R16.1.3. U.S. Code Annotated: If the U.S.C. cite is not available, then cite to the U.S. Code Annotated. The citation form is `<Name of Statute>, <title> U.S.C.A. § <section number> <(<Name of Publisher> <year published>)>`.

1.  Note: Electronic databases like Westlaw or LEXIS generally refer to the most recent unofficial code, such as "U.S.C.A" (United States Code Annotated).

2.  List of common unofficial codes. U.S.C.A. is preferred.
    - United States Code Annotated, "U.S.C.A." (published by West).
    - United States Code Service, "U.S.C.S." (published by LexisNexis).
    - Gould's United States Code Unannotated, "U.S.C.U." (published by Gould).

    **Examples:**

    - Stored Communications Act, 18 U.S.C.A. §§ 2701-2711 (West 2000).
    - Mineral Leasing Act of 1920, 30 U.S.C.S. §§ 181-287 (LexisNexis 2015).

R16.1.4. Pinpoint citations: To cite to an individual provision within a statute, use the following form: `<Name of Statute> <original section`

```
number>, <title> <Abbreviation for Name of Statutory Code> §
<section number> <(<Name of Publisher, but only if citing
unofficial code> <year published>)>
```

1. Include the original section number of the provision after the statute name.

2. "Original section number" refers to the section in the original act, whereas "section number" refers to the equivalent section as codified in the code.

   **Examples:**

   - Drug Price Competition and Patent Term Restoration Act § 202, 17 U.S.C. § 271(e) (2012).

   - Digital Millennium Copyright Act of 1998 § 103, 17 U.S.C.A. § 1201 (West 2008).

R16.1.5. Official Session Laws: If neither a U.S. Code or U.S. Code Annotated citation is available, then cite to official session laws, using the following forms:

1. Cite without pinpoint: <Name of Statute,> Pub. L. No. <____>, <volume> Stat. <page number> <(year passed)>.

2. Cite with pinpoint: <Name of Statute,> Pub. L. No. <____>, <original section number>, <volume> Stat. <page number>, <page pinpoint> <(year passed)>.

   **Examples:**

   - Family Sponsor Immigration Act of 2002, Pub. L. No. 107-150, 116 Stat. 74.

   - Patient Protection and Affordable Care Act, Pub. L. No. 111-148, § 1101, 124 Stat. 119, 141-43 (2010).

## R17. State Statutes

R17.1.  Official state codes: You should cite state statutes to official codes if at all possible. State code compilations are ranked by order of preference (in a manner that seems arbitrary); those rankings are available in Table T3.

R17.2.  The elements of a citation to a state code include: <Name of Code, abbreviated> § <section number> <(year published)>

**Examples:**

- Ala. Code § 13A-12-5(a)(1) (2000) ("A person commits the offense of unlawful bear exploitation if he or she knowingly . . . [p]romotes, engages in, or is employed at a bear wrestling match.").

- N.Y. Arts & Cult. Aff. Law § 60.03 (McKinney 2000) (prohibiting the sale of knowingly forged sports personality autographs).

# R18. Rules of Procedure and Evidence, Restatements, and Uniform Acts

R18.1.  Rules of Evidence and Procedure

R18.1.1.  Cite current or uniform rules of evidence or procedure by indicating the abbreviation of the source, followed by the rule number (no comma in between).

**Examples:**

- Fed. R. Civ. P. 12(b)(1).
- Fed. R. App. P. 1.
- Unif. R. Evid. 601.

R18.1.2.  We do not mandate specific abbreviations, but here are several suggestions:

- Federal Rules of Civil Procedure: Fed. R. Civ. P.
- Federal Rules of Criminal Procedure: Fed. R. Crim. P.
- Federal Rules of Appellate Procedure: Fed. R. App. P.
- Federal Rules of Evidence: Fed. R. Evid.

R18.2.  Restatements

R18.2.1.  Cite Restatements by indicating the title of the particular Restatement cited, followed by the number of the section containing the material you are referencing, followed by the name of the publisher and the year published in parentheses.

- Do not use a comma in between title and section number, or between the section number and the year parenthetical.
- You may in addition refer to a comment by its letter designation if the material you are citing is contained in a comment.
- Comments are abbreviated "cmt."

**Examples:**

- Restatement (Second) of Trusts § 46 (Am. Law Inst. 1959).
- Restatement (Third) of The Law Governing Lawyers § 2 cmt. e (Am. Law Inst. 2000).

- Restatement (Third) of Prop.: Servitudes § 7.1 (Am. Law Inst. 2000).

---

**INDIGO INKLING**

It is unclear whether *The Bluebook* requires citation to different volumes. In practice, it makes little difference since the section number will direct the reader to the appropriate volume.

---

R18.3. Uniform Commercial Code: Cites to the Uniform Commercial code take the following form: U.C.C. § <section number> (<publisher> <year published>).

   ◦ **Example:** U.C.C § 9-105 (Unif. Law Comm'n 2010).

R18.4. Uniform Laws Annotated: Citations to the Uniform Laws Annotated take the following form: <Title of Act> § <section number>, <volume> U.L.A. <page> <(year published)>.

   1. Use the abbreviations specified in Table T11; thus, "Uniform" becomes "Unif."

   2. Cite the title of the act in full, including year of enactment where it is included in the title.

   **Examples:**

   - Unif. Rules of Evidence (1974) § 702 note 24, 13E U.L.A. 114 (2011)
   - Unif. Mediation Act § 8, 7A Pt. III U.L.A. 137 (2006).

---

**INDIGO INKLING**

Judge Posner has criticized the long lists of uniform abbreviations mandated by *The Bluebook* as a contradiction in terms, since a non-obvious abbreviation (one you must learn from a predesignated list) will likely confuse the reader, and so should not be used at all. Still, we follow the system of abbreviations *The Bluebook* requires as a matter of consistency.

---

# R19. Administrative Rules and Regulations

R19.1. Citations to "administrative" rules and regulations—that is, those promulgated by an administrative agency (e.g., the Environmental Protection Agency or the Food and Drug Administration)—take the following form: `<title number of CFR provision>` C.F.R. § `<section number> <(year published)>`.

R19.2. If the regulation is generally referred to by name or listing the name and/or the name of the agency issuing the regulation would otherwise improve clarity, include it at the beginning of the citation. Citations to administrative rules and regulations that include the regulation name take the following form: `<Name of the Regulation and/or Name of the Agency Promulgating the Regulation>`, `<title no. of CFR provision>` C.F.R. § `<section number> <(year published)>`.

R19.3. Include a parenthetical to explain content of rule or regulation where that information would be helpful.

**Examples:**

- 36 C.F.R. § 272.1 (2014) (defining the Forest Service's iconic character as "a fanciful owl, who wears slacks (forest green when colored), a belt (brown when colored), and a Robin Hood style hat (forest green when colored) with a feather (red when colored), and who furthers the slogan, Give a Hoot, Don't Pollute").

- DOE Employee Privacy Standards, 10 C.F.R. § 1008.3 (2000).

---

INDIGO INKLING
There aren't specific rules for state agency citations—just cite them using approximately the same form as you would the federal rules.

---

## R20. Federal Taxation Materials

R20.1. Internal Revenue Code: Citations to the Internal Revenue Code take either of two forms:

R20.1.1. Citations to the code itself take the following form: I.R.C. § `<section number> <(year published)>`.

R20.1.2. Citations to Title 26 of the U.S. Code, which is where the Internal Revenue Code is codified, take the following form: 26 U.S.C. § `<section number> <(year published)>`.

**Examples:**

- I.R.C. § 312 (2014).
- 26 U.S.C. § 312 (2014).

R20.2. Treasury Regulations

- The Department of the Treasury issues Treasury Regulations pursuant to § 7805 of the Internal Revenue Code. Treasury Regulations are codified in Title 26 of the Code of Federal Regulations ("C.F.R."), but should be cited as "Treas. Reg." according to the following form: Treas. Reg. § `<section number> <(year published)>`. If the regulation is temporary, then begin the citation with Temp. Treas. Reg. instead.

  **Examples:**

- Treas. Reg. § 1.414(r)-8 (1994).
- Temp. Treas. Reg. § 1.274-5T(6) (1985).

R20.3. Treasury Determinations

- Cite Revenue Rulings ("Rev. Rul."), Revenue Procedures ("Rev. Proc."), and Treasury Decisions ("T.D.") to the following sources, in the following order of preference:

- Cumulative Bulletin ("C.B.")
- Internal Revenue Bulletin ("I.R.B.")
- Treasury Decisions Under Internal Revenue Laws ("Treas. Dec. Int. Rev.").

  - **Examples:**
- Rev. Rul. 81-225, 1981-2 C.B. 12.
- Rev. Proc. 97-27, 1997-21 I.R.B. 11.
- T.D. 2135, 17 Treas. Dec. Int. Rev. 39 (1915).

# R21. Legislative Materials

R21.1. Federal Bills and Resolutions
If unenacted, cite as follows: `<name of bill, if helpful>, <abbreviation from the list below> <bill number>, <number of the Congress> <section, if not citing the entire bill> <year of publication>`, with additional information when needed to distinguish between different versions of the bill in a given Congress, with names of subcommittees and committees abbreviated according to the form set out in Table T5, Table T11, and Table T12.

Select an abbreviation based on the type of bill or resolution:

| Type | Abbreviation |
| --- | --- |
| Senate Bill | S. |
| House Bill | H.R. |
| Senate Resolution | S. Res. |
| House Resolution | H.R. Res. |
| Senate Joint Resolution | S.J. Res. |
| House Joint Resolution | H.R.J. Res. |
| Senate Concurrent Resolution | S. Con. Res. |
| House Concurrent Resolution | H.R. Con. Res. |
| Senate Executive Resolution | S. Exec. Res. |

**Examples:**

- S. 812, 108th Cong. (2003).

- Clinical Social Work Medicare Equality Act of 2001, S. 1083, 107th Cong. § 2(b) (2001).

- ABLE Act of 2014, H.R. 647, 113th Cong. (as passed by House, Dec. 3, 2014).

- H.R. 1746, 111th Cong. § 2(c)(4) (as reported by H. Comm. on Transp. and Infrastructure, Apr. 23, 2009).

- H.R. Res. 431, 114th Cong. (2015).

- S.J. Res. 12, 109th Cong. (2005).

---

INDIGO INKLING
When citing Congressional legislation, you can include in your citation whether it was enacted in the first or second session of Congress.

---

R21.2. Enacted federal bills and resolutions

Once enacted, bills and joint resolutions are statutes and should be cited as such, except cite them as unenacted bills or resolutions when showing the legislation's history. Cite enacted simple resolutions and concurrent resolutions as if they were unenacted, but add an "(enacted)" parenthetical if it would be helpful.

R21.3. State bills and resolutions

Cite as follows: `<number of bill or resolution>, <number, or year if unnumbered, of the legislative body>, <number or designation of the legislative session> <name of state, abbreviated as in` <u>Table T12.1</u>`, and year of enactment or publication, if unenacted>`.

**Examples:**

◦ L.D. 3, 127th Leg., Reg. Sess. (Me. 2015).

R21.4. Committee Hearings

R21.4.1. Cite committee hearings as follows: `<full title of hearing>`: *Hearing on* `<bill number, if any>` *Before the* `<name of committee or subcommittee>, <number of the Congress> <optional pincite to page number> <year of publication> <name and title of speaker>`. For the names of subcommittees and committees, abbreviate according to the form set out in <u>Table T5</u>, <u>Table T11</u>, and <u>Table T12</u>. For the names of individuals, abbreviate using <u>Table T10</u>.

R21.4.2. For state committee hearings, cite as follows: `<full title of hearing>`: *Hearing on* `<bill number, if any>` *Before the* `<name of committee or subcommittee>, <number of the legislative session> <optional pincite to page number> <abbreviation for the state's name from` <u>Table T12.1</u>`> <year of publication> <name and title of speaker>`. For the names of subcommittees and committees, abbreviate according to the form set out in <u>Table T5</u>, <u>Table T11</u>, and <u>Table T12</u>. For the names of individuals, abbreviate using <u>Table T10</u>.

**Examples:**

▪ *Cell Tax Fairness Act of 2008: Hearing on H.R. 5793 Before the Subcomm. on Commercial and Administrative Law of the H. Comm. on the Judiciary*, 110th Cong. 12 (2008) (statement of Zoe Lofgren, Member, H. Comm. on the Judiciary).

▪ *Welfare and Poverty in America: Hearing before the S. Comm. on Fin.*, 114th Cong. (2015) (statement of Dr. Pamela Loprest, Senior Fellow, Urban Institute).

▪ *Testimony from invited guests addressing the use of eminent domain in the State: Hearing before the Assemb. Commerce and Econ. Dev. Com.*,

2006–2007 Sess. 5 (N.J. 2006) (statement of Guy R. Gregg, Assemblyman).

- *Hearing on L.D. 319 Before the Health and Human Servs. Comm.*, 127th Leg., Reg. Sess. (Me. 2015) (statement of Susan Lamb, Executive Director, Maine Chapter of the National Association of Social Workers).

R21.5.  Federal reports

R21.5.1.   Cite numbered federal reports as follows: `<name of house, in small caps>` Rep. No. `<number of the Congress, followed by a hyphen and the number of the report>`, `<at optional pincite> <year of publication> <parenthetical to indicate conference report, if applicable>`

**Examples:**

- S. Rep. No. 106-261, at 441 (2000).
- H.R. Rep. No. 110-803, at 105 (2008) (Conf. Rep.).

R21.5.2.   Citations to federal and state non-statutory legislative materials, including legislative history and unenacted bills, aren't expressed in a uniform manner, but generally include the following elements:

- title, if available,
- name of legislative body, abbreviated
- section number, page no. or number of report
- number of Congress and/or legislative session
- (publication year)
- (if the bill or resolution was enacted). Only include this additional parenthetical if the bill was enacted; if unenacted, you don't need to add anything extra.

**Examples:**

- Paycheck Fairness Act, H.R. 11, 111th Cong. § 203 (2009).
- American Clean Energy and Security Act, H.R. 2454, 111th Cong. (2009).
- S. 2318, 112th Cong. (2013) (enacted).

# R22. Short Form Citation of Legislative and Administrative Materials

R22.1.  The first time you mention a statute, rule, regulation, or legislative material, use the full citation.

R22.2.  For subsequent citations in the same general discussion, you may use any short form that clearly identifies the source.

R22.3. Use of "*id.*": see below . . .

| Full citation | id. citation for same provision | id. citation for different provision within same title |
|---|---|---|
| 7 U.S.C. § 7101 (2012). | *Id.* | *Id.* § 7102(26). |
| 9 C.F.R. § 54.1 (2014). | *Id.* | *Id.* § 151.9. |

# R23. Sources and Authorities: Constitutions

R23.1.  Citations to the U.S. Constitution follow a simple form, elaborated below:

- ◦ `<U.S. Const.> <cited section of constitution, abbreviated> <number of article or amendment in Roman numeral form> <§ and pinpoint, if applicable> <(additional information, if needed)>`.

R23.2. Use Table T12 and Table T13 to find abbreviations.

R23.3.  Citations to state constitutions are expressed the same format, substituting U.S. with the abbreviated name of the state.

- **Examples:**
  - ◦ U.S. Const. amend. XIII, § 1 (abolishing slavery in the United States).
  - ◦ U.S. Const. amend. XVIII (repealed 1933).
  - ◦ U.S. Const. pmbl.
  - ◦ Ariz. Const. art. XVI, § 2 (providing for the creation of a "National Guard of Arizona").

---

INDIGO INKLING
Perhaps because constitutions are considered Capital-I important, they should never be expressed in the short form **except** for *id.*

---

# D. COURT & LITIGATION DOCUMENTS

## R24. Citing Court or Litigation Documents from Your Case

The full citation for a court or litigation document includes:

R24.1.  Document title

- Use the tables to figure out what to abbreviate.

  - **Exception:** Never abbreviate if the abbreviation would confuse the reader.

  - Always abbreviate an official record, such as the appellate record, to "R."

  - **Example:** For their own profit and advantage, Defendants are misappropriating the non-transformed, copyrighted material in which each Plaintiff has invested heavily. Compl. for Copyright Infringement 11.

R24.2.  The exact page and line (or paragraph) you're referring to

- Use "at" if citing to an appellate record.

- Don't use "p." before the page number.

- Use commas only if necessary to avoid confusion.

- Use colon to separate page and line.

R24.3.  Date of document, if the date is particularly relevant or omitting the date could cause confusion

- Miller Aff. ¶ 8, Jan. 12, 2015.

- Pl.'s Br. 4–5, May 7, 2014.

- Trial Tr. vol. 3, 45, Mar. 5, 2015.

R24.4.  Electronic Case Filing number, if applicable :

- Include an ECF number in your own case whenever a document has been filed electronically. For other cases, the ECF number is optional unless it is necessary to find the document.

- Find the ECF number on PACER, a federal case management system that assigns each case document a document number.

- Use the page number on the original document, not the ECF page number.

R24.5.  Citations to court or litigation documents may also be enclosed in parentheses:

- (Mem. Opp'n 7)

**Examples:**

- Defendants' evidence in support of their "fraud on the copyright office" defense consists of nothing more than unsupported assertions in their Motion, multiple irrelevant affidavits from previously undisclosed third parties, inadmissible correspondence between counsel, and examples of prior lawsuits that all ended short of judicial determination. Pl.'s Resp. to Defs.' Mot. for Summ. J. at 14.

- Pl.'s Compl. ¶ 12, ECF No. 147.

- Sanchez Dep. 1:1–2, Jan. 3, 2005, ECF No. 8.

## R25. Citing Court or Litigation Documents from Another Case

R25.1.  After you cite to the document according to the rules set out directly above, add the full citation for the case where it comes from, and end with the case docket number in parentheses.

R25.2.  If there has been no decision in the case you're citing, then replace the year in parentheses with the date on which the filing was made.

**Examples:**

- Pl.'s Resp. to Defs.' Mot. for Summ. J. 14, *Martinez-Mendoza v. Champion Int'l Corp.*, 340 F.3d 1200 (11th Cir. 2003) (No. 06-19139).

- Compl. 5, *Parsell v. Shell Oil Co.*, 421 F. Supp. 1275 (D. Conn. 1976).

- Compl. 2, *Jones v. Smith*, No. 09-230 (9th Cir. Apr. 17, 2015)

## R26. Short Form Citation for Court Documents

Use a short form citation for court documents when:

1. there is no mistaking what the short citation refers to;

2. the full citation is not too far away (the full citation can be to the case itself, any other document from the case, or to the same document); and

3. the reader has easy access to the full citation.

Don't use "id." for court documents, unless it saves a lot of space. Unlike cases, court documents may be cited using *supra*.

**Examples:**

| Full Form (Original citation) | Short Form Citation (subsequent reference) |
|---|---|
| Pl.'s Resp. to Defs.' Mot. for Summ. J. at 14, *Martinez-Mendoza v. Champion Int'l Corp.*, 340 F.3d 1200 (11th Cir. 2003) (No. 06-19139). | Pl.'s Resp. to Defs.' Mot. for Summ. J. at 14, *Martinez-Mendoza*, 340 F.3d 1200 (No. 06-19139). |
| Decl. of Martha Woodmansee at 7, *Salinger v. Colting*, 641 F. Supp. 2d 250 (S.D.N.Y. 2010) (No. 09 Civ. 05095). | Decl. of Martha Woodmansee at 7, *Salinger*, 641 F. Supp. 2d 250 (No. 09 Civ. 05095). |

## R27. Capitalization Within the Text of Court Documents and Legal Memoranda

R27.1.  Capitalize "Court" if:

- you are referring to the U.S. Supreme Court.

- you are referring to the court you're sending the document to.

- you are naming the court in full.

**Example:** The U.S. Court of Appeals held that actress's performance satisfied minimum requirements for performance to be copyrightable.

**But:** The *Aalmuhammed* court explained that "the word author is traditionally used to mean the originator or the person who causes something to come into being."

R27.2.  Capitalize **"Plaintiff," "Defendant," "Appellant"** and **"Appellee,"** unless you are referring to parties from other litigation.

- **Example:** The Court concluded that it was unclear whether the Plaintiff had a copyright interest in her acting performance.

- **But, if referring to parties from other litigation:** In *Bobbs-Merrill* the plaintiff-copyright owner sold its book with a printed notice announcing that any retailer who sold the book for less than one dollar was liable for copyright infringement.

R27.3.  Capitalize **court document titles** if:

- the document is filed in your dispute and

- you're using the exact title or short form. (Do not abbreviate court documents within the text.)

R27.4.  Do not capitalize the name for a type of court document, such as an injunction, petition, etc.

# E. BOOKS & NON-PERIODICALS

## R28. Full Citation for Books & Non-Periodicals

A full citation to a book or other non-periodical is made up of the following elements:

1. Volume number (if there is more than one volume).

2. Names of the authors, as listed on the publication.

   ◦ For two authors, list in the same order and use an "&."

   ◦ For more than two authors, use an "et al." after the first name and stop there. (If you're bored, feel free to list out all the authors with an "&" before the last.)

   ◦ Use titles that follow an author's name (Sr.) but not titles that precede them (Hon.)

3. Italicized title of the publication, capitalized as necessary.

   ◦ For law review articles, use small caps for both the title and author, and do not italicize the title.

4. The exact page number you are referring to. If you are citing a work organized using sections or paragraphs, use those instead, adding a page number only if helpful.

5. Year of publication, name of editor or translator (if applicable), edition (if more than one), all in parentheses.

   ◦ If listing an editor or a translator, then follow the name with ed., or trans., respectively. Include that comma before the year of publication.

   ◦ Cite the most recent edition, unless you have a really good (read: substantive) reason for citing older.

**Examples:**

- Marc A. Franklin et al., *Mass Media Law Cases and Materials* 472 (8th ed. 2011).

- 1 Melville B. Nimmer & David Nimmer, *Nimmer on Copyright* § 1.01[B][1][a] at 1–14–15 (2011).

- Gabriel García Márquez, *One Hundred Years of Solitude* (Gregory Rabassa trans., Harper & Row 2003) (1967).

- Roger Angell, *This Old Man, in The Best American Essays 2015* (Ariel Levy & Robert Atwan eds.,2015).

## R29. Short Form Citation for Books & Non-Periodicals

R29.1. *Id.*: References to books or non-periodical material cited in the immediately preceding citation (when that citation contains only one source) should be followed by "*id.*"

- Update the page number you're referring to within that source, as needed.

- Do not use for internal cross references, or for citing back to a body of collected works when you are really supposed to be citing a single work from that body.

R29.2. *supra*: Can be used instead of "*id.*" Supra should include:

- last name of the author

- italicize "supra", but not the comma that follows

- update the specific page you're referring to

**Examples:**

| Full: | *Id.:* | Supra |
|---|---|---|
| B.F. Skinner, *Beyond Freedom and Dignity* 32 (2002). | *Id.* at 21. | Skinner, *supra*, at 21. |
| 3 Melville Nimmer & David Nimmer, *Nimmer on Copyright* § 12.01 (Rev. ed. 2015) | *See id.* § 14.02. | *See* Nimmer & Nimmer, *supra*, § 14.02 |
| Graham C. Lilly et al., *Principles of Evidence* 122 (6th ed. 2012) | *Id.* At 88–103 | Lilly, *supra*, at 90 |

# F. JOURNALS, MAGAZINES, & NEWSPAPER ARTICLES

## R30. Full Citation for Journals, Magazines & Newspaper Articles

R30.1. Citations to **consecutively paginated journals** (that is, journals in which page numbering is continued from the last issue) take the following form: `<Author's Name(s)>, <Italicized Title of the Article>, <volume number, if applicable> <Name of Publication, abbreviated> <page number of first page of article cited>, <pincite, if citing to specific point> <(year published)>.`

- **Example:** Liz Brown, *Bridging The Gap: Improving Intellectual Property Protection for the Look and Feel of Websites*, 3 N.Y.U. J. Intell. Prop. & Ent. L. 310, 351 (2014).

R30.2. Citations to **journals and magazines with standard pagination** (that is, where pagination re-starts for every issue) take the following form:

`<Author's Name(s)>, <Italicized Title of the Article>, <Name of Publication, abbreviated>, <full date of publication>, at <page number of first page of article cited>`. You may add a pincite to the end of the citation, if you are citing to a particular point in the article, in the following form: `, <pincite>`.

- **Example:** Jack Dickey, *The Power of Taylor Swift*, Time, Nov. 24, 2014, at 13, 17.

R30.3. Citations to material written by students in law journals take the following form: `<Author's Name(s), if signed with more than initials>, <Designation of Piece>, <Italicized Title of the Article>, <volume number, if applicable> <Name of Publication, abbreviated> <page number of first page of article cited>, <pincite, if citing to specific point> <(year published)>`.

**Examples:**

- Amanda Levendowski, Note, *Using Copyright to Combat Revenge Porn*, 3 N.Y.U. J. Intell. Prop. & Ent. L. 422 (2014).

- Victoria Nemiah, Note, *License and Registration, Please: Using Copyright "Conditions" To Protect Free/Open Source Software*, 3 N.Y.U. J. Intell. Prop. & Ent. L. 358, 361 (2014).

- Comment, *Law and Lawns: Mandatory Water Restrictions and Substantive Due Process*, 7 Calif. L. Rev. 138 (1972).

R30.4. Citations to **newspaper articles** take the following form: `<Author's Name(s), if signed>, <Italicized Title of the Article>, <Name of Publication, abbreviated>, <full date of publication>, at <number of first page of article>`.

**Examples:**

- Vikas Bajaj, *Rules for the Marijuana Market*, N.Y. Times, Aug. 5, 2014, at A20.

- Charlie Savage, *U.N. Commission Presses U.S. on Torture*, N.Y. Times, Nov. 14, 2014, at A6.

- Peter Baker & Julie Hirschfeld Davis, *Obama, Down But Not Out, Presses Ahead*, N.Y. Times, Nov. 14, 2014, at A1.

## R31. Short Form Citation for Journals, Magazines & Newspaper Articles

If you have already cited a work from a periodical in full . . .

R31.1.  Use *"id."* to avoid placing two full citations that are exactly the same right next to each other.

  ◦ **Example:** The 24-year-old pop star spoke with TIME this fall as she readied for the release of her new album and again as she watched its record reception. Jack Dickey, *The Power of Taylor Swift*, Time, Nov. 24, 2014, at 13. 'Other women who are killing it should motivate you,' she says. *Id.*

R31.2.  Use *"supra"* when you've used the full citation before, but it's not right next to the sentence you will provide the citation for now. Use a shortened title if you cite to multiple sources from the same author.

  ◦ **Example:** Brown, *Bridging The Gap, supra*, at 320.

## G. INTERNET SOURCES

## R32. General Principles for Internet Sources

R32.1.  When an authenticated, official, or exact copy of a document is available online, *cite* as if to the equivalent print source (i.e., URL information should not be included).

  ◦ Exact copy: unaltered online reproduction of the entirety of a printed source, including pagination.

  ◦ Official copy: version of document designated "official" by a federal, state, or local government.

  ◦ Authenticated copy: source that uses some authenticating tool, such as a digital signature. This is generally the preferred version.

R32.2.  For sources that are available in a non-internet source, append the URL to the end of the citation if doing so would make accessing the source significantly easier.

  ◦ **Example:** Daniel E. Ho & Frederick Schauer, *Testing the Marketplace of Ideas*, 90 N.Y.U. L. Rev. 1160, 1175 (2015), http://www.nyulawreview.org/sites/default/files/pdf/NYULawReview-90-4-Ho_Schauer.pdf

R32.3.  For Internet sources that have the characteristics of a print source, cite as if you were citing the print source, and append the URL to the end of the citation. Internet sources have the characteristics of a print source if the source has all the information needed to cite it according to another rule and the source has a fixed, permanent pagination (such as a PDF).

R32.4. For cites directly to webpages and other Internet sources, follow the formula in Rule 33, below.

---

INDIGO INKLING

Note that many of the Internet citation rules are little more than common sense (that's a compliment, not a dig). For example: include the URL that most directly links your reader to the authority, as you don't want to send readers on a wild goose chase through the recesses of the Internet in search of a source. For completeness sake, we include these rules below, even though most people would probably intuit them.

---

## R33. Basic Formula for Internet Sources

Citations to Internet sources follow this form: `<Author Name>, <Title of Website Page>, <Main Website Title>, <pincite> <(Date & Time Accessed)>, <URL>`.

R33.1. Author Name(s)

R33.1.1. Actual authors: When available, use the name(s) of the actual authors(s) of the source.

R33.1.2. Institutional authors: When the name of the actual author is unavailable, use the name of the institution associated with the source if one is clearly apparent.

- Institutional authors should be omitted if the website's title makes the domain's owner clear.

- Institutional authors should be abbreviated (see Table T11 and Table T12 for abbreviations).

R33.1.3. Forum authors: For web posts and comments, use the actual name of the post author, or the username of the post author if the actual name is not available.

- For comments, the author of the comment should be included if available, but the author of the original post need not be cited.

R33.1.4. If the name of the author is unavailable in each of the above forms, it may be omitted from the basic formula.

R33.2. Title of Specific Website Page

R33.2.1. Include the particular cited page within the website. This title should be based on either the title bar or the heading of that page as viewed in the browser.

R33.2.2. The included title should be informative but not unduly long, if possible.

R33.2.3. Include the title of certain pages linked from main website when relevant, including postings, comments, and titles of subheadings (in italics). Where relevant, as in comments, subheadings should indicate their relationship to the page to which they are responsive.

- **Example:** Mike Masnick, *Left Shark Bites Back: 3D Printer Sculptor Hires Lawyer To Respond to Katy Perry's Bogus Takedown*, TechDirt (Feb. 9, 2015, 12:27 PM), https://www.techdirt.com/articles/20150209/11373729960/left-shark-bites-back-3d-printer-sculptor-hires-lawyer-to-respond-to-katy-perrys-bogus-takedown.shtml.

- **Example:** Nasch, Re: Costumes, IP, and Ownership Rights, Comment to *Left Shark Bites Back*, TechDirt (Feb. 14, 2015, 9:55 AM), https://www.techdirt.com/articles/20150209/11373729960/left-shark-bites-back-3d-printer-sculptor-hires-lawyer-to-respond-to-katy-perrys-bogus-takedown.shtml.

R33.2.4. Descriptive titles (not italicized) may also be used where page headings alone are not clear.

- **Example:** Parker Higgins & Sarah Jeong, Archive of 5 Useful Articles Newsletter, 5 Useful Articles, http://tinyletter.com/5ua (last visited March 2, 2015).

R33.3. Main Website Title

R33.3.1. Include the domain name/ homepage where the citation may be found.

R33.3.2. Title should be abbreviated (see Table T12, Table T15, and Table T18 for abbreviations).

---

INDIGO INKLING
Think of a *webpage* as the page in your Internet browser (Chrome, Firefox, Safari, etc.) where you can scroll up and down. Think of a *website* as a group of webpages that work together. For example, abovethelaw.com is a website. Once you click on an article or a tab, then you're on a webpage.

---

R33.4. Pincite

R33.4.1. Include when an electronic document preserves the pagination of a printed version. Cite to pages as they would appear on the document if printed.

- **Example:** James Huguenin-Love, *Song on Wire: A Technical Analysis of* ReDigi *and the Pre-Owned Digital Media Marketplace*, 4 N.Y.U. J. Intell. Prop. & Ent. L. 1, 4 (2014), http://jipel.law.nyu.edu/wp-content/uploads/2015/02/JIPEL-Winter-2014-Edition.pdf.

## R33.5. Date & Time

R33.5.1. Omit time (i) if the source is not updated throughout the day or (ii) if there is no time listed

R33.5.2. If no date is provided cite to the *last modified* or *last updated* date for the URL, or, if none of the above are provided, use the *last visited* date. Any date cited in one of these three formats should be placed after the URL in the citation.

- **Example:** ESPN, http://www.espn.go.com/ (last visited Apr. 8, 2015).

## R33.6. URL

R33.6.1. Cite in its entirety unless the URL is especially long or unwieldy.

R33.6.2. If the URL is too long and unwieldy, cite just to the root URL and include a parenthetical directing the user to the specific material cited.

R33.6.3. When helpful, include URL to an archived version of the webpage in brackets

R33.6.4. When a website is served by multiple URLs, use the primary one.

- **Example:** Chris Cillizza, *Winners and Losers of the 2014 Midterm Elections*, Wash. Post Blogs (Nov. 5, 2014, 10:25 AM), http://www.washingtonpost.com/blogs/the-fix/wp/2014/11/04/winners-and-losers-of-the-2014-election-early-edition/

- **Example:** Laura Moy, *Public Knowledge & Consumers Petition Copyright Office for Right to Unlock Access to Their Own Stuff*, Public Knowledge Blogs (Nov. 3, 2014), https://www.publicknowledge.org/news-blog/blogs/public-knowledge-consumers-petition-copyright-office-for-right-to-unlock-ac.

- **Example:** *Google Books Ngram Viewer*, Google, https://books.google.com/ngrams (select corpus "English Fiction"; then search for "Arrakis") (last visited Apr. 17, 2012).

- **Example:** Kevin Underhill, *Gollum Experts to Testify, Says Court*, Lowering the Bar (Dec. 4, 2015), http://www.loweringthebar.net/2015/12/gollum-experts.html [https://web.archive.org/web/20151208124302/http://www.loweringthebar.net/2015/12/gollum-experts.html]

---

INDIGO INKLING

When a document is available in multiple formats, cite to the format that best preserves the document as it would display if printed. This will allow citations to specific page numbers (for pincites) regardless of whether it is being viewed digitally or in print. For example, PDF is preferred over HTML.

---

## R34. Short Form Citations for Internet Sources

*Id.* and *supra* can be used, together with the author name, as a short form citation following the full citation of an Internet source. Note: if no author is provided, use the title of the source (see section [NUMBER], above).

**Examples:**

- Full cite: Chris Cillizza, *Winners and Losers of the 2014 Midterm Elections*, Wash. Post Blogs (Nov. 5, 2014, 10:25 AM), http://www.washingtonpost.com/blogs/the-fix/wp/2014/11/04/winners-and-losers-of-the-2014-election-early-edition/

- Short form: Cillizza, *supra*.

- Full cite: Superfan Suits, http://www.superfansuits.com/ (last visited Feb. 21, 2015) (motto: "Tight and Bright. Since 2008").

- Short form: Superfan Suits, *supra*.

# H. EXPLANATORY PARENTHETICALS

Sometimes, it is helpful to include extra information to explain the relevance of certain citations. This information goes at the end of your citation but before any citation indicating subsequent history. Explanatory parentheticals may consist of present participles, direct quotations, or short statements.

## R35. General Principles for Explanatory Parentheticals

R35.1. If not quoting the authority, do not begin parenthetical with capital letter.

- **Example:** *Dr. Seuss Enters., L.P. v. Penguin Books USA, Inc.*, 109 F.3d 1394 (9th Cir. 1997) (holding that publisher's parody of O.J. Simpson murder trial was substantially similar to copyrighted work).

R35.2. If quoting the authority, only begin parenthetical with capital letter and end with a period when the parenthetical quoted is or reads as a complete sentence.

- **Example:** *See Ty, Inc. v. Publ'ns Int'l Ltd.*, 292 F.3d 512, 520 (7th Cir. 2002) ("[T]he shortage that creates the secondary market stampedes children into nagging their parents to buy them the latest Beanie Babies, lest they be humiliated by not possessing the Beanie Babies that their peers possess.").

## R36. Order of parentheticals

(date) [hereinafter <short name>] (en banc) (<Lastname, J.>, concurring) (plurality opinion) (per curiam) (alteration in original) (emphasis added) (footnote omitted) (citations omitted) (quoting <another source>) (internal quotation marks omitted) (citing <another source>), http://www.domainname.com (explanatory parenthetical), prior or subsequent history.

When citing directly to Internet sources, the "hereinafter" parenthetical should come right after the URL or, if one exists, the "last visited" parenthetical.

# I. QUOTATIONS

## R37. General Principles for Quotations

R37.1. Quotations should be designated with quotation marks, except for block quotations.

R37.2. The quotation should flow with the rest of the text *unless* it is a block quotation (see below).

R37.3. Punctuation that is part of the quoted text should appear inside the quotation marks. Commas and periods that are not part of the quoted text should also appear inside the quotation marks.

R37.4. Insert the citation sentence for the quoted material directly after the close of the quotation marks.

## R38. Alterations of Quotations

R38.1. Omission of Letters from a Common Root Word: Place an empty bracket at the end of a common root word to indicate the change.

- ◦ **Example:** "The court dismissed the claim[]."

R38.2. Mistakes in the Original Quotation: To acknowledge a significant mistake in the original quotation, keep the problematic word or phrase and follow it with [sic] to indicate this to the reader.

- ◦ **Example:** "The Copyright Office are [sic] a department of the Library of Congress."

R38.3. Substitution of Letters or Words: Any substitutions into quoted material should be bracketed. This includes . . .

- ◦ words which might add clarity and context
- ◦ changes to the capitalization of letters
- ▪ **Example:** "[T]he [Copyright] Office is a department of the Library of Congress."

R38.4. Use of Parenthetical Clauses to Indicate Changes to Quotation

- ◦ (emphasis added)
- ◦ (alteration in original)
- ◦ (citation omitted)
- ◦ (emphasis omitted)
- ◦ (internal quotation marks omitted)
- ◦ (footnote omitted)

R38.5. When using a quotation within a quotation, you can either (1) attribute it to the original source with a parenthetical, or (2) acknowledge it by signalling that its citation has been omitted.

---

INDIGO INKLING

The following should not be indicated in a parenthetical:

- Emphasis (indicated by italics/underline) in a quotation that was copied from the original source.

- Omission of a citation or footnote call number that follows a quotation.

---

# R39. Omissions in Quotations

R39.1. Generally

- ◦ Omissions are indicated by an ellipsis [ . . . ]

- ◦ The ellipsis in legal writing is represented by three periods, with a space after the last letter of the preceding phrase, a space between each period, and a space before the first letter of the following phrase.

- ◦ An ellipsis never begins a quotation.

R39.2. When omitting the beginning of a quoted sentence, do not use an ellipsis. Instead, capitalize the first letter and place it in brackets.

- ◦ **Example:** "[T]he actual knowledge provision turns on whether the provider actually or *subjectively* knew of specific infringement, while the red flag provision turns on whether the provider was subjectively aware of facts that would have made the specific infringement *objectively* obvious to a reasonable person."

R39.3. When omitting the middle of a quoted sentence, insert an ellipsis to indicate the omission

- ◦ **Example:** "The difference between actual and red flag knowledge is . . . between a subjective and an objective standard."

R39.4. When Using a Quotation as a Complete Sentence

- ◦ **Example:** "The difference between actual and red flag knowledge is thus not between specific and generalized knowledge, but instead between a subjective and an objective standard. In other words, the actual knowledge provision turns on whether the provider actually or *subjectively* knew of specific infringement, while the red flag provision turns on whether the provider was subjectively aware of facts that would have made the specific infringement *objectively* obvious to a reasonable person." *Viacom Int'l, Inc. v. YouTube, Inc.*, 676 F.3d 19, 31 (2d Cir. 2012).

R39.5. When Using a Quotation as a Phrase or Clause: If there is an omission within the quotation, mark the omission with an ellipsis.

- ◦ **Example:** *Exxon Mobil Corp. v. Allapattah Servs., Inc.*, 545 U.S. 546, 571 (2005) (noting that "[t]he distinguished jurists who drafted the Subcommittee Working Paper . . . agree that this provision, on its face, overrules *Zahn*.").

R39.6. When omitting material at the end of one sentence and the beginning of the next sentence, use one ellipsis to mark the omission but include the final punctuation mark of the first sentence as well as bracket and capitalize the first letter of the following sentence.

- **Example:** "The difference between actual and red flag knowledge is thus not between specific and generalized knowledge . . . . [T]he red flag provision turns on whether the provider was subjectively aware of facts that would have made the specific infringement *objectively* obvious to a reasonable person."

R39.7. When omitting the end of a quoted sentence, insert an ellipsis between the last letter quoted and the punctuation mark of the original quote.

- **Example:** "The difference between actual and red flag knowledge is thus not between specific and generalized knowledge . . . ."

R39.8. When omitting a footnote or citation, insert a parenthetical indicating the omission immediately after the citation to the quoted source (see above).

R39.9. When omitting material following a *final punctuation mark*, do not use an ellipsis.

- **Example:** "The difference between actual and red flag knowledge is thus not between specific and generalized knowledge, but instead between a subjective and an objective standard."

R39.10.When omitting material following a *final punctuation mark* but including material in the next sentence use an ellipsis to connect the final punctuation with the beginning of the new quote and capitalize and bracket the next letter.

- **Example:** "The difference between actual and red flag knowledge is thus not between specific and generalized knowledge, but instead between a subjective and an objective standard. . . . [T]he red flag provision turns on whether the provider was subjectively aware of facts that would have made the specific infringement *objectively* obvious to a reasonable person."

## R40. Special Rules for Block Quotations

R40.1. Basic form: Set off quotations consisting of 50+ words into a block quotation, which appears as in the example below:

> Here is where the block quotation should begin and here is where it should end. See the indentations on the right and left sides? This is how it should appear in your writing. The reasoning behind this set-

up is to offset the lengthy quotations from the rest of the text and to clearly indicate that this is all directly cited material.

R40.2. Formatting of block quotations.

- Block quotations are single spaced.
- Indent both left and right.
- Block quotations should be formatted with "full justification"—that is, all lines in a paragraph are expanded so they butt up against both the left and right text margins. Note that this is not a Bluebook requirement, but it is required by many law reviews.
- DO NOT use quotation marks surrounding the block quotation.
- Internal quotation marks should appear as in the original.
- The citation following a block quotation should start at the line's left margin, without any indentation.

**Example:** Judge Patterson explains the excellence of the *Harry Potter* series:

> Plaintiff J.K. Rowling is the author of the highly acclaimed *Harry Potter* book series [. . .] Written for children but enjoyed by children and adults alike, the *Harry Potter* series chronicles the lives and adventures of Harry Potter and his friends as they come of age at the Hogwarts School of Witchcraft and Wizardry and face the evil Lord Voldemort. [. . .] It is a tale of a fictional world filled with magical spells, fantastical creatures, and imaginary places and things [. . .]

*Warner Bros. Entm't Inc. v. RDR Books*, 575 F. Supp. 2d 513, 518 (S.D.N.Y. 2008) (describing an excellent book series).

INDIGO INKLING

Here is where some have noted that *The Bluebook* rules sometime produce odd results. *The Bluebook* makes no exception for quotations of 50 or more words in parentheticals (unless used in a footnote in a law review article), meaning that the following footnote is formatted correctly, if bizarrely:

*See id. (*

To perhaps a greater extent than even the legal scholars, modern economists assume that property consists of an ad hoc collection of rights in resources. Indeed there is a tendency among economists to use the term property to describe virtually every device—public or private, common-law or regulatory, contractual or governmental, formal or informal—by which divergences between private and social costs or benefits are reduced.

(citations omitted)).

[Source: http://prawfsblawg.blogs.com/prawfsblawg/2005/05/ the_bluebook_is.html]

# J. TABLES

## T1. Federal Judicial and Legislative Materials

| Materials | Date | Citation |
| --- | --- | --- |
| Supreme Court (U.S.): Cite to U.S., if possible. If not, cite to S. Ct. If that's not possible, cite to L. Ed. If you can cite to none of the above, cite to U.S.L.W. | | |
| United States Reports | | |
| 91 U.S. to date | 1875–date | U.S. |
| Wallace | 1863–1874 | e.g., 68 U.S. (1 Wall.) |
| Black | 1861–1862 | e.g., 66 U.S. (1 Black) |
| Howard | 1843–1860 | e.g., 42 U.S. (1 How.) |
| Peters | 1828–1842 | e.g., 26 U.S. (1 Pet.) |
| Wheaton | 1816–1827 | e.g., 14 U.S. (1 Wheat.) |
| Cranch | 1801–1815 | e.g., 5 U.S. (1 Cranch) |
| Dallas | 1790–1800 | e.g., 1 U.S. (1 Dall.) |
| Supreme Court Reporter | 1882–date | S. Ct. |
| United States Supreme Court Reports, Lawyers' Edition | 1790–date | L. Ed., L. Ed. 2d |
| United States Law Week | 1933–date | U.S.L.W. |
| Circuit Justices (e.g., Burger, Circuit Justice): Cite to U.S., else, cite to S. Ct., L. Ed., or U.S.L.W. in that order of preference. | | |
| United States Reports | 1893–date | U.S. |
| Supreme Court Reporter | 1893–date | S. Ct. |
| United States Supreme Court Reports, Lawyers' Edition | 1790–date | L. Ed., L. Ed. 2d |
| United States Law Week | 1933–date | U.S.L.W. |

Some cases presided over by Circuit Justices are found in other reporters. Cite to these cases in the following manner:

- *Williamson v. United States*, 184 F.2d 280 (Jackson, Circuit Justice, 2d Cir. 1950).

Courts of Appeals (e.g., 2d Cir., D.C. Cir.), previously Circuit Courts of Appeals (e.g., 2d Cir.), and Court of Appeals of/for the District of Columbia (D.C. Cir.): Cite to F., F.2d, or F.3d.

| | | |
| --- | --- | --- |
| Federal Reporter | 1891–date | F., F.2d, F.3d |
| Federal Appendix | 2001–date | F. App'x |

Circuit Courts (e.g., C.C.S.D.N.Y., C.C.D. Cal.) (abolished 1912): Cite to F. or F. Cas.

| | | |
| --- | --- | --- |
| Federal Reporter | 1880–1912 | F. |

| Materials | Date | Citation |
|---|---|---|
| Federal Cases | 1789–1880 | F. Cas. |

Temporary Emergency Court of Appeals (Temp. Emer. Ct. App.) (1971–1993), Emergency Court of Appeals (Emer. Ct. App.) (created 1942, abolished 1961), and Commerce Court (Comm. Ct.) (created 1910, abolished 1913): Cite to F. or F.2d.

| Materials | Date | Citation |
|---|---|---|
| Federal Reporter | 1910–1993 | F., F.2d |

For United States Court of Appeals for the Federal Circuit (Fed. Cir.) (created 1982), successor to the United States Court of Customs and Patent Appeals (C.C.P.A.) (previously the Court of Customs Appeals (Ct. Cust. App.)) and the appellate jurisdiction of the Court of Claims (Ct. Cl.): Cite to F., F.2d, or F.3d; else, cite to the official reporter.

| Materials | Date | Citation |
|---|---|---|
| Federal Reporter | 1910–date | F., F.2d, F.3d |
| Court of Claims Reports | 1956–1982 | Ct. Cl. |
| Court of Customs and Patent Appeals Reports | 1929–1982 | C.C.P.A. |
| Court of Customs Appeals Reports | 1910–1929 | Ct. Cust. |

United States Court of Federal Claims (Fed. Cl.) (created 1992), formerly United States Claims Court (Cl. Ct.) (created 1982), and successor to the original jurisdiction of the Court of Claims (Ct. Cl.): Cite to one of the following reporters:

| Materials | Date | Citation |
|---|---|---|
| Federal Claims Reporter | 1992–date | Fed. Cl. |
| United States Claims Court Reporter | 1983–1992 | Cl. Ct. |
| Federal Reporter | 1930–1932 | F.2d |
| | 1960–1982 | F.2d |
| Federal Supplement | 1932–1960 | F. Supp. |
| Court of Claims Reports | 1863–1982 | Ct. Cl. |

For United States Court of International Trade (Ct. Int'l Trade) (created 1980), formerly United States Customs Court (Cust. Ct.) (created 1926): Cite to the official reporters, if possible; if not, in the following order, cite to F. Supp., F. Supp. 2d, or F. Supp. 3d to Cust. B. & Dec. (an official publication), or to I.T.R.D. (BNA).

| Materials | Date | Citation |
|---|---|---|
| Court of International Trade Reports | 1980–date | Ct. Int'l Trade |
| Customs Court Reports | 1938–1980 | Cust. Ct. |
| Federal Supplement | 1980–date | F. Supp., F. Supp. 2d, F. Supp. 3d |
| Customs Bulletin and Decisions | 1967–date | Cust. B. & Dec. |
| International Trade Reporter Decisions | 1980–date | I.T.R.D. (BNA) |

For District Courts (e.g., D. Mass., S.D.N.Y.): For cases after 1932, cite to F. Supp., F. Supp. 2d, F. Supp. 3d, F.R.D., or B.R.; else, cite to Fed. R. Serv.,Fed. R. Serv. 2d, or Fed. R. Serv. 3d. For prior cases, cite to F., F.2d, or F. Cas.

| Materials | Date | Citation |
|---|---|---|
| Federal Supplement | 1932–date | F. Supp., F. Supp. 2d, F. Supp. 3d |
| Federal Rules Decisions | 1938–date | F.R.D. |
| West's Bankruptcy Reporter | 1979–date | B.R. |

| Materials | Date | Citation |
|---|---|---|
| Federal Rules Service | 1938–date | Fed. R. Serv. (Callaghan), Fed. R. Serv. 2d (Callaghan), Fed. R. Serv. 3d (West) |
| Federal Reporter | 1880–1932 | F., F.2d |
| Federal Cases | 1789–1880 | F. Cas. |

Citations to F. Cas. should give the case number parenthetically.

- *Davey v. The Mary Frost*, 7 F. Cas. 11 (E.D. Tx. 1876) (No. 3591).

For Bankruptcy Courts (e.g., Bankr. N.D. Cal.) and Bankruptcy Appellate Panels (e.g., B.A.P. 1st Cir.), cite to B.R.; else, cite to a service.

| | | |
|---|---|---|
| Bankruptcy Reporter | 1979–date | B.R. |

Judicial Panel on Multidistrict Litigation (J.P.M.L.) (created 1968) and Special Court, Regional Rail Reorganization Act (Reg'l Rail Reorg. Ct.) (created 1973): Cite to F. Supp., F. Supp. 2d., or F. Supp. 3d.

| | | |
|---|---|---|
| Federal Supplement | 1968–date | F. Supp., F. Supp. 2d, F. Supp. 3d |

For Tax Court (T.C.) (created 1942), previously Board of Tax Appeals (B.T.A.), cite to T.C. or B.T.A.; else, cite to T.C.M. (CCH), T.C.M. (P-H), T.C.M. (RIA), or B.T.A.M. (P-H).

| Materials | Date | Citation |
|---|---|---|
| United States Tax Court Reports | 1942–date | T.C. |
| Reports of the United States Board of Tax Appeals | 1924–1942 | B.T.A. |
| Tax Court Memorandum Decisions | 1942–date | T.C.M. (CCH) |
| | 1942–1991 | T.C.M. (P-H) |
| | 1991–date | T.C.M. (RIA) |
| Board of Tax Appeals Memorandum Decisions | 1928–1942 | B.T.A.M. (P-H) |

For United States Court of Appeals for Veterans Claims (Vet. App.), previously United States Court of Veterans Appeals (Vet. App.) (created 1988), cite to Vet. App.

| | | |
|---|---|---|
| West's Veterans Appeals Reporter | 1990–date | Vet. App. |

United States Court of Appeals for the Armed Forces (C.A.A.F.), previously United States Court of Military Appeals (C.M.A.): Cite to C.M.A..

| | | |
|---|---|---|
| Decisions of the United States Court of Military Appeals | 1951–1975 | C.M.A. |
| West's Military Justice Reporter | 1978–date | M.J. |
| Court Martial Reports | 1951–1975 | C.M.R. |

Military Service Courts of Criminal Appeals (A. Ct. Crim. App., A.F. Ct. Crim. App., C.G. Ct. Crim. App., N-M. Ct. Crim. App.), previously Courts of Military Review (e.g., A.C.M.R.), previously Boards of Review (e.g., A.B.R.): For cases after 1950, cite to M.J. or C.M.R. For earlier cases, cite to the official reporter.

| | | |
|---|---|---|
| West's Military Justice Reporter | 1975–date | M.J. |
| Court Martial Reports | 1951–1975 | C.M.R. |

For statutory compilations, cite to U.S.C.

| Materials | Date | Citation |
|---|---|---|
| United States Code (26 U.S.C. may be abbreviated as I.R.C.) | | `<tit. no.>` U.S.C. § x (`<year>`) |
| United States Code Annotated | | `<tit. no.>` U.S.C.A. § x (West `<year>`) |
| United States Code Service | | `<tit. no.>` U.S.C.S. § x (LexisNexis `<year>`) |
| Gould's United States Code Unannotated | | `<tit. no.>` U.S.C.U. § x (Gould `<year>`) |
| Session laws | | |
| United States Statutes at Large | | `<vol. no.>` Stat. `<page no.>` (`<year>`) |

For public laws before 1957, cite by by chapter number; for subsequent public laws, cite by public law number.

## T2. Federal Administrative and Executive Materials

| Administrative Materials | Citation |
|---|---|

**Armed Services Board of Contract Appeals (ASBCA)**

**Decisions:** Cite decisions as: `<case name>`, ASBCA No. `<decision number>`, `<citation to services>` For citations to the *Board of Contract Appeals Decisions* (BCA), published by Commerce Clearing House, the publisher is not indicated and the volume number should be used to indicate the year of the decision.

> RMTC Sys., Inc., ASBCA No. 43466, 93-1 BCA ¶ 25,508.

**Civilian Board of Contract Appeals (CBCA)**

**Decisions:** Cite the same way as a citation for the Armed Services Board of Contract Appeals, but include the opposing agency in the case name.

> G2G, LLC v. Dept. of Commerce, CBCA 4845-R, 15-1 BCA ¶ 36,163.

**Armed Services Board of Contract Appeals (ASBCA)**

**Decisions:** Cite decisions as: `<case name>`, ASBCA No. `<decision number>`, `<citation to services>` For citations to the *Board of Contract Appeals Decisions* (BCA), published by Commerce Clearing House, the publisher is not indicated and the volume number should be used to indicate the year of the decision.

**Commodity Futures Trading Commission (CFTC)**

**Decisions:** Cite as `<case name>`, CFTC No. `<docket number>`, `<secondary source if available>` (`<date>`).

> Windjammer Capital LLC v. Glob. Futures Exch. & Trading Co., Inc., CFTC No. 14-R1, 2015 WL 9434227 (Dec. 22, 2015).

**Interpretive Letters, No-Action Letters, and Exemptive Letters:** Cite a service or an electronic database. Include the full name of the correspondent if available, the CFTC docket number, and the full date on which the letter became publicly available.

**Consumer Financial Protection Bureau (CFPB)**

**Decisions:** Cite as `<case name>`, CFPB No. `<decision number>`, `<secondary source if available>` (`<date>`).

| Administrative Materials | Citation |
|---|---|
| American Express Travel Related Servs., Inc., CFPB No. 2013-CFPB-0013 (Dec. 24, 2013). | |

## Department of Agriculture (USDA)

**Decisions:** Cite to the Agriculture Decisions (Agric. Dec).

Arizona Livestock Auction, Inc., *55 Agric Dec.* 1121 (U.S.D.A. 1996).

**Directives**: Cite as: `<issuing agency abbreviated according to table below> <directive number>, <directive title>` (U.S.D.A. `<year>`).

| | |
|---|---|
| Agricultural Marketing Service | AMS |
| Agricultural Research Service | ARS 218 |
| Animal and Plant Health Inspection Service | APHIS |
| Center for Nutrition Policy and Promotion | CNPP |
| Cooperative State Research, Education, and Extension Service | CSREES |
| Economic Research Service | ERS |
| Farm Service Agency | FSA |
| Food and Nutrition Service | FNS |
| Food Safety and Inspection Service | FSIS |
| Foreign Agricultural Service | FAS |
| Forest Service | FS |
| Grain Inspection, Packers, and Stockyards Administration | GIPSA |
| National Agricultural Library | NAL |
| National Agricultural Statistics Service | NASS |
| National Institute of Food and Agriculture | NIFA |
| National Resources Conservation Service | NRCS |
| Risk Management Agency | RMA |
| Rural Development | RD |
| Rural Housing Service | RHS |
| Rural Utilities Service | RUS |

## Department of Commerce, National Oceanic and Atmospheric Administration (NOAA)

**Decisions in Consistency Appeals Under the Coastal Zone Management Act:** Citation format for decisions of the Secretary of Commerce under the Coastal Zone Management Act: Decision and Findings in the Consistency Appeal of `<party name>`, from an objection by `<state or relevant state agency's name>` (Sec'y of Commerce `<date>`). If these decisions are not published in an official reporter; indicate the source where the decision is located.

**Other NOAA Decisions:** For decisions of administrative law judges in civil administrative law cases, cite to the *Ocean Resources and Wildlife Reporter* (O.R.W.); else cite to an appropriate secondary source.

*Decisions of the Administrator for Appeals* (NOAA App.) should so specify.

| Administrative Materials | Citation |
|---|---|

**Department of Commerce, Patent and Trademark Office (USPTO)**

**Decisions:** For decisions of the Commissioner of Patents, cite to *Decisions of the Commissioner of Patents* (Dec. Comm'r Pat.) following Rule 19, except that if the party name includes a procedural phrase, it should be included.

For decisions by the Board of Patent Appeals and Interferences (B.P.A.I.), cite as: <party name>, No. <docket number>, <citation to secondary source if available> (B.P.A.I. <date>).

For decisions of the Trademark Trial and Appeal Board (T.TA.B.), cite as: <case name>, <citation to secondary source> (T.T.A.B. <year>).

**Patents:**

If relevant, cite the patent number and the date the patent was filed.

> U.S. Patent No. 8,112,504 B2 (filed Mar. 4, 2009)

The patent name and/or issuing date may be included if relevant.

> System for disseminating media content representing episodes in a serialized sequence, U.S. Patent No. 8,112,504 B2 (filed Mar. 4, 2009) (issued Feb. 7, 2012)

For citations to a specific field of the title page, include the field code in brackets:

> U.S. Patent No. 8,112,504 B2, at [75] (filed Mar. 4, 2009)

For citations to a specific portion of patent text, a patent figure, or an item within a figure:

> U.S. Patent No. 8,112,504 B2, fig. 1, item 141 (filed Mar. 4, 2009)

Short form patent ctiations include an apostrophe followed by the last three digits of the patent number:

> '504 Patent.

**Trademarks:**

For registered trademarks, cite as <TRADEMARK NAME>, Registration No. <registration number>.

> THE BLUEBOOK A UNIFORM SYSTEM OF CITATION, Registration No. 3,886,986.

For trademarks that have been filed, but not approved, cite as U.S. Trademark Application Serial No. <Serial Number> (filed <date>).

> U.S. Trademark Application Serial No. 86,680,743 (filed Jul. 1, 2015).

| | |
|---|---|
| Official Gazette of the United States Patent Office (1872–1971) | Off. Gaz. Pat. Office |
| Official Gazette of the United States Patent and Trademark Office (1975–2002) | Off. Gaz. Pat. & Trademark Office |
| Trademark Manual of Examining Procedure | TMEP (5th ed. Sept. 2007) |
| Manual of Patent Examining Procedure | MPEP (8th ed. Rev. 7, Sept. 2008) |

**Department of Education**

**Reports:** Cite *Institution of Education Sciences* reports as Institution of Education Sciences, <title> <page> (<date>).

| Administrative Materials | Citation |
|---|---|

Institute of Education Sciences, National Board for Education Sciences Annual Report 12 (2014).

**Reports:** Cite federal student aid proceedings as <case name>, U.S. Dep't of Educ., No. <docket number> (<date>).

Lincoln Univ., U.S. Dep't of Educ., No. 13-68-SF (Mar. 16, 2015).

## Department of Homeland Security, Bureau of Customs and Border Protection

The two official reporters of the Bureau of Customs and Border Protection and its predecessors are the *Administrative Decisions Under Immigration and Nationality Laws* (I. & N. Dec.) and the *Customs Bulletin and Decisions* (Cust. B. & Dec).

## Department of Justice

**Advisory Opinions:** For published, formal advisory opinions, cite in the same manner as adjudications. Cite opinions from the Attorney General as *Opinions of the Attorneys General* (Op. Att'y Gen.).

Cite opinions from the Office of Legal Counsel as *Opinions of the Office of Legal Counsel of the Department of Justice* (Op. O.L.C.).

Authority of Sec'y of Treasury to Compromise Final Judgments, 36 U.S. Op. Att' Gen. 40 (1929)

Diversion of Water From Niagara River, 30 Op. Att'y Gen. 217 (1913).

U.S. Assistance to Countries That Shoot Down Civil Aircraft Involved in Drug Trafficking, 18 Op. O.L.C. 148, 165 (1994).

Cite precedent decisions of the Board of Immigration Appeals (BIA) to *Administrative Decisions Under Immigration and Nationality Laws* (I. & N. Dec.) as published by the Department of Justice Executive Office for Immigration Review (EOIR).

## Department of Labor

**Decisions in Petition for Modification Cases Under Section 101(c) of the Mine Act, 30 U.S.C. § 811(c):** Cite as <description of decision>, <case name>, Docket No. <docket number> (Dep't of Labor <date>).

Note that these decisions have not been reported in any official reporter or service.

**Decisions in Enforcement Actions Brought by the Office of Federal Contract Compliance Programs:** Cite as <case name>, <docket number>, <description of decision> (Dep't of Labor <date>).

Note that these decisions have not been reported in any official reporter or service.

OFCCP v. Bank of Am., 97-OFC-16, Secretary's Decision and Order of Remand (Dep't of Labor Mar. 31, 2003).

**Decisions by the Benefits Review Board:** Cite to a service.

Jones v. I.T.O. Corp. of Baltimore, 9 Ben. Rev. Bd. Serv. (MB) 583, 585 (1979).

## Department of the Interior

Cite agency decisions to *Interior Decisions* (Interior Dec.) or *Interior and General Land Office Cases Relating to Public Lands* (Pub. Lands Dec.). Where a board within the agency issues the opinion, note the board in the same parenthetical as the date, using these abbreviations:

| Administrative Materials | Citation |
|---|---|
| Interior Board of Land Appeals | IBLA |
| Interior Board of Indian Appeals | DBIA |
| Interior Board of Contract Appeals | IBCA |
| Shell Offshore, Inc., 94 Interior Dec. 69 (IBLA 1987). | |

## Department of State

**Reports:** For reports of the Bureau of Democracy, Human Rights, and Labor, cite as: U.S. Dep't of State, Bureau of Democracy, H.R. and Lab., <title> <page> (<date>).

U.S. Dep't of State, Bureau of Democracy, H.R. and Lab., International Religious Freedom Report 14 (2014).

## Department of the Treasury

**Regulations:** For Department of Treasury regulations, cite as <Treas. Reg.>, despite the fact that they are published under Title 26 of the C.F.R.

For unamended regulations, cite the year:

Treas. Reg. § 1.41-2 (1989).

Indicate if the regulation is a temnporary regulation by beginning the citation with Temp:

Temp. Treas. Reg. § 5e.274-8 (1982).

For specific questions and answers, cite as:

Treas. Reg. § 1.72-16(a), Q&A (3)(a) (1963).

If any subsection of the cited section has been amended or appears in substantially different versions, give the year of the most recent amendment. Follow this rule even if the particular subsection you are citing has never been amended.

Treas. Reg. § 1.41-2 (as amended in 2001).

Indicate when the source of the amendment is relevant.

Treas. Reg. § 1.41-2 (as amended by T.D. 8930, 65 FR 287).

For proposed Treasury regulations to the *Federal Register*, cite in the following manner:

Prop. Treas. Reg. § 1.704-1, 48 Fed. Reg. 9871, 9872 (Mar. 9, 1983).

**Treasury Determinations:** Cite Revenue Rulings, Revenue Procedures, and Treasury Decisions to the *Cumulative Bulletin* (C.B.) or its advance sheet, the Internal Revenue Bulletin (I.R.B.), or to *Treasury Decisions Under Internal Revenue Laws* (Treas. Dec. Int. Rev.), in that order of preference.

The numbering of the *Cumulative Bulletin* is as follows:

1. By volume number from 1919 to 1921.

2. By volume number and part number from 1921 to 1936.

3. By year and part number from 1937 to date.

The abbreviations used are explained in the introductory pages of each volume of the *Cumulative Bulletin*.

| Administrative Materials | Citation |
|---|---|

**Private Letter Rulings:** Cite by number and the date issued, if available.

**Technical Advice Memoranda:** Cite by number and the date issued, if available.

**General Counsel Memoranda:** Cite by number and the date on which the memorandum was approved.

**Other Treasury Determinations:** For all other Treasury materials, cite to the *Cumulative Bulletin*, *Internal Revenue Bulletin*, or *Internal Revenue Manual* (IRM).

> Delegation Orders (Deleg. Order)
>
> Treasury Orders (Treas. Order)
>
> Treasury Directives (Treas. Dir.)
>
> Notices, Announcements, and News Releases

Otherwise cite by number and date issued.

**Cases:** For the Tax Court and Board of Tax Appeals, cite as those of a court, not of an agency.

**Acquiescence:** The following may be indicated in the case citation if the Commissioner of the Internal Revenue Service has published an acquiescence (*acq.*), acquiescence in result only (*acq. In result*), or nonacquiescence *(nonacq.)* in a decision of the Tax Court or Board of Tax Appeals.

**Action on Decision:** To cite an action on decision (*action on dec*) as subsequent history, include its identifying number, if any, and its full date.

Environmental Protection Agency (EPA)

**Decisions:** For *Environmental Administrative Decisions* (E.A.D.) indicate the decision maker—either the Environmental Appeals Board (EAB) or an administrative law judge—if the source does not make it obvious.

> Donald Cutler, 11 E.A.D. 622, 623 (EAB 2004).

Equal Employment Opportunity Commission (EEOC)

**Decisions:** For EEOC decisions that do not have readily identifiable titles, cite using the decision number in place of the title. Otherwise cite per Rule 19.

> Budnik v. Chertoff, EEOC DOC 0520070154 (2006).

For EEOC Federal Sector decisions that have party names, cite in accordance with Rule 11.2.

Executive Office of the President

**Executive Orders, Presidential Proclamations, and Reorganization Plans:** Cite by page number to 3 C.F.R. However, since all executive orders are not reprinted in successive years of the C.F.R., cite to the original year, rather than the most recent edition of the C.F.R.

Where relevant, include a parallel citation to the U.S.C.

> Exec. Order 13,136, 3 C.F.R. 216 (Sep. 3, 1999).

If the material is not in the C.F.R., cite to the Federal Register.

> Exec. Order 12,900, 59 FR 9061 (Feb. 22, 1994).

A parallel citation to the *Statutes at Large* may also be given.

| Administrative Materials | Citation |
|---|---|

**Other Presidential Papers:** Cite to *Public Papers of the Presidents* (Papers) if found there. If not recorded in the *Public Papers*, cite the *Weekly Compilation of Presidential Documents* (Weekly Comp. Pres. Doc.), published from 1965 to January 29, 2009, the *Daily Compilation of Presidential Documents* (Daily Comp. Pres. Doc.), published from January 29, 2009 to date, or the *U.S. Code Congressional and Administrative News* (U.S.C.C.A.N.).

**Budgets:** Use the structure of book citations for governmental budgets.

> Office of Mgmt. & Budget, Exec. Office of the President, Budget of the United States Government, Fiscal Year 2014 (2013).

### Federal Aviation Administration (FAA)

**Decisions:** For decisions of administrative law judges in civil penalty enforcement matters adjudicated under 14 C.F.R. Part 13, Section 13.16 and subpart G, cite per Rule 12.4.2 as slip opinions.

For Decisions of the Administrator or his delegate, cite using an order number, not a docket number.

For Decisions of the Office of Dispute Resolution for Acquisition (ODRA) adjudicated under 14 C.F.R. Part 17, the citation should incorporate the type of dispute.

For other FAA decisions and orders, the citation should indicate the nature of the decision, followed by the date.

> Federal Express Corporation, FAA Order No. 2002-20, 2002 WL 31777976 (F.A.A.).
>
> Envirosolve, LLC, FAA Order No. 2006-2, 2006 WL 465371 (Feb. 7, 2006).
>
> Aerocomp, Inc., FAA Order No. 2006-1, Order Dismissing Appeal (Jan. 12, 2006).

### Federal Communications Commission (FCC)

Cite to the *Federal Communications Commission Reports* (F.C.C., F.C.C.2d), published 1934-1986, or the *Federal Communications Commission Record* (FCC Rcd.), published since 1986.

> Protecting and Promoting the Open Internet, GN Docket No. 14-28, Notice of Proposed Rulemaking, 29 FCC Rcd 5561 (2014).

### Federal Energy Regulatory Commission (FERC)

Cite decisions to the *Federal Energy Guidelines: FERC Reports* (FERC).

> Filing of Privileged Materials and Answers to Motions, Order No. 769, 141 FERC ¶ 61,049 (2012).

### Federal Labor Relations Authority (FLRA)

Cite decisions to the *Decisions of the Federal Labor Relations Authority* (F.L.R.A.).

### Federal Mine Safety and Health Review Commission (FMSHRC)

Cite decisions to the *Federal Mine Safety and Health Review Commission Decisions* (FMSHRC).

### Federal Reserve System

**Enforcement Actions:** Cite written agreements resulting from enforcement actions as: Written Agreement between <private bank name> and <Federal Reserve Bank name>, Docket no. <docket number> (<date>).

| Administrative Materials | Citation |
| --- | --- |

Written Agreement Between Allied First Bancorp, Inc. and Federal Reserve Bank of Chicago, Docket No. 14-006-WA/RB-HC (2014).

**Federal Trade Commission (FTC)**

Cite decisions to the *Federal Trade Commission* (F.T.C.).

**Government Accountability Office (GAO)**

**Bid Protest Decisions:** Cite to *Decisions of the Comptroller General of the United States* (Comp. Gen.).

Space Communications Co., 66 Comp. Gen. 2 (1987).

For unpublished decisions to a readily accessible source, cite as: <protesting party>, <docket number>, <volume number or year> <source> <location within source volume or year> (Comp. Gen. <date>).

Do not indicate the publisher when citing these cases to the *Comptroller General's Procurement Decision*, published by West.

HP Enterprise Services, LLC, B-405692, 2012 CPD ¶ 13 (Comp. Gen. Dec. 14, 2011).

Phoenix Environmental Design, Inc., B-412503, 2016 WL 873296 (Comp. Gen. Mar. 7, 2016).

Insert "et al." after the docket number where a decision resolves multiple bid protests, each having its own docket number.

IAP-Hill, LLC, B-406289 et al, 2012 CPD ¶ 151 (Comp. Gen. Apr. 4, 2012).

**International Trade Commission (USITC)**

**Trade Remedy Investigations:** Cite as: <investigation name>, Inv. No. <number>, USITC Pub. <number> (<date>) (<status>).

Indicate where a single decision contains multiple investigation numbers.

Trade and Investment Polices in India, 2014–2015, Inv. No. 332-550, USITC Pub. 4566 (Sep. 2015).

The Year in Trade 2014: Operation of the Trade Agreements Program, USITC Pub. 4543 (July 2015).

Polyvinyl Alcohol from China, Japan, and Taiwan, Inv. Nos. 701-TA-309, 731-TA-528, 731-TA-529, USITC Pub. 4067 (Mar. 27, 2009) (Review).

**Merit Systems Protection Board (MSPB)**

Cite decisions to the *Decisions of the United States Merit Systems Protection Board* (M.S.P.B.).

**National Labor Relations Board (NLRB)**

Cite decisions and orders to the *Decisions and Orders of the National Labor Relations Board* (N.L.R.B.).

**National Mediation Board (NMB)**

Cite decisions to the *Decisions of the National Mediation Board* (N.M.B.).

**National Transportation Safety Board (NTSB)**

Cite decisions to the *National Transportation Safety Board Decisions* (N.T.S.B.), published from 1967-1977.

| Administrative Materials | Citation |
| --- | --- |

### Nuclear Regulatory Commission (NRC)

For decisions of the Nuclear Regulatory Commission, cite to the *Nuclear Regulatory Commission Issuances* (N.R.C.).

For decisions of its predecessor, the Atomic Energy Commission (1956–1975), cite to the *Atomic Energy Commission Reports* (A.E.C.).

### Occupational Safety and Health Review Commission (OSHRC)

**Decisions:** For commission decisions reported in a service, cite as: `<party name>, <service volume number> <publisher> <service, abbreviated as below> <page/paragraph number> (No. <docket number>, <year>).`

> US Pagoda, Inc., CCH OSHD ¶ 33123 (No. 10-2035, 2011).

At the end of a citation, indicate parenthetically when an administrative law judge issued the decision, rather than the commission.

> Miller Construction Co., 24 BNA OSHC 1817 (No. 13-0323, 2013) (ALJ).

The abbreviations OSHRC uses for services reporting its decisions vary from those in Table T4 as follows:

| | |
| --- | --- |
| Occupational Safety & Health Cases (BNA) | OSHC |
| Occupational Safety & Health Decisions | OSHD |

A decision that is not cited in any service or database may be cited as a slip opinion using Rule 12.4.2(b).

> Prime Roofing Corp., No. 07-1409 (OSHRC Feb. 5, 2008).

### Securities and Exchange Commission (SEC)

**Interpretive Letters, No-Action Letters, and Exemptive Letters:** Cite a service or an electronic database (Rule 12.4.1). In the citation, include the correspondent's full name and the date that the letter became publicly available.

> Poplogix LLC, SEC No-Action Letter, 2010 WL 4472794 (Nov. 5, 2010).

> MP Environmental Funding LLC, SEC Interprative Letter, 2007 WL 2838964 (Sep. 19, 2007)

**Releases:** Cite the *Federal Register*, SEC Docket, or a service (Rule 19). Releases that have subject-matter title may be presented in a short form. Make sure to include the act under which the release was issued, the release number, and the date.

> SEC Whistleblower Rules, Exchange Act Release No. 75592, 80 Fed. Reg 47829 (Aug. 10, 2015).

If the release is an adjudication, abbreviate the parties' names according to Rule 11.

> Midas Securities, LLC., Exchange Act Release No. 66200, 102 SEC Docket 3123, 102 SEC Docket 3137 (Jan. 20, 2012).

If the adjudication occurred before an administrative law judge, indicate this fact in the date parenthetical.

If a particular release is issued under the Securities Act, the Exchange Act, or the Investment Company Act, a parallel citation should be given in that order.

| Administrative Materials | Citation |
|---|---|

**Staff Interpretations:** Cite SEC Staff Accounting Bulletins, Staff Legal Bulletins, and Telephone Interpretations as follows:

> SEC Staff Accounting Bulletin No. 99, 64 Fed. Reg. 45150 (Aug. 19, 1999).

**SEC Filings:** For annual reports, proxy statements, and other company filings required under federal securities laws, provide the name of the company (abbreviated according to Rule 15.1), the title as given in the document, the form type in parentheses, the page number if applicable, and the full date of filing with the SEC.

> Apple Inc., Annual Report (Form 10-K), (Oct. 28, 2015).

If citing annual reports, proxy statements, or other documents in a form other than that filed with the SEC, treat as books under Rule 15.

> Facebook, Inc., 2014 Annual Report (2014).

---

## Small Business Administration (SBA)

**Decisions:** Cite decisions as: <party name>, SBA No. <docket number> (<date>).

> OxyHeal Medical Systems, Inc., SBA No. SIZ-5707 (Jan. 19 2016).

The docket number indicates the type of decision:

| | |
|---|---|
| Small disadvantaged business | SDBA |
| Size determination | SIZ |
| Service disabled veteran owned business | VET |
| Business development program | BDP |
| North American Industry Classification System | NAICS |

## Social Security Administration (SSA)

**Rulings and Acquiescence Rulings:** For Social Security Rulings, cite as SSR; for Social Security Acquiescence Rulings, cite as SSAR.

Cite to the *Social Security Rulings, Cumulative Edition* (S.S.R. Cum. Ed.). If not published there, cite to another official source, such as the *Code of Federal Regulations* or the *Federal Register*. Otherwise, cite a commercial database or other source.

> SSR 62-2, 1960-1974 Soc. Sec. Rep. Serv. 69 (Jan. 1, 1962).

## Surface Transportation Board (STB)

For materials from the Surface Transportation Board, cite to the *Surface Transportation Board Reporter* (S.T.B.). For materials from its predecessor, cite to the Interstate Commerce Commission (ICC), to the *Interstate Commerce Commission Reporter* (I.C.C., I.C.C. 2d).

The official date for unpublished decisions is the date on which the decision was served on the parties or otherwise filed by the STB (or ICC). Do not cite the date of the decision.

# T3. U.S. States and Other Jurisdictions

| Category | Dates | Abbreviation |
|---|---|---|
| **Alabama** | | |
| **Supreme Court (Ala.):** Cite to So., So. 2d, or So. 3d. | | |
| Southern Reporter | 1886–date | So., So. 2d, So. 3d |
| Alabama Reports | 1840–1976 | Ala. |
| Porter | 1834–1839 | Port. |
| Stewart and Porter | 1831–1834 | Stew. & P. |
| Stewart | 1827–1831 | Stew. |
| Minor | 1820–1826 | Minor |
| **Court of Civil Appeals (Ala. Civ. App.) and Court of Criminal Appeals (Ala. Crim. App.), before 1969 Court of Appeals (Ala. Ct. App.):** Cite to So., So. 2d, or So. 3d. | | |
| Southern Reporter | 1911–date | So., So. 2d, So. 3d |
| Alabama Appellate Courts Reports | 1911–1974 | Ala. App. |
| **Statutory compilations:** Cite to Ala. Code (published by West). | | |
| Code of Alabama, 1975 (West) | | Ala. Code § x-x-x (<year>) |
| Michie's Alabama Code, 1975 (LexisNexis) | | Ala. Code § x-x-x (LexisNexis <year>) |
| **Session laws:** Cite to Ala. Laws. | | |
| Alabama Laws | | <year> Ala. Laws <page no.> |
| West's Alabama Legislative Service | | <year> Ala. Legis. Serv. <page no.> (West) |
| Michie's Alabama Code <year> Advance Legislative Service (LexisNexis) | | <year>-<pamph. no.> Ala. Adv. Legis. Serv. <page no.> (LexisNexis) |
| **Administrative compilation** | | |
| Alabama Administrative Code | | Ala. Admin. Code r. x-x-x.x (<year>) |
| **Administrative register** | | |
| Alabama Administrative Monthly | | <vol. no.> Ala. Admin. Monthly <page no.> (<month day, year>) |
| **Alaska** | | |
| **Supreme Court (Alaska):** Cite to P.2d or P.3d. | | |

| Category | Dates | Abbreviation |
|---|---|---|
| Pacific Reporter | 1960–date | P.2d, P.3d |

**Court of Appeals (Alaska Ct. App.):** Cite to P.2d or P.3d.

| | | |
|---|---|---|
| Pacific Reporter | 1980–date | P.2d, P.3d |

**District Courts of Alaska (D. Alaska):** These courts had local jurisdiction from 1884 to 1959. Cite to F. Supp., F., or F.2d; else, cite to Alaska or Alaska Fed., in that order of preference.

| | | |
|---|---|---|
| Federal Supplement | 1946–1959 | F. Supp. |
| Federal Reporter | 1886–1932 | F., F.2d |
| Alaska Reports | 1887–1958 | Alaska |
| Alaska Federal Reports | 1869–1937 | Alaska Fed. |

**United States District Courts for California and Oregon, and District Courts of Washington (D. Cal., D. Or., D. Wash.):** These courts had local jurisdiction in Alaska until 1884. Cite to F. or F. Cas.

| | | |
|---|---|---|
| Federal Reporter | 1880–1884 | F. |
| Federal Cases | 1867–1880 | F. Cas. |
| Alaska Federal Reports | 1869–1937 | Alaska Fed. |

**Statutory compilations:** Cite to Alaska Stat.

| | |
|---|---|
| Alaska Statutes (LexisNexis) | Alaska Stat. § x.x.x (<year>) |
| West's Alaska Statutes Annotated | Alaska Stat. Ann. § x.x.x (West <year>) |

**Session laws:** Cite to Alaska Sess. Laws.

| | |
|---|---|
| Session Laws of Alaska | <year> Alaska Sess. Laws <page no.> |
| Alaska Statutes <year> Advance Legislative Service | <year>-<pamph. no.> Alaska Adv. Legis. Serv. <page no.> (LexisNexis) |
| West's Alaska Legislative Service | <year> Alaska Legis. Serv. <page no.> (West) |

**Administrative compilation**

| | |
|---|---|
| Alaska Administrative Code (LexisNexis) | Alaska Admin. Code tit. x, § x.x (<year>) |

## Arizona

**Supreme Court (Ariz.):** Cite to P., P.2d, or P.3d.

| | | |
|---|---|---|
| Pacific Reporter | 1883–date | P., P.2d, P.3d |
| Arizona Reports | 1866–date | Ariz. |

**Court of Appeals (Ariz. Ct. App.):** Cite to P.2d or P.3d.

| Category | Dates | Abbreviation |
|---|---|---|
| Pacific Reporter | 1965–date | P.2d, P.3d |
| Arizona Reports | 1976–date | Ariz. |
| Arizona Appeals Reports | 1965–1977 | Ariz. App. |

**Tax Court (Ariz. Tax Ct.):** Cite to P.2d or P.3d.

| Pacific Reporter | 1988–date | P.2d, P.3d |
|---|---|---|

**Statutory compilations:** Cite to Ariz. Rev. Stat. Ann..

| Arizona Revised Statutes Annotated (West) | | Ariz. Rev. Stat. Ann. § x-x (<year>) |
|---|---|---|
| Arizona Revised Statutes (LexisNexis) | | Ariz. Rev. Stat. § x-x (LexisNexis <year>) |

**Session laws:** Cite to Ariz. Sess. Laws.

| Session Laws, Arizona | | <year> Ariz. Sess. Laws <page no.> |
|---|---|---|
| Arizona Legislative Service (West) | | <year> Ariz. Legis. Serv. <page no.> (West) |

**Administrative compilation**

| Arizona Administrative Code | | Ariz. Admin. Code § x-x-x (<year>) |
|---|---|---|

**Administrative register**

| Arizona Administrative Register | | <vol. no.> Ariz. Admin. Reg. <page no.> (<month day, year>) |
|---|---|---|

### Arkansas

**Public domain citation format:** Arkansas has adopted a public domain citation format for cases after February 13, 2009. For additional instruction, consult Arkansas Supreme Court Rule 5-2. The format is:

- *Smith v. Hickman*, 2009 Ark. 12, at 1, 273 S.W.3d 340, 343.
- *Doe v. State*, 2009 Ark. App. 318, at 7, 2009 WL 240613, at *8.

**Supreme Court (Ark.):** Cite to S.W., S.W.2d, or S.W.3d.

| South Western Reporter | 1886–date | S.W., S.W.2d, or S.W.3d |
|---|---|---|
| Arkansas Reports | 1837–2009 | Ark. |

**Court of Appeals (Ark. Ct. App.):** Cite to S.W.2d or S.W.3d.

| South Western Reporter | 1979–date | S.W.2d, S.W.3d |
|---|---|---|

| Category | Dates | Abbreviation |
|---|---|---|
| Arkansas Appellate Reports | 1981–2009 | Ark. App. |
| Arkansas Reports | 1979–1981 | Ark. |

**Statutory compilations:** Cite to Ark. Code Ann. (published by LexisNexis).

| Category | Dates | Abbreviation |
|---|---|---|
| Arkansas Code of 1987 Annotated (LexisNexis) | | Ark. Code Ann. § x-x-x (\<year\>) |
| West's Arkansas Code Annotated | | Ark. Code Ann. § x-x-x (West \<year\>) |

**Session laws:** Cite to Ark. Acts.

| Category | Dates | Abbreviation |
|---|---|---|
| Acts of Arkansas (West) | | \<year\> Ark. Acts \<page no.\> |
| Arkansas Code of 1987 Annotated \<year\> Advance Legislative Service (LexisNexis) | | \<year\>-\<pamph. no.\> Ark. Adv. Legis. Serv. \<page no.\> (LexisNexis) |
| West's Arkansas Legislative Service | | \<year\> Ark. Legis. Serv. \<page no.\> (West) |

**Administrative compilation**

| Category | Dates | Abbreviation |
|---|---|---|
| Code of Arkansas Rules (LexisNexis) | | x-x-x Ark. Code R. § x (LexisNexis \<year\>) |

**Administrative registers:** Cite to Ark. Reg..

| Category | Dates | Abbreviation |
|---|---|---|
| Arkansas Register | | \<vol. no.\> Ark. Reg. \<page no.\> (\<month year\>) |
| Arkansas Government Register | | \<iss. no.\> Ark. Gov't Reg. \<page no.\> (LexisNexis \<month year\>) |

## California

**Supreme Court (Cal.):** Cite to P., P.2d, or P.3d.

| Category | Dates | Abbreviation |
|---|---|---|
| Pacific Reporter | 1883–date | P., P.2d, P.3d |
| California Reports | 1850–date | Cal., Cal. 2d, Cal. 3d, Cal. 4th |
| West's California Reporter | 1959–date | Cal. Rptr., Cal. Rptr. 2d, Cal. Rptr. 3d |
| California Unreported Cases | 1855–1910 | Cal. Unrep. |

**Court of Appeal (Cal. Ct. App.), previously District Court of Appeal (Cal. Dist. Ct. App.):** Cite to P. or P.2d (before 1960) or Cal. Rptr., Cal. Rptr. 2d (after 1959), or Cal. Rptr. 3d.

| Category | Dates | Abbreviation |
|---|---|---|
| West's California Reporter | 1959–date | Cal. Rptr., Cal. Rptr. 2d, Cal. Rptr. 3d |
| Pacific Reporter | 1905–1959 | P., P.2d |
| California Appellate Reports | 1905–date | Cal. App., Cal. App. 2d, Cal. App. 3d, Cal. App. 4th |

| Category | Dates | Abbreviation |
|---|---|---|

**Appellate Divisions of the Superior Court (Cal. App. Dep't Super. Ct.):** Cite to P. or P.2d (before 1960) or to Cal. Rptr., Cal. Rptr. 2d (after 1959), or Cal. Rptr. 3d.

| West's California Reporter | 1959–date | Cal. Rptr., Cal. Rptr. 2d, Cal. Rptr. 3d |
| Pacific Reporter | 1929–1959 | P., P.2d |
| California Appellate Reports Supplement (bound with Cal. App.) | 1929–date | Cal. App. Supp., Cal. App. 2d Supp., Cal. App. 3d Supp., Cal. App. 4th Supp. |

**Statutory compilations:** Cite to either the West or the Deering subject-matter code.

| West's Annotated California Codes | | Cal. <Subject> Code § x (West <year>) |
| Deering's California Codes, Annotated (LexisNexis) | | Cal. <Subject> Code § x (Deering <year>) |
|     Agricultural (renamed "Food and Agricultural" in 1972) | | Agric. |
|     Business and Professions | | Bus. & Prof. |
|     Civil | | Civ. |
|     Civil Procedure | | Civ. Proc. |
|     Commercial | | Com. |
|     Corporations | | Corp. |
|     Education | | Educ. |
|     Elections | | Elec. |
|     Evidence | | Evid. |
|     Family | | Fam. |
|     Financial | | Fin. |
|     Fish and Game | | Fish & Game |
|     Food and Agricultural (formerly "Agricultural") | | Food & Agric. |
|     Government | | Gov't |
|     Harbors and Navigation | | Harb. & Nav. |
|     Health and Safety | | Health & Safety |
|     Insurance | | Ins. |
|     Labor | | Lab. |
|     Military and Veterans | | Mil. & Vet. |
|     Penal | | Penal |

| Category | Dates | Abbreviation |
|---|---|---|
| Probate | | Prob. |
| Public Contract | | Pub. Cont. |
| Public Resources | | Pub. Res. |
| Public Utilities | | Pub. Util. |
| Revenue and Taxation | | Rev. & Tax. |
| Streets and Highways | | Sts. & High. |
| Unemployment Insurance | | Unemp. Ins. |
| Vehicle | | Veh. |
| Water | | Water |
| Welfare and Institutions | | Welf. & Inst. |

**Session laws:** Cite to Cal. Stat..

| | |
|---|---|
| Statutes of California | `<year>` Cal. Stat. `<page no.>` |
| West's California Legislative Service | `<year>` Cal. Legis. Serv. `<page no.>` (West) |
| Deering's California Advance Legislative Service (LexisNexis) | `<year>-<pamph. no.>` Cal. Adv. Legis. Serv. `<page no.>` (LexisNexis) |

**Administrative compilation**

| | |
|---|---|
| California Code of Regulations (West) | Cal. Code Regs. tit. x, § x (`<year>`) |

**Administrative register**

| | |
|---|---|
| California Regulatory Notice Register | `<iss. no.>` Cal. Regulatory Notice Reg. `<page no.>` (`<month day, year>`) |

## Colorado

**Public domain citation format:** Colorado has adopted a public domain citation format for cases after January 3, 2012. For additional information, consult Rules of the Supreme Court of Colorado, Chief Justice Directive 12-01. The format is:

- *Smith v. Jones*, 2012 CO 22.

- *Smith v. Jones*, 2012 CO 22, ¶¶ 13–14.

- *Jones v. Smith*, 2012 COA 35.

**Supreme Court (Colo.):** Cite to P., P.2d, or P.3d, if found there; else, cite to Colo., if found there, or to Colo. Law. or Brief Times Rptr.

| | | |
|---|---|---|
| Pacific Reporter | 1883–date | P., P.2d, P.3d |
| Colorado Reports | 1864–1980 | Colo. |
| Colorado Lawyer | 1972–date | Colo. Law. |

| Category | Dates | Abbreviation |
|---|---|---|
| Brief Times Reporter | 1977–1996 | Brief Times Rptr. |
| Colorado Journal | 1996–2002 | Colo. J. |
| Law Week Colorado | 2002–date | L. Week Colo. |

**Court of Appeals (Colo. App.):** Cite to P., P.2d, or P.3d, if found there; else, cite to Colo. App., if found there, or else to one of the other reporters listed below.

| | | |
|---|---|---|
| Pacific Reporter | 1970–date | P.2d, P.3d |
| | 1912–1915 | P. |
| | 1891–1905 | P. |
| Colorado Court of Appeals Reports | 1891–1905 | Colo. App. |
| | 1912–1915 | Colo. App. |
| | 1970–1980 | Colo. App. |
| Colorado Lawyer | 1972–date | Colo. Law. |
| Brief Times Reporter | 1977–1996 | Brief Times Rptr. |
| Colorado Journal | 1996–2002 | Colo. J. |
| Law Week Colorado | 2002–date | L. Week Colo. |

**Statutory compilations:** Cite to Colo. Rev. Stat..

| | |
|---|---|
| Colorado Revised Statutes (LexisNexis) | Colo. Rev. Stat. § x-x-x (<year>) |
| West's Colorado Revised Statutes Annotated | Colo. Rev. Stat. Ann. § x-x-x (West <year>) |

**Session laws:** Cite to Colo. Sess. Laws.

| | |
|---|---|
| Session Laws of Colorado (LexisNexis) | <year> Colo. Sess. Laws <page no.> |
| Colorado Legislative Service (West) | <year> Colo. Legis. Serv. <page no.> (West) |

**Administrative compilations:** Cite to Colo. Code Regs..

| | |
|---|---|
| Colorado Code of Regulations | Colo. Code Regs. § x-x (<year>) |
| Code of Colorado Regulations (LexisNexis) | <vol. no.> Colo. Code Regs. § x-x (LexisNexis <year>) |

**Administrative register**

| Category | Dates | Abbreviation |
|---|---|---|
| Colorado Register | | `<iss. no.>` Colo. Reg. `<page no.>` (`<month year>`) |

Connecticut

**Supreme Court (Conn.), previously Supreme Court of Errors (Conn.):** Cite to A., A.2d, or A.3d.

| Category | Dates | Abbreviation |
|---|---|---|
| Atlantic Reporter | 1885–date | A., A.2d, A.3d |
| Connecticut Reports | 1814–date | Conn. |
| Day | 1802–1813 | Day |
| Root | 1789–1798 | Root |
| Kirby | 1785–1789 | Kirby |

**Appellate Court (Conn. App. Ct.):** Cite to A.2d or A.3d.

| Category | Dates | Abbreviation |
|---|---|---|
| Atlantic Reporter | 1983–date | A.2d, A.3d |
| Connecticut Appellate Reports | 1983–date | Conn. App. |

**Superior Court (Conn. Super. Ct.) and Court of Common Pleas (Conn. C.P.):** Cite to A.2d or A.3d, if found there; else, cite to Conn. Supp., if found there, or else to one of the other reporters listed below.

| Category | Dates | Abbreviation |
|---|---|---|
| Atlantic Reporter | 1954–date | A.2d, A.3d |
| Connecticut Supplement | 1935–date | Conn. Supp. |
| Connecticut Law Reporter | 1990–date | Conn. L. Rptr. |
| Connecticut Superior Court Reports | 1986–1994 | Conn. Super. Ct. |

**Circuit Court (Conn. Cir. Ct.):** Cite to A.2d or A.3d.

| Category | Dates | Abbreviation |
|---|---|---|
| Atlantic Reporter | 1961–1974 | A.2d, A.3d |
| Connecticut Circuit Court Reports | 1961–1974 | Conn. Cir. Ct. |

**Statutory compilations:** Cite to Conn. Gen. Stat..

| Category | Dates | Abbreviation |
|---|---|---|
| General Statutes of Connecticut | | Conn. Gen. Stat. § x-x (`<year>`) |
| Connecticut General Statutes Annotated (West) | | Conn. Gen. Stat. Ann. § x-x (West `<year>`) |

**Session laws:** Cite to Conn. Acts, Conn. Pub. Acts, or Conn. Spec. Acts.

| Category | Dates | Abbreviation |
|---|---|---|
| Connecticut Public & Special Acts | 1972–date | `<year>` Conn. Acts `<page no.>` ([Reg. or Spec.] Sess.) |
| Connecticut Public Acts | 1650–1971 | `<year>` Conn. Pub. Acts `<page no.>` |

| Category | Dates | Abbreviation |
|---|---|---|
| Connecticut Special Acts (Resolves & Private Laws, Private & Special Laws, Special Laws, Resolves & Private Acts, Resolutions & Private Acts, Private Acts & Resolutions, and Special Acts & Resolutions) | 1789–1971 | \<year> Conn. Spec. Acts \<page no.> |
| Connecticut Legislative Service (West) | | \<year> Conn. Legis. Serv. \<page no.> (West) |

**Administrative compilation**

| | | |
|---|---|---|
| Regulations of Connecticut State Agencies | | Conn. Agencies Regs. § x-x-x (\<year>) |

**Administrative registers:** Cite to Conn. L.J..

| | | |
|---|---|---|
| Connecticut Law Journal | | \<vol. no.> Conn. L.J. \<page no.> (\<month day, year>) |
| Connecticut Government Register (LexisNexis) | | \<iss. no.> Conn. Gov't Reg. \<page no.> (LexisNexis \<month year>) |

Delaware

**Supreme Court (Del.), previously Court of Errors and Appeals (Del.):** Cite to A., A.2d, or A.3d.

| | | |
|---|---|---|
| Atlantic Reporter | 1886–date | A., A.2d, A.3d |
| Delaware Reports | | |
| 31 Del. to 59 Del. | 1919–1966 | Del. |
| Boyce | 1909–1920 | e.g., 24 Del. (1 Boyce) |
| Pennewill | 1897–1909 | e.g., 17 Del. (1 Penne.) |
| Marvel | 1893–1897 | e.g., 15 Del. (1 Marv.) |
| Houston | 1855–1893 | e.g., 6 Del. (1 Houst.) |
| Harrington | 1832–1855 | e.g., 1 Del. (1 Harr.) |
| Delaware Cases | 1792–1830 | Del. Cas. |

**Court of Chancery (Del. Ch.):** Cite to A., A.2d, or A.3d.

| | | |
|---|---|---|
| Atlantic Reporter | 1886–date | A., A.2d, A.3d |
| Delaware Chancery Reports | 1814–1968 | Del. Ch. |
| Delaware Cases | 1792–1830 | Del. Cas. |

| Category | Dates | Abbreviation |
|---|---|---|

**Superior Court (Del. Super. Ct.), previously Superior Court and Orphans' Court (Del. Super. Ct. & Orphans' Ct.):** Cite to A.2d or A.3d, if found there; else, cite to one of the official reporters listed under Supreme Court (Del.).

| | | |
|---|---|---|
| Atlantic Reporter | 1951–date | A.2d, A.3d |

**Family Court (Del. Fam. Ct.):** Cite to A.2d or A.3d.

| | | |
|---|---|---|
| Atlantic Reporter | 1977–date | A.2d, A.3d |

**Statutory compilations:** Cite to Del. Code Ann..

| | |
|---|---|
| Delaware Code Annotated (LexisNexis) | Del. Code Ann. tit. x, § x (<year>) |
| West's Delaware Code Annotated | Del. Code Ann. tit. x, § x (West <year>) |

**Session laws:** Cite to Del. Laws.

| | |
|---|---|
| Laws of Delaware | <vol. no.> Del. Laws <page no.> (<year>) |
| Delaware Code Annotated <year> Advance Legislative Service (LexisNexis) | <year>-<pamph. no.> Del. Code. Ann. Adv. Legis. Serv. <page no.> (LexisNexis) |
| West's Delaware Legislative Service | <year> Del. Legis. Serv. <page no.> (West) |

**Administrative compilations:** Cite to Del. Admin. Code.

| | |
|---|---|
| Delaware Administrative Code | x-x-x Del. Admin. Code § x (<year>) |
| Code of Delaware Regulations (LexisNexis) | x-x-x Del. Code Regs. § x (LexisNexis <year>) |

**Administrative registers:** Cite to Del. Reg. Regs..

| | |
|---|---|
| Delaware Register of Regulations | <vol. no.> Del. Reg. Regs. <page no.> (<month day, year>) |
| Delaware Government Register (LexisNexis) | <iss. no.> Del Gov't Reg. <page no.> (LexisNexis <month year>) |

District of Columbia

**Court of Appeals (D.C.), previously Municipal Court of Appeals (D.C.):** Cite to A.2d or A.3d.

| | | |
|---|---|---|
| Atlantic Reporter | 1943–date | A.2d, A.3d |

**United States Court of Appeals for the District of Columbia Circuit (D.C. Cir.), previously Court of Appeals of/for the District of Columbia (D.C. Cir.), previously Supreme Court of the District of Columbia (D.C.):** Cite to F., F.2d, or F.3d.

| | | |
|---|---|---|
| Federal Reporter | 1919–date | F., F.2d, F.3d |

| Category | Dates | Abbreviation |
|---|---|---|
| United States Court of Appeals Reports | 1941–date | U.S. App. D.C. |
| Appeal Cases, District of Columbia | 1893–1941 | App. D.C. |
| District of Columbia Reports | | |
| Tucker and Clephane | 1892–1893 | 21 D.C. (Tuck. & Cl.) |
| Mackey | 1880–1892 | <12–20> D.C. (Mackey <1–9>) |
| MacArthur and Mackey | 1879–1880 | 11 D.C. (MacArth. & M.) |
| MacArthur | 1873–1879 | <8–10> D.C. (MacArth. <1–3>) |
| District of Columbia Reports (reported by Mackey) | 1863–1872 | <6–7> D.C. |
| Hayward & Hazleton, Circuit Court (Circuit Court Reports, vols. 6–7) | 1840–1863 | <1–2> Hay. & Haz. |
| Cranch, Circuit Court | 1801–1840 | <1–5> D.C. (Cranch <1–5>) |

**Superior Court (D.C. Super. Ct.), previously Municipal Court (D.C. Mun. Ct.):** Cite to Daily Wash. L. Rptr.

| | | |
|---|---|---|
| Daily Washington Law Reporter | 1971–date | Daily Wash. L. Rptr. |

**Statutory compilations:** Cite to D.C. Code.

| | |
|---|---|
| District of Columbia Official Code (LexisNexis) | D.C. Code § x-x (<year>) |
| West's District of Columbia Code Annotated (West) | D.C. Code Ann. § x-x (West <year>) |

**Session laws:** Cite to Stat., D.C. Reg., or D.C. Code Adv. Leg. Serv..

| | |
|---|---|
| United States Statutes at Large | <vol. no.> Stat. <page no.> (<year>) |
| District of Columbia Register | <vol. no.> D.C. Reg. <page no.> (<month day, year>) |
| District of Columbia Official Code Lexis Advance Legislative Service | <year>-<pamph. no.> D.C. Code Adv. Leg. Serv. <page no.> |

| Category | Dates | Abbreviation |
|---|---|---|
| District of Columbia Session Law Service West | | \<year> D.C. Sess. L. Serv. \<page no.> (West) |

**Municipal regulations:** Cite to D.C. Mun. Regs..

| Category | Dates | Abbreviation |
|---|---|---|
| Code of D.C. Municipal Regulations | | D.C. Mun. Regs. tit. x, § x (\<year>) |
| Code of District of Columbia Municipal Regulations (LexisNexis) | | D.C. Code Mun. Regs. tit. x § x (LexisNexis \<year>) |

**Administrative register**

| Category | Dates | Abbreviation |
|---|---|---|
| District of Columbia Register | | \<vol. no.> D.C. Reg. \<page no.> (\<month day, year>) |

## Florida

**Supreme Court (Fla.):** Cite to So., So. 2d, or So. 3d.

| Category | Dates | Abbreviation |
|---|---|---|
| Southern Reporter | 1886–date | So., So. 2d, So. 3d |
| Florida Reports | 1846–1948 | Fla. |
| Florida Law Weekly | 1978–date | Fla. L. Weekly |

**District Court of Appeal (Fla. Dist. Ct. App.):** Cite to So. 2d or So. 3d.

| Category | Dates | Abbreviation |
|---|---|---|
| Southern Reporter | 1957–date | So. 2d, So. 3d |
| Florida Law Weekly | 1978–date | Fla. L. Weekly |

**Circuit Court (Fla. Cir. Ct.), County Court (e.g., Fla. Orange County Ct.), Public Service Commission (Fla. P.S.C.), and other lower courts of record:** Cite to Fla. Supp. or Fla. Supp. 2d.

| Category | Dates | Abbreviation |
|---|---|---|
| Florida Supplement | 1950–1991 | Fla. Supp., Fla. Supp. 2d |
| Florida Law Weekly Supplement | 1992–date | Fla. L. Weekly Supp. |

**Statutory compilations:** Cite to Fla. Stat..

| Category | Dates | Abbreviation |
|---|---|---|
| Florida Statutes | | Fla. Stat. § x.x (\<year>) |
| West's Florida Statutes Annotated | | Fla. Stat. Ann. § x.x (West \<year>) |
| LexisNexis Florida Statutes Annotated | | Fla. Stat. Ann. § x.x (LexisNexis \<year>) |

**Session laws:** Cite to Fla. Laws.

| Category | Dates | Abbreviation |
|---|---|---|
| Laws of Florida | | \<year> Fla. Laws \<page no.> |

| Category | Dates | Abbreviation |
| --- | --- | --- |
| West's Florida Session Law Service | | <year> Fla. Sess. Law Serv. <page no.> (West) |

**Administrative compilation**

| | | |
| --- | --- | --- |
| Florida Administrative Code Annotated (LexisNexis) | | Fla. Admin. Code Ann. r. x-x.x (<year>) |

**Administrative register:** Cite to Fla. Admin. Reg..

| | | |
| --- | --- | --- |
| Florida Administrative Register | 2012–date | <vol. no.> Fla. Admin. Reg. <page no.> (<month day, year>) |
| Florida Administrative Weekly (LexisNexis) | 1996–2012 | <vol. no.> Fla. Admin. Weekly <page no.> (<month day, year>) |

Georgia

**Supreme Court (Ga.):** Cite to S.E. or S.E.2d.

| | | |
| --- | --- | --- |
| South Eastern Reporter | 1887–date | S.E., S.E.2d |
| Georgia Reports | 1846–date | Ga. |

**Court of Appeals (Ga. Ct. App.):** Cite to S.E. or S.E.2d.

| | | |
| --- | --- | --- |
| South Eastern Reporter | 1907–date | S.E., S.E.2d |
| Georgia Appeals Reports | 1907–date | Ga. App. |

**Statutory compilations:** Cite to Ga. Code Ann. (published by LexisNexis).

| | | |
| --- | --- | --- |
| Official Code of Georgia Annotated (LexisNexis) | | Ga. Code Ann. § x-x-x (<year>) |
| West's Code of Georgia Annotated | | Ga. Code Ann. § x-x-x (West <year>) |

**Session laws:** Cite to Ga. Laws.

| | | |
| --- | --- | --- |
| Georgia Laws | | <year> Ga. Laws <page no.> |
| Georgia <year> Advance Legislative Service (LexisNexis) | | <year>-<pamph. no.> Ga. Code Ann. Adv. Legis. Serv. <page no.> (LexisNexis) |
| West's Georgia Legislative Service | | <year> Ga. Code Ann. Adv. Legis. Serv. <page no.> (West) |

**Administrative compilation**

| | | |
| --- | --- | --- |
| Official Compilation Rules | | Ga. Comp. R. & Regs. x-x-x.x (<year>) |

| Category | Dates | Abbreviation |
|---|---|---|
| and Regulations of the State of Georgia | | |
| **Administrative register** | | |
| Georgia Government Register (LexisNexis) | | `<iss. no.>` Ga. Gov't Reg. `<page no.>` (LexisNexis `<month year>`) |

Hawaii

**Supreme Court (Haw.):** Cite to P.2d or P.3d.

| | | |
|---|---|---|
| Pacific Reporter | 1959–date | P.2d, P.3d |
| West's Hawaii Reports (begins with vol. 76) | 1994–date | Haw. |
| Hawaii Reports (ends with vol. 75) | 1847–1994 | Haw. |

**Intermediate Court of Appeals (Haw. Ct. App.):** Cite to P.2d or P.3d.

| | | |
|---|---|---|
| Pacific Reporter | 1980–date | P.2d, P.3d |
| West's Hawaii Reports | 1994–date | Haw. |
| Hawaii Appellate Reports | 1980–1994 | Haw. App. |

**Statutory compilations:** Cite to Haw. Rev. Stat..

| | |
|---|---|
| Hawaii Revised Statutes | Haw. Rev. Stat. § x-x (`<year>`) |
| Michie's Hawaii Revised Statutes Annotated (LexisNexis) | Haw. Rev. Stat. Ann. § x-x (LexisNexis `<year>`) |
| West's Hawai'i Revised Statutes Annotated | Haw. Rev. Stat. Ann. § x-x (West `<year>`) |

**Session laws:** Cite to Haw. Sess. Laws.

| | |
|---|---|
| Session Laws of Hawaii | `<year>` Haw. Sess. Laws `<page no.>` |
| Michie's Hawaii Revised Statutes Annotated Advance Legislative Service (LexisNexis) | `<year>`-`<pamph. no.>` Haw. Rev. Stat. Ann. Adv. Legis. Serv. `<page no.>` (LexisNexis) |
| West's Hawai'i Legislative Service | `<year>` Haw. Legis. Serv. `<page no.>` (West) |

**Administrative compilation**

| Category | Dates | Abbreviation |
|---|---|---|
| Code of Hawaii Rules (LexisNexis) | | Haw. Code R. § x-x-x (LexisNexis \<year\>) |
| **Administrative register** | | |
| Hawaii Government Register (LexisNexis) | | \<iss. no.\> Haw. Gov't Reg. \<page no.\> (LexisNexis \<month year\>) |

### Idaho

**Supreme Court (Idaho):** Cite to P., P.2d, or P.3d.

| | | |
|---|---|---|
| Pacific Reporter | 1883–date | P., P.2d, P.3d |
| Idaho Reports | 1866–date | Idaho |

**Court of Appeals (Idaho Ct. App.):** Cite to P.2d or P.3d.

| | | |
|---|---|---|
| Pacific Reporter | 1982–date | P.2d, P.3d |
| Idaho Reports | 1982–date | Idaho |

**Statutory compilations:** Cite to Idaho Code (published by LexisNexis).

| | | |
|---|---|---|
| Idaho Code (LexisNexis) | | Idaho Code § x-x (\<year\>) |
| West's Idaho Code Annotated | | Idaho Code Ann. § x-x (West \<year\>) |

**Session laws:** Cite to Idaho Sess. Laws.

| | | |
|---|---|---|
| Idaho Session Laws | | \<year\> Idaho Sess. Laws \<page no.\> |
| Idaho Code Annotated Advance Legislative Service (LexisNexis) | | \<year\>-\<pamph. no.\> Idaho Code Ann. Adv. Legis. Serv. \<page no.\> (LexisNexis) |
| West's Idaho Legislative Service | | \<year\> Idaho Legis. Serv. \<page no.\> (West) |

**Administrative compilation:** http://adminrules.gov/rules/current

| | | |
|---|---|---|
| Idaho Administrative Code | | Idaho Admin. Code r. x.x.x.x (\<year\>) |
| **Administrative register** | | |
| Idaho Administrative Bulletin | | \<vol. no.\> Idaho Admin. Bull. \<page no.\> (\<month day, year\>) |

### Illinois

**Public domain format:** Illinois has adopted a public domain citation format for cases effective July 1, 2011. *See* Illinois Supreme Court Rule 6. The format is:

- *People v. Doe*, 2011 IL 102345

| Category | Dates | Abbreviation |
|----------|-------|--------------|

- *People v. Doe*, 2011 IL App (1st) 101234

**Supreme Court (Ill.):** Cite to N.E., N.E.2d, or N.E.3d.

| | | |
|----------|-------|--------------|
| North Eastern Reporter | 1884–date | N.E., N.E.2d, N.E.3d |
| Illinois Official Reports | 2011–date | `<year> IL <docket no.>` |
| Illinois Reports | | |
| 11 Ill. to date | 1849–2011 | Ill., Ill. 2d |
| Gilman | 1844–1849 | e.g., 6 Ill. (1 Gilm.) |
| Scammon | 1832–1843 | e.g., 2 Ill. (1 Scam.) |
| Breese | 1819–1831 | 1 Ill. (Breese) |
| West's Illinois Decisions | 1976–date | Ill. Dec. |

**Appellate Court (Ill. App. Ct.):** Cite to N.E.2d, N.E.3d.

| | | |
|----------|-------|--------------|
| North Eastern Reporter | 1936–date | N.E.2d, N.E.3d |
| Illinois Official Reports | 2011–date | `<year> IL App. (<court no.>)` |
| Illinois Appellate Court Reports | 1877–2011 | Ill. App., Ill. App. 2d, Ill. App. 3d |
| West's Illinois Decisions | 1976–date | Ill. Dec. |

**Illinois Circuit Court (Ill. Cir. Ct.), previously Court of Claims (Ill. Ct. Cl.):** Cite to Ill. Ct. Cl..

| | | |
|----------|-------|--------------|
| Illinois Court of Claims Reports | 1889–date | Ill. Ct. Cl. |

**Statutory compilations:** Cite to Ill. Comp. Stat..

| | | |
|----------|-------|--------------|
| Illinois Compiled Statutes | | `<ch. no.> Ill. Comp. Stat. <act no.> / <sec. no.> (<year>)` |
| West's Smith-Hurd Illinois Compiled Statutes Annotated | | `<ch. no.> Ill. Comp. Stat. Ann. <act no.> / <sec. no.> (West <year>)` |
| Illinois Compiled Statutes Annotated (LexisNexis) | | `<ch. no.> Ill. Comp. Stat. Ann. <act no.> / <sec. no.> (LexisNexis <year>)` |

**Session laws:** Cite to Ill. Laws.

| | | |
|----------|-------|--------------|
| Laws of Illinois | | `<year> Ill. Laws <page no.>` |
| Illinois Legislative Service (West) | | `<year> Ill. Legis. Serv. <page no.> (West)` |

| Category | Dates | Abbreviation |
|---|---|---|
| Illinois Compiled Statutes Annotated Advance Legislative Service (LexisNexis) | | `<year>-<pamph. no.>` Ill. Comp. Stat. Ann. Adv. Legis. Serv. `<page no.>` (LexisNexis) |

**Administrative compilations:** Cite to Ill. Admin. Code.

| Category | Dates | Abbreviation |
|---|---|---|
| Illinois Administrative Code | | Ill. Admin. Code tit. x, § x (`<year>`) |
| Code of Illinois Rules (LexisNexis) | | `<vol. no.>` Ill. Code R. `<rule no.>` (LexisNexis `<year>`) |

**Administrative register**

| Category | Dates | Abbreviation |
|---|---|---|
| Illinois Register | | `<vol. no.>` Ill. Reg. `<page no.>` (`<month day, year>`) |

Indiana

**Supreme Court (Ind.):** Cite to N.E., N.E.2d, N.E.3d.

| Category | Dates | Abbreviation |
|---|---|---|
| North Eastern Reporter | 1885–date | N.E., N.E.2d, N.E.3d |
| Indiana Reports | 1848–1981 | Ind. |
| Blackford | 1817–1847 | Blackf. |

**Court of Appeals (Ind. Ct. App.), previously Appellate Court (Ind. App.):** Cite to N.E., N.E.2d, or N.E.3d.

| Category | Dates | Abbreviation |
|---|---|---|
| North Eastern Reporter | 1891–date | N.E., N.E.2d, N.E.3d |
| Indiana Court of Appeals Reports (prior to 1972, Indiana Appellate Court Reports) | 1890–1979 | Ind. App. |

**Tax Court (Ind. T.C.):** Cite to N.E.2d or N.E.3d.

| Category | Dates | Abbreviation |
|---|---|---|
| North Eastern Reporter | 1986–date | N.E., N.E.2d, N.E.3d |

**Statutory compilations:** Cite to Ind. Code.

| Category | Dates | Abbreviation |
|---|---|---|
| Indiana Code | | Ind. Code § x-x-x-x (`<year>`) |
| West's Annotated Indiana Code | | Ind. Code Ann. § x-x-x-x (West `<year>`) |
| Burns Indiana Statutes Annotated (LexisNexis) | | Ind. Code Ann. § x-x-x-x (LexisNexis `<year>`) |

**Session laws:** Cite to Ind. Acts.

| Category | Dates | Abbreviation |
|---|---|---|
| Acts, Indiana | | `<year>` Ind. Acts `<page no.>` |
| West's Indiana Legislative Service | | `<year>` Ind. Legis. Serv. `<page no.>` (West) |

| Category | Dates | Abbreviation |
|---|---|---|
| Burns Indiana Statutes Annotated Advance Legislative Service (LexisNexis) | | `<year>`-`<pamph. no.>` Ind. Stat. Ann. Adv. Legis. Serv. `<page no.>` (LexisNexis) |

**Administrative compilations:** Cite to Ind. Admin. Code.

| | | |
|---|---|---|
| Indiana Administrative Code | | `<tit. no.>` Ind. Admin. Code `<rule no.>` (`<year>`) |
| West's Indiana Administrative Code | | `<tit. no.>` Ind. Admin. Code `<rule no.>` (West `<year>`) |

**Administrative register**

| | | |
|---|---|---|
| Indiana Register | | `<vol. no.>` Ind. Reg. `<page no.>` (`<month day, year>`) |

Iowa

**Supreme Court (Iowa):** Cite to N.W. or N.W.2d.

| | | |
|---|---|---|
| North Western Reporter | 1879–date | N.W., N.W.2d |
| Iowa Reports (Cite to edition published by Clarke for vols. 1–8.) | 1855–1968 | Iowa |
| Greene | 1847–1854 | Greene |
| Morris | 1839–1846 | Morris |
| Bradford | 1838–1841 | Bradf. |

**Court of Appeals (Iowa Ct. App.):** Cite to N.W.2d.

| | | |
|---|---|---|
| North Western Reporter | 1977–date | N.W.2d |

**Statutory compilations:** Cite to Iowa Code.

| | | |
|---|---|---|
| Code of Iowa | | Iowa Code § x.x (`<year>`) |
| West's Iowa Code Annotated | | Iowa Code Ann. § x.x (West `<year>`) |

**Session laws:** Cite to Iowa Acts.

| | | |
|---|---|---|
| Acts of the State of Iowa | | `<year>` Iowa Acts `<page no.>` |
| Iowa Legislative Service (West) | | `<year>` Iowa Legis. Serv. `<page no.>` (West) |

**Administrative compilation**

| | | |
|---|---|---|
| Iowa Administrative Code | | Iowa Admin. Code r. x-x.x (`<year>`) |

| Category | Dates | Abbreviation |
|---|---|---|
| **Administrative register** | | |
| Iowa Administrative Bulletin | | <vol. no.> Iowa Admin. Bull. <page no.> (<month day, year>) |

### Kansas

**Supreme Court (Kan.):** Cite to P., P.2d, or P.3d.

| | | |
|---|---|---|
| Pacific Reporter | 1883–date | P., P.2d, P.3d |
| Kansas Reports | 1862–date | Kan. |
| McCahon | 1858–1868 | McCahon |

**Court of Appeals (Kan. Ct. App.):** Cite to P., P.2d, or P.3d.

| | | |
|---|---|---|
| Pacific Reporter | 1895–1901 | P. |
| | 1977–date | P.2d, P.3d |
| Kansas Court of Appeals Reports | 1895–1901 | Kan. App. |
| | 1977–date | Kan. App. 2d |

**Statutory compilations:** Cite to Kan. Stat. Ann..

| | | |
|---|---|---|
| Kansas Statutes Annotated | | Kan. Stat. Ann. § x-x (<year>) |
| West's Kansas Statutes Annotated | | Kan. Stat. Ann. § x-x (West <year>) |

**Session laws:** Cite to Kan. Sess. Laws.

| | | |
|---|---|---|
| Session Laws of Kansas | | <year> Kan. Sess. Laws <page no.> |
| West's Kansas Legislative Service | | <year> Kan. Legis. Serv. <page no.> (West) |

**Administrative compilation**

| | | |
|---|---|---|
| Kansas Administrative Regulations (updated by supplements) | | Kan. Admin. Regs. § x-x-x (<year>) |

**Administrative register**

| | | |
|---|---|---|
| Kansas Register | | <vol. no.> Kan. Reg. <page no.> (<month day, year>) |

### Kentucky

**Supreme Court (Ky.):** before 1976 the Court of Appeals (Ky.) was the highest state court. Cite to S.W., S.W.2d, or S.W.3d.

| | | |
|---|---|---|
| South Western Reporter | 1886–date | S.W., S.W.2d, S.W.3d |
| Kentucky Reports | | |

| Category | Dates | Abbreviation |
|---|---|---|
| 78 Ky. to 314 Ky. | 1879–1951 | Ky. |
| Bush | 1866–1879 | e.g., 66 Ky. (3 Bush) |
| Duvall | 1863–1866 | e.g., 62 Ky. (1 Duv.) |
| Metcalf | 1858–1863 | e.g., 58 Ky. (1 Met.) |
| Monroe, Ben | 1840–1857 | e.g., 53 Ky. (14 B. Mon.) |
| Dana | 1833–1840 | e.g., 35 Ky. (5 Dana) |
| Marshall, J.J. | 1829–1832 | e.g., 27 Ky. (4 J.J. Marsh.) |
| Monroe, T.B. | 1824–1828 | e.g., 19 Ky. (3 T.B. Mon.) |
| Littell | 1822–1824 | e.g., 13 Ky. (3 Litt.) |
| Littell's Selected Cases | 1795–1821 | e.g., 16 Ky. (1 Litt. Sel. Cas.) |
| Marshall, A.K. | 1817–1821 | e.g., 10 Ky. (3 A.K. Marsh.) |
| Bibb | 1808–1817 | e.g., 6 Ky. (3 Bibb) |
| Hardin | 1805–1808 | 3 Ky. (Hard.) |
| Sneed | 1801–1805 | 2 Ky. (Sneed) |
| Hughes | 1785–1801 | 1 Ky. (Hughes) |
| Kentucky Opinions | 1864–1886 | Ky. Op. |
| Kentucky Law Reporter | 1880–1908 | Ky. L. Rptr. |
| Kentucky Appellate Reporter | 1994–2000 | Ky. App. |
| Kentucky Attorneys Memo | 2001–2007 | Ky. Att'y Memo |
| Kentucky Law Summary | 1966–date | Ky. L. Summ. |

**Court of Appeals (Ky. Ct. App.) (for decisions before 1976, see Kentucky Supreme Court):** Cite to S.W.2d or S.W.3d.

| Category | Dates | Abbreviation |
|---|---|---|
| South Western Reporter | 1976–date | S.W.2d, S.W.3d |
| Kentucky Appellate Reporter | 1994–2000 | Ky. App. |
| Kentucky Attorneys Memo | 2001–2007 | Ky. Att'y Memo |
| Kentucky Law Summary | 1966–date | Ky. L. Summ. |

**Statutory compilations:** Cite to one of the following codes.

| | | |
|---|---|---|
| Baldwin's Kentucky Revised | | Ky. Rev. Stat. Ann. § x.x (West <year>) |

| Category | Dates | Abbreviation |
|---|---|---|
| Statutes Annotated (West) | | |
| Michie's Kentucky Revised Statutes Annotated (LexisNexis) | | Ky. Rev. Stat. Ann. § x.x (LexisNexis <year>) |
| **Session laws:** Cite to Ky. Acts. | | |
| Acts of Kentucky | | <year> Ky. Acts <page no.> |
| Kentucky Revised Statutes and Rules Service (West) | | <year> Ky. Rev. Stat. & R. Serv. <page no.> (West) |
| Michie's Kentucky Revised Statutes Advance Legislative Service (LexisNexis) | | <year>-<pamph. no.> Ky. Rev. Stat. Adv. Legis. Serv. <page no.> (LexisNexis) |
| **Administrative compilation** | | |
| Kentucky Administrative Regulations Service | | <tit. no.> Ky. Admin. Regs. <rule no.> (<year>) |
| **Administrative register** | | |
| Administrative Register of Kentucky | | <vol. no.> Ky. Admin. Reg. <page no.> (<month year>) |

Louisiana

**Public domain citation format:** Louisiana has adopted a public domain citation format for cases after December 31, 1993. *See* Rules of the Supreme Court of Louisiana, part G, section 8. The format is:

- *Smith v. Jones*, 93-2345 (La. 7/15/94); 650 So.2d 500

- *Smith v. Jones*, 93-2345 (La. App. 1 Cir. 7/15/94); 660 So.2d 400

- *Smith v. Jones*, 94-2345, p. 7 (La. 7/15/94); 650 So.2d 500, 504

**Supreme Court (La.), before 1813 the Superior Court of Louisiana (La.) and the Superior Court of the Territory of Orleans (Orleans):** Cite to So., So. 2d, or So. 3d.

| | | |
|---|---|---|
| Southern Reporter | 1886–date | So., So. 2d, So. 3d |
| Louisiana Reports | 1901–1972 | La. |
| Louisiana Annual Reports | 1846–1900 | La. Ann. |
| Robinson | 1841–1846 | Rob. |
| Louisiana Reports | 1830–1841 | La. |
| Martin (Louisiana Term Reports) | 1809–1830 | Mart. (o.s.), Mart. (n.s.) |

| Category | Dates | Abbreviation |
|---|---|---|
| **Court of Appeal (La. Ct. App.):** Cite to So., So. 2d, or So. 3d. | | |
| Southern Reporter | 1928–date | So., So. 2d, So. 3d |
| Louisiana Court of Appeals Reports | 1924–1932 | La. App. |
| Peltier's Decisions, Parish at Orleans | 1917–1924 | Pelt. |
| Teissier, Orleans Court of Appeals | 1903–1917 | Teiss. |
| Gunby's Reports | 1885 | Gunby |
| McGloin | 1881–1884 | McGl. |
| **Statutory compilations:** Cite to one of the following codes. | | |
| West's Louisiana Statutes Annotated | | La. Stat. Ann. § x:x (<year>) |
| West's Louisiana Children's Code Annotated | | La. Child. Code Ann. art. x (<year>) |
| West's Louisiana Civil Code Annotated | | La. Civ. Code Ann. art. x (<year>) |
| West's Louisiana Code of Civil Procedure Annotated | | La. Code Civ. Proc. Ann. art. x (<year>) |
| West's Louisiana Code of Criminal Procedure Annotated | | La. Code Crim. Proc. Ann. art. x (<year>) |
| West's Louisiana Code of Evidence Annotated | | La. Code Evid. Ann. art. x (<year>) |
| West's Louisiana Constitution Annotated | | La. Const. Ann. art. x (<year>) |
| **Session laws:** Cite to La. Acts. | | |
| **State of Louisiana:** Acts of the Legislature <year> La. Acts <page no.> | | |
| West's Louisiana Session Law Service | | <year> La. Sess. Law Serv. <page no.> (West) |
| **Administrative compilation** | | |
| Louisiana Administrative Code | | La. Admin. Code tit. x, § x (<year>) |
| **Administrative register** | | |

| Category | Dates | Abbreviation |
|---|---|---|
| Louisiana Register | | <vol. no.> La. Reg. <page no.> (<month day, year>) |

### Maine

**Public domain citation format:** Maine has adopted a public domain citation format for cases after December 31, 1996. *See* Administrative Order of the Supreme Judicial Court—New Citation Form (Aug. 20, 1996). The format is:

- *Estate of Hoch v. Stifel*, 2011 ME 24, 16 A.3d 137
- *Estate of Hoch v. Stifel*, 2011 ME 24, ¶ 11, 16 A.3d 137
- *Saucier v. State Tax Assessor*, 1998 ME 61, 708 A.2d 28

**Supreme Judicial Court (Me.):** Cite to A., A.2d or A.3d.

| | | |
|---|---|---|
| Atlantic Reporter | 1885–date | A., A.2d, A.3d |
| Maine Reports | 1820–1965 | Me. |

**Statutory compilations:** Cite to Me. Stat..

| | |
|---|---|
| West's Maine Statutes | Me. Stat. tit. x, § x (<year>) |
| Maine Revised Statutes Annotated (West) | Me. Rev. Stat. Ann. tit. x, § x (<year>) |

**Session laws:** Cite to Me. Laws.

| | |
|---|---|
| Laws of the State of Maine | <year> Me. Laws <page no.> |
| Maine Legislative Service (West) | <year> Me. Legis. Serv. <page no.> (West) |

**Administrative compilation**

| | |
|---|---|
| Code of Maine Rules (LexisNexis) | x-x-x Me. Code R. § x (LexisNexis <year>) |

**Administrative register**

| | |
|---|---|
| Maine Government Register (LexisNexis) | <iss. no.> Me. Gov't Reg. <page no.> (LexisNexis <month year>) |

### Maryland

**Court of Appeals (Md.):** Cite to A., A.2d or A.3d.

| | | |
|---|---|---|
| Atlantic Reporter | 1885–date | A., A.2d, A.3d |
| Maryland Reports | 1851–date | Md. |
| Gill | 1843–1851 | Gill |
| Gill and Johnson | 1829–1842 | G. & J. |
| Harris and Gill | 1826–1829 | H. & G. |
| Harris and Johnson | 1800–1826 | H. & J. |

| Category | Dates | Abbreviation |
|---|---|---|
| Harris and McHenry | 1770–1774 1780–1799 | H. & McH. |

**Court of Special Appeals (Md. Ct. Spec. App.):** Cite to A.2d or A.3d.

| | | |
|---|---|---|
| Atlantic Reporter | 1967–date | A.2d, A.3d |
| Maryland Appellate Reports | 1967–date | Md. App. |

**Statutory compilations:** Cite by subject to either Michie's Md. Code Ann. or West's Md. Code Ann..

| | |
|---|---|
| Michie's Annotated Code of Maryland (LexisNexis) | Md. Code Ann., \<subject\> § x-x (LexisNexis \<year\>) |
| West's Annotated Code of Maryland | Md. Code Ann., \<subject\> § x-x (West \<year\>) |
| Agriculture | Agric. |
| Business Occupations and Professions | Bus. Occ. & Prof. |
| Business Regulation | Bus. Reg. |
| Commercial Law | Com. Law |
| Constitutions | Const. |
| Corporations and Associations | Corps. & Ass'ns |
| Correctional Services | Corr. Servs. |
| Courts and Judicial Proceedings | Cts. & Jud. Proc. |
| Criminal Law | Crim. Law |
| Criminal Procedure | Crim. Proc. |
| Economic Development | Econ. Dev. |
| Education | Educ. |
| Election Law | Elec. Law |
| Environment | Envir. |
| Estates and Trusts | Est. & Trusts |
| Family Law | Fam. Law |
| Financial Institutions | Fin. Inst. |
| Health–General | Health–Gen. |
| Health Occupations | Health Occ. |
| Housing and Community Development | Hous. & Cmty. Dev. |
| Human Services | Hum. Servs. |
| Insurance | Ins. |

| Category | Dates | Abbreviation |
|---|---|---|
| Labor and Employment | | Lab. & Empl. |
| Land Use | | Land Use |
| Local Government | | Local Gov't |
| Natural Resources | | Nat. Res. |
| Public Safety | | Pub. Safety |
| Public Utility | | Pub. Util. |
| Real Property | | Real Prop. |
| State Finance and Procurement | | State Fin. & Proc. |
| State Government | | State Gov't |
| State Personnel and Pensions | | State Pers. & Pens. |
| Tax–General | | Tax–Gen. |
| Tax–Property | | Tax–Prop. |
| Transportation | | Transp. |

**Session laws:** Cite to Md. Laws.

| | | |
|---|---|---|
| Laws of Maryland | | `<year>` Md. Laws `<page no.>` |
| Michie's Annotated Code of Maryland Advance Legislative Service (LexisNexis) | | `<year>-<pamph. no.>` Md. Code Ann. Adv. Legis. Serv. `<page no.>` (LexisNexis) |
| West's Maryland Legislative Service | | `<year>` Md. Legis. Serv. `<page no.>` (West) |

**Administrative compilation**

| | | |
|---|---|---|
| Code of Maryland Regulations | | Md. Code Regs. `<reg. no.>` (`<year>`) |

**Administrative register**

| | | |
|---|---|---|
| Maryland Register | | `<vol. no.>` Md. Reg. `<page no.>` (`<month day, year>`) |

Massachusetts

**Supreme Judicial Court (Mass.):** Cite to N.E., or N.E.2d, N.E.3d..

| | | |
|---|---|---|
| North Eastern Reporter | 1885–date | N.E., N.E.2d, N.E.3d |

Massachusetts Reports

| | | |
|---|---|---|
| 97 Mass. to date | 1867–date | Mass. |
| Allen | 1861–1867 | e.g., 83 Mass. (1 Allen) |
| Gray | 1854–1860 | e.g., 67 Mass. (1 Gray) |
| Cushing | 1848–1853 | e.g., 55 Mass. (1 Cush.) |

| Category | Dates | Abbreviation |
|---|---|---|
| Metcalf | 1840–1847 | e.g., 42 Mass. (1 Met.) |
| Pickering | 1822–1839 | e.g., 18 Mass. (1 Pick.) |
| Tyng | 1805–1822 | e.g., 2 Mass. (1 Tyng) |
| Williams | 1804–1805 | 1 Mass. (1 Will.) |

**Appeals Court (Mass. App. Ct.):** Cite to N.E.2d, N.E.3d.

| Category | Dates | Abbreviation |
|---|---|---|
| North Eastern Reporter | 1972–date | N.E.2d, N.E.3d |
| Massachusetts Appeals Court Reports | 1972–date | Mass. App. Ct. |

**Lower Courts (Mass. Dist. Ct., Bos. Mun. Ct.):** Cite to Mass. App. Div., if found there; else cite to Mass. Supp. or Mass. App. Dec..

| Category | Dates | Abbreviation |
|---|---|---|
| Reports of Massachusetts | 1936–1950 | Mass. App. Div. |
| Appellate Division | 1980–date | |
| Massachusetts Reports Supplement | 1980–1983 | Mass. Supp. |
| Massachusetts Appellate Decisions | 1941–1977 | Mass. App. Dec. |
| Appellate Division Advance Sheets | 1975–1979 | `<year>` Mass. App. Div. Adv. Sh. `<page no.>` |

**Statutory compilations:** Cite to Mass. Gen. Laws.

| Category | Abbreviation |
|---|---|
| General Laws of Massachusetts (Mass. Bar Ass'n/West) | Mass. Gen. Laws ch. x, § x (`<year>`) |
| Massachusetts General Laws Annotated (West) | Mass. Gen. Laws Ann. ch. x, § x (West `<year>`) |
| Annotated Laws of Massachusetts (LexisNexis) | Mass. Ann. Laws ch. x, § x (LexisNexis `<year>`) |

**Session laws:** Cite to Mass. Acts.

| Category | Abbreviation |
|---|---|
| Acts and Resolves of Massachusetts | `<year>` Mass. Acts `<page no.>` |
| Massachusetts Legislative Service (West) | `<year>` Mass. Legis. Serv. `<page no.>` (West) |
| Massachusetts Advance Legislative Service (LexisNexis) | `<year>`-`<pamph. no.>` Mass. Adv. Legis. Serv. `<page no.>` (LexisNexis) |

| Category | Dates | Abbreviation |
|---|---|---|
| **Administrative compilations:** Cite to official Mass. Code Regs.. | | |
| Code of Massachusetts Regulations | | `<tit. no.>` Mass. Code Regs. `<sec. no.>` (`<year>`) |
| Code of Massachusetts Regulations (LexisNexis) | | `<tit. no.>` Mass. Code Regs. `<sec. no.>` (LexisNexis `<year>`) |
| **Administrative register** | | |
| Massachusetts Register | | `<iss. no.>` Mass. Reg. `<page no.>` (`<month day, year>`) |

Michigan

| Category | Dates | Abbreviation |
|---|---|---|
| **Supreme Court (Mich.):** Cite to N.W. or N.W.2d. | | |
| North Western Reporter | 1879–date | N.W., N.W.2d |
| Michigan Reports | 1847–date | Mich. |
| Douglass | 1843–1847 | Doug. |
| Blume, Unreported Opinions | 1836–1843 | Blume Unrep. Op. |
| Blume, Supreme Court Transactions | 1836–1843 | Blume Sup. Ct. Trans. |
| **Court of Appeals (Mich. Ct. App.):** Cite to N.W.2d. | | |
| North Western Reporter | 1965–date | N.W.2d |
| Michigan Appeals Reports | 1965–date | Mich. App. |
| **Court of Claims (Mich. Ct. Cl.):** Cite to Mich. Ct. Cl. | | |
| Michigan Court of Claims Reports | 1939–1942 | Mich. Ct. Cl. |
| **Statutory compilations:** Cite to Mich. Comp. Laws. | | |
| Michigan Compiled Laws (1979) | | Mich. Comp. Laws § x.x (`<year>`) |
| Michigan Compiled Laws Annotated (West) | | Mich. Comp. Laws Ann. § x.x (West `<year>`) |
| Michigan Compiled Laws Service (LexisNexis) | | Mich. Comp. Laws Serv. § x.x (LexisNexis `<year>`) |

**Session laws:** Cite to Mich. Pub. Acts.

| Category | Dates | Abbreviation |
|---|---|---|
| Public and Local Acts of the Legislature of the State of Michigan | | `<year>` Mich. Pub. Acts `<page no.>` |
| Michigan Legislative Service (West) | | `<year>` Mich. Legis. Serv. `<page no.>` (West) |
| Michigan Advance Legislative Service (LexisNexis) | | `<year>-<pamph. no.>` Mich. Adv. Legis. Serv. `<page no.>` (LexisNexis) |
| **Administrative compilation** | | |
| Michigan Administrative Code | | Mich. Admin. Code r. x.x (`<year>`) |
| **Administrative register** | | |
| Michigan Register | | `<iss. no.>` Mich. Reg. `<page no.>` (`<month day, year>`) |

## Minnesota

**Supreme Court (Minn.):** Cite to N.W. or N.W.2d.

| | | |
|---|---|---|
| North Western Reporter | 1879–date | N.W., N.W.2d |
| Minnesota Reports | 1851–1977 | Minn. |

**Court of Appeals (Minn. Ct. App.):** Cite to N.W.2d.

| | | |
|---|---|---|
| North Western Reporter | 1983–date | N.W.2d |

**Statutory compilations:** Cite to Minn. Stat..

| | | |
|---|---|---|
| Minnesota Statutes | | Minn. Stat. § x.x (`<year>`) |
| Minnesota Statutes Annotated (West) | | Minn. Stat. Ann. § x.x (West `<year>`) |

**Session laws:** Cite to Minn. Laws.

| | | |
|---|---|---|
| Laws of Minnesota | | `<year>` Minn. Laws `<page no.>` |
| Minnesota Session Law Service (West) | | `<year>` Minn. Sess. Law Serv. `<page no.>` (West) |

**Administrative compilation**

| | | |
|---|---|---|
| Minnesota Rules | | Minn. R. `<rule no.>` (`<year>`) |

**Administrative register**

| | | |
|---|---|---|
| Minnesota State Register | | `<vol. no.>` Minn. Reg. `<page no.>` (`<month day, year>`) |

## Mississippi

**Public domain citation format:** Mississippi has adopted a public domain citation format for cases after July 1, 1997. *See* <u>Mississippi Rules of Appellate Procedure, Rule 28(f)</u>. The format is:

| Category | Dates | Abbreviation |
|----------|-------|--------------|

- *Smith v. Jones*, 95-KA-01234-SCT (Miss. 1997)
- *Smith v. Jones*, 95-KA-01234-SCT (¶1) (Miss. 1997)

**Supreme Court (Miss.):** Cite to So., So. 2d, or So. 3d.

| | | |
|----------|-----------|----------------------|
| Southern Reporter | 1886–date | So., So. 2d, So. 3d |
| Mississippi Reports | | |
| 23 Miss. to 254 Miss. | 1851–1966 | Miss. |
| Smedes and Marshall | 1843–1850 | e.g., 9 Miss. (1 S. & M.) |
| Howard | 1834–1843 | e.g., 2 Miss. (1 Howard) |
| Walker | 1818–1832 | 1 Miss. (1 Walker) |
| Mississippi Decisions | 1820–1885 | Miss. Dec. |

**Court of Appeals (Miss. Ct. App.):** Cite to So. 2d or So. 3d.

| | | |
|----------|-----------|----------------|
| Southern Reporter | 1995–date | So. 2d, So. 3d |

**Statutory compilations:** Cite to Miss. Code Ann. (published by LexisNexis).

| | |
|----------|----------------------|
| Mississippi Code 1972 Annotated (LexisNexis) | Miss. Code Ann. § x-x-x (<year>) |
| West's Annotated Mississippi Code | Miss. Code Ann. § x-x-x (West <year>) |

**Session laws:** Cite to Miss. Laws.

| | |
|----------|----------------------|
| General Laws of Mississippi | <year> Miss. Laws <page no.> |
| Mississippi General Laws Advance Sheets (LexisNexis) | <year>-<pamph. no.> Miss. Laws Adv. Sh. <page no.> (LexisNexis) |
| West's Mississippi Legislative Service | <year> Miss. Legis. Serv. <page no.> (West) |

**Administrative compilation**

| | |
|----------|----------------------|
| Code of Mississippi Rules (LexisNexis) | <tit. no.>-<ch. no.> Miss. Code R. § x (LexisNexis <year>) |

**Administrative register**

| | |
|----------|----------------------|
| Mississippi Government Register (LexisNexis) | <iss. no.> Miss. Gov't Reg. <page no.> (LexisNexis <month year>) |

| Category | Dates | Abbreviation |
|---|---|---|
| Missouri | | |
| **Supreme Court (Mo.):** Cite to S.W., S.W.2d, or S.W.3d. | | |
| South Western Reporter | 1886–date | S.W., S.W.2d, S.W.3d |
| Missouri Reports | 1821–1956 | Mo. |
| **Court of Appeals (Mo. Ct. App.):** Cite to S.W., S.W.2d, or S.W.3d. | | |
| South Western Reporter | 1902–date | S.W., S.W.2d, S.W.3d |
| Missouri Appeals Reports | 1876–1954 | Mo. App. |
| **Statutory compilations:** Cite to Mo. Rev. Stat.. | | |
| Missouri Revised Statutes | | Mo. Rev. Stat. § x.x (<year>) |
| Vernon's Annotated Missouri Statutes (West) | | Mo. Ann. Stat. § x.x (West <year>) |
| **Session laws:** Cite to Mo. Laws. | | |
| Session Laws of Missouri | | <year> Mo. Laws <page no.> |
| Missouri Legislative Service (West) | | <year> Mo. Legis. Serv. <page no.> (West) |
| **Administrative compilation** | | |
| Missouri Code of State Regulations Annotated | | Mo. Code Regs. Ann. tit. x, § x-x.x (<year>) |
| **Administrative register** | | |
| Missouri Register | | <vol. no.> Mo. Reg. <page no.> (<month day, year>) |
| Montana | | |

**Public domain citation format:** Montana has adopted a public domain citation format for cases after December 31, 1997. *See*:

- AF 06-0632 (02-25-10) Order In re: Opinion Forms and Citation Standards of the Supreme Court of Montana

- Adoption of Public Domain and Neutral-Format Citation (Dec. 16, 1997)

- AF 07-0064 (01-22-09) Order in the Matter of Amending Citations Standards for the Montana Supreme Court

The format is:

- *Doe v. Roe*, 1998 MT 12, ¶¶ 44-45, 286 Mont. 175, 989 P.2d 1312

| Category | Dates | Abbreviation |
|---|---|---|
| **Supreme Court (Mont.):** Cite to P., P.2d, or P.3d. | | |
| Pacific Reporter | 1883–date | P., P.2d, P.3d |
| Montana Reports | 1868–date | Mont. |
| State Reporter | 1945–date | State Rptr. |
| **Statutory compilations:** Cite to Mont. Code Ann.. | | |
| Montana Code Annotated | | Mont. Code Ann. § x-x-x (<year>) |
| West's Montana Code Annotated | | Mont. Code Ann. § x-x-x (West <year>) |
| Session laws | | |
| Laws of Montana | | <year> Mont. Laws <page no.> |
| **Administrative compilation** | | |
| Administrative Rules of Montana | | Mont. Admin. R. <rule no.> (<year>) |
| **Administrative register** | | |
| Montana Administrative Register | | <iss. no.> Mont. Admin. Reg. <page no.> (<month day, year>) |
| Nebraska | | |
| **Supreme Court (Neb.):** Cite to N.W. or N.W.2d. | | |
| North Western Reporter | 1879–date | N.W., N.W.2d |
| Nebraska Reports | 1860–date | Neb. |
| **Court of Appeals (Neb. Ct. App.):** Cite to N.W.2d. | | |
| North Western Reporter | 1992–date | N.W.2d |
| Nebraska Appellate Reports | 1992–date | Neb. App. |
| **Statutory compilations:** Cite to Neb. Rev. Stat.. | | |
| Revised Statutes of Nebraska | | Neb. Rev. Stat. § x-x (<year>) |
| Revised Statutes of Nebraska Annotated (LexisNexis) | | Neb. Rev. Stat. Ann. § x-x (LexisNexis <year>) |
| West's Revised Statutes of Nebraska Annotated | | Neb. Rev. Stat. Ann. § x-x (West <year>) |

**Session laws:** Cite to Neb. Laws.

| Category | Dates | Abbreviation |
|---|---|---|
| Laws of Nebraska | | <year> Neb. Laws <page no.> |
| West's Nebraska Legislative Service | | <year> Neb. Legis. Serv. <page no.> (West) |
| **Administrative compilation** | | |
| Nebraska Administrative Code | | <tit. no.> Neb. Admin. Code § x-x (<year>) |

Nevada

**Supreme Court (Nev.):** Cite to P., P.2d, or P.3d.

| | | |
|---|---|---|
| Pacific Reporter | 1883–date | P., P.2d, P.3d |
| Nevada Reports | 1865–date | Nev. |

**Statutory compilations:** Cite to Nev. Rev. Stat..

| | | |
|---|---|---|
| Nevada Revised Statutes | | Nev. Rev. Stat. § x.x (<year>) |
| Michie's Nevada Revised Statutes Annotated (LexisNexis) | | Nev. Rev. Stat. Ann. § x.x (LexisNexis <year>) |
| West's Nevada Revised Statutes Annotated | | Nev. Rev. Stat. Ann. § x.x (West <year>) |

**Session laws:** Cite to Nev. Stat..

| | | |
|---|---|---|
| Statutes of Nevada | | <year> Nev. Stat. <page no.> |
| West's Nevada Legislative Service | | <year> Nev. Legis. Serv. <page no.> (West) |
| **Administrative compilation** | | |
| Nevada Administrative Code | | Nev. Admin. Code § x.x (<year>) |
| **Administrative register** | | |
| Nevada Register of Administrative Regulations | | <vol. no.> Nev. Reg. Admin. Regs. <reg. no.> (<month day, year>) |

New Hampshire

**Supreme Court (N.H.):** Cite to A., A.2d, or A.3d.

| | | |
|---|---|---|
| Atlantic Reporter | 1885–date | A., A.2d, A.3d |
| New Hampshire Reports | 1816–date | N.H. |

**Statutory compilations:** Cite to N.H. Rev. Stat. Ann. (published by West).

| Category | Dates | Abbreviation |
|---|---|---|
| New Hampshire Revised Statutes Annotated (West) | | N.H. Rev. Stat. Ann. § x:x (<year>) |
| Lexis New Hampshire Revised Statutes Annotated | | N.H. Rev. Stat. Ann. § x:x (LexisNexis <year>) |

**Session laws:** Cite to N.H. Laws or N.H. Legis. Serv..

| | | |
|---|---|---|
| Laws of the State of New Hampshire (West) | | <year> N.H. Laws <page no.> |
| New Hampshire Legislative Service (West) | | <year> N.H. Legis. Serv. <page no.> |
| Lexis New Hampshire Revised Statutes Annotated <year> Advance Legislative Service (LexisNexis) | | <year>-<pamph. no.> N.H. Rev. Stat. Ann. Adv. Legis. Serv. <page no.> (LexisNexis) |

**Administrative compilations:** Cite to N.H. Code Admin. R. Ann..

| | | |
|---|---|---|
| New Hampshire Code of Administrative Rules Annotated (LexisNexis) | | N.H. Code Admin. R. Ann. <dep't name as abbreviated in Rules> <rule no.> (<year>) |
| Code of New Hampshire Rules (LexisNexis) | | N.H. Code R. <dep't name as abbreviated in Rules> <rule no.> (LexisNexis <year>) |

**Administrative registers:** Cite to N.H. Rulemaking Reg..

| | | |
|---|---|---|
| New Hampshire Rulemaking Register | | <vol. no.> N.H. Rulemaking Reg. <page no.> (<month day, year>) |
| New Hampshire Government Register (LexisNexis) | | <iss. no.> N.H. Gov't Reg. <page no.> (LexisNexis <month year>) |

## New Jersey

**Supreme Court (N.J.), previously Court of Errors and Appeals (N.J.):** Cite to A., A.2d, or A.3d.

| Category | Dates | Abbreviation |
|---|---|---|
| Atlantic Reporter | 1885–date | A., A.2d, A.3d |
| New Jersey Reports | 1948–date | N.J. |
| New Jersey Law Reports | 1790–1948 | N.J.L. |
| New Jersey Equity Reports | 1845–1948 | N.J. Eq. |

| Category | Dates | Abbreviation |
|---|---|---|
| New Jersey Miscellaneous Reports | 1923–1948 | N.J. Misc. |

**Superior Court (N.J. Super. Ct. App. Div., N.J. Super. Ct. Ch. Div., N.J. Super. Ct. Law Div.), previously Court of Chancery (N.J. Ch.), Supreme Court (N.J. Sup. Ct.), and Prerogative Court (N.J. Prerog. Ct.):** Cite to A., A.2d, or A.3d.

| | | |
|---|---|---|
| Atlantic Reporter | 1885–date | A., A.2d, A.3d |
| New Jersey Superior Court Reports | 1948–date | N.J. Super. |
| New Jersey Law Reports | 1790–1948 | N.J.L. |
| New Jersey Equity Reports | 1830–1948 | N.J. Eq. |
| New Jersey Miscellaneous Reports | 1923–1948 | N.J. Misc. |

**County Court (e.g., Essex County Ct.) and other lower courts:** Cite to A.2d.

**Tax Court (N.J. Tax Ct.):** Cite to N.J. Tax.

| | | |
|---|---|---|
| New Jersey Tax Court Reports | 1979–date | N.J. Tax |

**Statutory compilations:** Cite to N.J. Stat. Ann..

| | | |
|---|---|---|
| New Jersey Statutes Annotated (West) | | N.J. Stat. Ann. § x:x (West \<year>) |
| New Jersey Revised Statutes (2013) | | N.J. Rev. Stat. § x:x (\<year>) |

**Session laws:** Cite to N.J. Laws.

| | | |
|---|---|---|
| Laws of New Jersey | | \<year> N.J. Laws \<page no.> |
| New Jersey Session Law Service (West) | | \<year> N.J. Sess. Law Serv. \<page no.> (West) |

**Administrative compilation**

| | | |
|---|---|---|
| New Jersey Administrative Code (LexisNexis) | | N.J. Admin. Code § x:x-x.x (\<year>) |

**Administrative register**

| | | |
|---|---|---|
| New Jersey Register (LexisNexis) | | \<vol. no.> N.J. Reg. \<page no.> (\<month day, year>) |

**Administrative report**

| | | |
|---|---|---|
| New Jersey Administrative Reports | 1979–date | N.J. Admin., N.J. Admin. 2d |

| Category | Dates | Abbreviation |
|---|---|---|

New Mexico

**Public domain citation format:** New Mexico has adopted a public domain citation format for cases effective July 1, 2013. *See* New Mexico Supreme Court Rule 23-112 (effective June 4, 2004). The format is:

- *Bianco v. Horror One Prods.*, 2009-NMSC-006, ¶ 10, 145 N.M. 551.

- *Bianco v. Horror One Prods.*, 2009-NMSC-006, ¶ 10, 145 N.M. 551, 202 P.3d 810.

- *State v. Dickert*, 2012-NMCA-004, ¶ 28.

- *State v. Dickert*, 2012-NMCA-004, ¶ 28, 268 P.3d 515.

**Supreme Court (N.M.):** Cite to P., P.2d, or P.3d.

| | | |
|---|---|---|
| Pacific Reporter | 1883–date | P., P.2d, P.3d |
| New Mexico Reports | 1852–2012 | N.M. |

**Court of Appeals (N.M. Ct. App.):** Cite to P.2d or P.3d.

| | | |
|---|---|---|
| Pacific Reporter | 1967–date | P.2d, P.3d |
| New Mexico Reports | 1967–2012 | N.M. |

**Statutory compilations:** Cite to N.M. Stat. Ann..

| | | |
|---|---|---|
| New Mexico Statutes Annotated 1978 (Conway Greene) | | N.M. Stat. Ann. § x-x-x (<year>) |
| West's New Mexico Statutes Annotated | | N.M. Stat. Ann. § x-x-x (West <year>) |
| Michie's Annotated Statutes of New Mexico (LexisNexis) | | N.M. Stat. Ann. § x-x-x (LexisNexis <year>) |

**Session laws:** Cite to N.M. Laws.

| | | |
|---|---|---|
| Laws of the State of New Mexico | | <year> N.M. Laws <page no.> |
| New Mexico Advance Legislative Service (Conway Greene) | | <year> N.M. Adv. Legis. Serv. <page no.> |
| West's New Mexico Legislative Service | | <year> N.M. Legis. Serv. <page no.> (West) |

**Administrative compilation**

| | | |
|---|---|---|
| Code of New Mexico Rules (LexisNexis) | | N.M. Code R. § x.x.x.x (LexisNexis <year>) |

**Administrative register**

| Category | Dates | Abbreviation |
|---|---|---|
| New Mexico Register | | `<vol. no.>` **N.M. Reg.** `<page no.> (<month day, year>)` |

New York

**Court of Appeals (N.Y.) after 1847:** Cite to N.E., N.E.2d, or N.E.3d.

| Category | Dates | Abbreviation |
|---|---|---|
| North Eastern Reporter | 1885–date | N.E., N.E.2d, N.E.3d |
| New York Reports (The first series of N.Y. is reprinted in N.Y.S. and N.Y.S.2d without separate pagination. Do not include a parallel cite to N.Y.S. or N.Y.S.2d in citations to the first series of N.Y.) | 1847–date | N.Y., N.Y.2d |
| West's New York Supplement | 1956–date | N.Y.S.2d |

**Court for the Correction of Errors (N.Y.) and Supreme Court of Judicature (N.Y. Sup. Ct.) (highest state courts of law before 1847):** Cite to one of the following reporters.

| Category | Dates | Abbreviation |
|---|---|---|
| Lockwood's Reversed Cases | 1799–1847 | Lock. Rev. Cas. |
| Denio's Reports | 1845–1848 | Denio |
| Hill and Denio Supplement (Lalor) | 1842–1844 | Hill & Den. |
| Hill's Reports | 1841–1844 | Hill |
| Edmond's Select Cases | 1834–1853 | Edm. Sel. Cas. |
| Yates' Select Cases | 1809 | Yates Sel. Cas. |
| Anthon's Nisi Prius Cases | 1807–1851 | Ant. N.P. Cas. |
| Wendell's Reports | 1828–1841 | Wend. |
| Cowen's Reports | 1823–1829 | Cow. |
| Johnson's Reports | 1806–1823 | Johns. |
| Caines' Reports | 1803–1805 | Cai. |
| Caines' Cases | 1796–1805 | Cai. Cas. |
| Coleman & Caines' Cases | 1794–1805 | Cole. & Cai. Cas. |
| Johnson's Cases | 1799–1803 | Johns. Cas. |
| Coleman's Cases | 1791–1800 | Cole. Cas. |

| Category | Dates | Abbreviation |
|----------|-------|--------------|

**Court of Chancery (N.Y. Ch.) (highest state court of equity before 1848):** Cite to one of the following reporters.

| Category | Dates | Abbreviation |
|----------|-------|--------------|
| Edwards' Chancery Reports | 1831–1850 | Edw. Ch. |
| Barbour's Chancery Reports | 1845–1848 | Barb. Ch. |
| Sandford's Chancery Reports | 1843–1847 | Sand. Ch. |
| Saratoga Chancery Sentinel | 1841–1847 | Sarat. Ch. Sent. |
| Paige's Chancery Reports | 1828–1845 | Paige Ch. |
| Clarke's Chancery Reports | 1839–1841 | Cl. Ch. |
| Hoffman's Chancery Reports | 1839–1840 | Hoff. Ch. |
| Hopkins' Chancery Reports | 1823–1826 | Hopk. Ch. |
| Lansing's Chancery Reports | 1824–1826 | Lans. Ch. |
| Johnson's Chancery Reports | 1814–1823 | Johns. Ch. |
| New York Chancery Reports Annotated | 1814–1847 | N.Y. Ch. Ann. |

**Supreme Court, Appellate Division (N.Y. App. Div.), previously Supreme Court, General Term (N.Y. Gen. Term):** Cite to N.Y.S. or N.Y.S.2d.

| Category | Dates | Abbreviation |
|----------|-------|--------------|
| West's New York Supplement | 1888–date | N.Y.S., N.Y.S.2d |
| Appellate Division Reports | 1896–date | A.D., A.D.2d, A.D.3d |
| Supreme Court Reports | 1874–1896 | N.Y. Sup. Ct. |
| Lansing's Reports | 1869–1873 | Lans. |
| Barbour's Supreme Court Reports | 1847–1877 | Barb. |

**Other lower courts (e.g., N.Y. App. Term, N.Y. Sup. Ct., N.Y. Ct. Cl., N.Y. Civ. Ct., N.Y. Crim. Ct., N.Y. Fam. Ct.):** Cite to N.Y.S. or N.Y.S.2d.

| Category | Dates | Abbreviation |
|----------|-------|--------------|
| West's New York Supplement | 1888–date | N.Y.S., N.Y.S.2d |
| New York Miscellaneous Reports | 1892–date | Misc., Misc. 2d |

| Category | Dates | Abbreviation |
|---|---|---|
| **Other lower courts before 1888:** Cite to one of the following reporters. | | |
| Abbott's New Cases | 1876–1894 | Abb. N. Cas. |
| Abbott's Practice Reports | 1854–1875 | Abb. Pr., Abb. Pr. (n.s.) |
| Howard's Practice Reports | 1844–1886 | How. Pr., How. Pr. (n.s.) |
| **Statutory compilations:** Cite to one of the following sources. | | |
| McKinney's Consolidated Laws of New York Annotated (West) | | N.Y. \<subject\> Law § x (McKinney \<year\>) |
| New York Consolidated Laws Service (LexisNexis) | | N.Y. \<subject\> Law § x (Consol. \<year\>) |
| New York Consolidated Laws Unannotated (LexisNexis) | | N.Y. \<subject\> Law § x (LexisNexis \<year\>) |
| Abandoned Property | | Aband. Prop. |
| Agricultural Conservation | | Agric. Conserv. |
| Agriculture and Markets | | Agric. & Mkts. |
| Alcoholic Beverage Control | | Alco. Bev. Cont. |
| Alternative County Government | | Alt. County Gov't |
| Arts and Cultural Affairs | | Arts & Cult. Aff. |
| Banking | | Banking |
| Benevolent Orders | | Ben. Ord. |
| Business Corporation | | Bus. Corp. |
| Canal | | Canal |
| Civil Practice Law and Rules | | N.Y. C.P.L.R. \<rule no.\> (McKinney \<year\>) or: N.Y. C.P.L.R. \<rule no.\> (Consol. \<year\>) |
| Civil Rights | | Civ. Rights |
| Civil Service | | Civ. Serv. |
| Commerce | | Com. |
| Cooperative Corporations | | Coop. Corp. |
| Correction | | Correct. |
| County | | County |

| Category | Dates | Abbreviation |
| --- | --- | --- |
| Criminal Procedure | | Crim. Proc. |
| Debtor and Creditor | | Debt. & Cred. |
| Domestic Relations | | Dom. Rel. |
| Economic Development | | Econ. Dev. |
| Education | | Educ. |
| Elder | | Elder |
| Election | | Elec. |
| Eminent Domain Procedure | | Em. Dom. Proc. |
| Employers' Liability | | Empl'rs Liab. |
| Energy | | Energy |
| Environmental Conservation | | Envtl. Conserv. |
| Estates, Powers and Trusts | | Est. Powers & Trusts |
| Executive | | Exec. |
| Financial Services | | Fin. Serv. |
| General Associations | | Gen. Ass'ns |
| General Business | | Gen. Bus. |
| General City | | Gen. City |
| General Construction | | Gen. Constr. |
| General Municipal | | Gen. Mun. |
| General Obligations | | Gen. Oblig. |
| Highway | | High. |
| Indian | | Indian |
| Insurance | | Ins. |
| Judiciary | | Jud. |
| Judiciary Court Acts | | Jud. Ct. Acts |
| Labor | | Lab. |
| Legislative | | Legis. |
| Lien | | Lien |
| Limited Liability Company | | Ltd. Liab. Co. |
| Local Finance | | Local Fin. |
| Mental Hygiene | | Mental Hyg. |
| Military | | Mil. |

| Category | Dates | Abbreviation |
| --- | --- | --- |
| Multiple Dwelling | | Mult. Dwell. |
| Multiple Residence | | Mult. Resid. |
| Municipal Home Rule and Statute of Local Governments | | Mun. Home Rule |
| Navigation | | Nav. |
| Not-for-Profit Corporation | | Not-for-Profit Corp. |
| Optional County Government | | Opt. Cty. Gov't |
| Parks, Recreation and Historic Preservation | | Parks Rec. & Hist. Preserv. |
| Partnership | | P'ship |
| Penal | | Penal |
| Personal Property | | Pers. Prop. |
| Private Housing Finance | | Priv. Hous. Fin. |
| Public Authorities | | Pub. Auth. |
| Public Buildings | | Pub. Bldgs. |
| Public Health | | Pub. Health |
| Public Housing | | Pub. Hous. |
| Public Lands | | Pub. Lands |
| Public Officers | | Pub. Off. |
| Public Service | | Pub. Serv. |
| Racing, Pari-Mutuel Wagering and Breeding | | Rac. Pari-Mut. Wag. & Breed. |
| Railroad | | R.R. |
| Rapid Transit | | Rapid Trans. |
| Real Property | | Real Prop. |
| Real Property Actions and Proceedings | | Real Prop. Acts. |
| Real Property Tax | | Real Prop. Tax |
| Religious Corporations | | Relig. Corp. |
| Retirement and Social Security | | Retire. & Soc. Sec. |
| Rural Electric Cooperative | | Rural Elec. Coop. |
| Second Class Cities | | Second Class Cities |
| Social Services | | Soc. Serv. |

| Category | Dates | Abbreviation |
|---|---|---|
| Soil and Water Conservation Districts | | Soil & Water Conserv. Dist. |
| State | | State |
| State Administrative Procedure Act | | A.P.A. |
| State Finance | | State Fin. |
| State Printing and Public Documents | | State Print. & Pub. Docs. |
| State Technology | | State Tech. |
| Statutes | | Stat. |
| Surrogate's Court Procedure Act | | Surr. Ct. Proc. Act |
| Tax | | Tax |
| Town | | Town |
| Transportation | | Transp. |
| Transportation Corporations | | Transp. Corp. |
| Unconsolidated | | Unconsol. |
| Uniform Commercial Code | | U.C.C. |
| Vehicle and Traffic | | Veh. & Traf. |
| Village | | Village |
| Volunteer Ambulance Workers' Benefit | | Vol. Ambul. Workers' Ben. |
| Volunteer Firefighters' Benefit | | Vol. Fire. Ben. |
| Workers' Compensation | | Workers' Comp. |

**Uncompiled laws:** Cite to one of the following sources. For the user's convenience, the McKinney's volume in which the law appears is indicated parenthetically below.

| | |
|---|---|
| McKinney's Consolidated Laws | N.Y. \<law> § x (McKinney \<year>) |
| Consolidated Laws Service | N.Y. \<law> § x (Consol. \<year>) |
| LexisNexis New York Consolidated Laws Unannotated | N.Y. \<law> § x (LexisNexis \<year>) |
| New York City Civil Court Act (29A) | City Civ. Ct. Act |

| Category | Dates | Abbreviation |
|---|---|---|
| New York City Criminal Court Act (29A) | | City Crim. Ct. Act |
| Code of Criminal Procedure (11A) | | Code Crim. Proc. |
| Court of Claims Act (29A) | | Ct. Cl. Act |
| Family Court Act (29A) | | Fam. Ct. Act |
| Uniform City Court Act (29A) | | Uniform City Ct. Act |
| Uniform District Court Act (29A) | | Uniform Dist. Ct. Act |
| Uniform Justice Court Act (29A) | | Uniform Just. Ct. Act |

**Session laws:** Cite to official N.Y. Laws, if found there; else, cite to N.Y. Sess. Laws.

| Category | Dates | Abbreviation |
|---|---|---|
| Laws of New York | | \<year\> N.Y. Laws \<page no.\> |
| McKinney's Session Laws of New York (West) (McKinney) | | \<year\> N.Y. Sess. Laws \<page no.\> |
| New York Consolidated Laws Service | | \<year\>-\<pamph. no.\> N.Y. Consol. Laws Adv. |
| Advance Legislative Service (LexisNexis) | | Legis. Serv. \<page no.\> (LexisNexis) |

**Administrative compilation**

| Category | Dates | Abbreviation |
|---|---|---|
| Official Compilation of Codes, Rules & Regulations of the State of New York (West) | | N.Y. Comp. Codes R. & Regs. tit. x, § x (\<year\>) |

**Administrative register**

| Category | Dates | Abbreviation |
|---|---|---|
| New York State Register | | \<vol. no.\> N.Y. Reg. \<page no.\> (\<month day, year\>) |

North Carolina

**Supreme Court (N.C.):** Cite to S.E. or S.E.2d.

| Category | Dates | Abbreviation |
|---|---|---|
| South Eastern Reporter | 1887–date | S.E., S.E.2d |

North Carolina Reports

| Category | Dates | Abbreviation |
|---|---|---|
| 63 N.C. to date | 1868–date | N.C. |

| Category | Dates | Abbreviation |
|---|---|---|
| Phillips' Equity | 1866–1868 | 62 N.C. (Phil. Eq.) |
| Phillips' Law | 1866–1868 | 61 N.C. (Phil.) |
| Winston | 1863–1864 | 60 N.C. (Win.) |
| Jones' Equity (54–59) | 1853–1863 | e.g., 54 N.C. (1 Jones Eq.) |
| Jones' Law (46–53) | 1853–1862 | e.g., 46 N.C. (1 Jones) |
| Busbee's Equity | 1852–1853 | 45 N.C. (Busb. Eq.) |
| Busbee's Law | 1852–1853 | 44 N.C. (Busb.) |
| Iredell's Equity (36–43) | 1840–1852 | e.g., 36 N.C. (1 Ired. Eq.) |
| Iredell's Law (23–35) | 1840–1852 | e.g., 23 N.C. (1 Ired.) |
| Devereux & Battle's Equity (21–22) | 1834–1839 | e.g., 21 N.C. (1 Dev. & Bat. Eq.) |
| Devereux & Battle's Law (18–20) | 1834–1839 | e.g., 20 N.C. (3 & 4 Dev. & Bat.) |
| Devereux's Equity (16–17) | 1826–1834 | e.g., 16 N.C. (1 Dev. Eq.) |
| Devereux's Law (12–15) | 1826–1834 | e.g., 12 N.C. (1 Dev.) |
| Hawks (8–11) | 1820–1826 | e.g., 8 N.C. (1 Hawks) |
| Murphey (5–7) | 1804–1813 1818–1819 | e.g., 5 N.C. (1 Mur.) |
| Taylor's North Carolina Term Reports | 1816–1818 | 4 N.C. (Taylor) |
| Carolina Law Repository | 1813–1816 | 4 N.C. (Car. L. Rep.) |
| Haywood (2–3) | 1789–1806 | e.g., 2 N.C. (1 Hayw.) |
| Conference by Cameron & Norwood | 1800–1804 | 1 N.C. (Cam. & Nor.) |
| Taylor | 1798–1802 | 1 N.C. (Tay.) |
| Martin | 1778–1797 | 1 N.C. (Mart.) |
| **Court of Appeals (N.C. Ct. App.):** Cite to S.E.2d. | | |
| South Eastern Reporter | 1968–date | S.E.2d |
| North Carolina Court of Appeals Reports | 1968–date | N.C. App. |

| Category | Dates | Abbreviation |
|---|---|---|
| **Statutory compilations:** Cite to N.C. Gen. Stat. (published by LexisNexis). | | |
| General Statutes of North Carolina (LexisNexis) | | N.C. Gen. Stat. § x-x (`<year>`) |
| West's North Carolina General Statutes Annotated | | N.C. Gen. Stat. Ann. § x-x (West `<year>`) |
| **Session laws:** Cite to N.C. Sess. Laws. | | |
| Session Laws of North Carolina | | `<year>` N.C. Sess. Laws `<page no.>` |
| North Carolina `<year>` Advance Legislative Service (LexisNexis) | | `<year>`-`<pamph. no.>` N.C. Adv. Legis. Serv. `<page no.>` (LexisNexis) |
| North Carolina Legislative Service (West) | | `<year>` N.C. Legis. Serv. `<page no.>` (West) |
| **Administrative compilation** | | |
| North Carolina Administrative Code (West) | | `<tit. no.>` N.C. Admin. Code `<rule no.>` (`<year>`) |
| **Administrative register** | | |
| North Carolina Register (LexisNexis) | | `<vol. no.>` N.C. Reg. `<page no.>` (`<month day, year>`) |

North Dakota

**Public Domain Citation Format:** North Dakota has adopted a public domain citation format for cases after December 31, 1996. *See* North Dakota Rules of Court, Rule 11.6. The format is:

- *Smith v. Jones*, 1997 ND 15
- *Smith v. Jones*, 1997 ND 15, 600 N.W.2d 900
- *Smith v. Jones*, 1997 ND 15, ¶ 21
- *Smith v. Jones*, 1997 ND 15, ¶ 21, 600 N.W.2d 900

**Supreme Court (N.D.):** Cite to N.W. or N.W.2d.

| | | |
|---|---|---|
| North Western Reporter | 1890–date | N.W., N.W.2d |
| North Dakota Reports | 1890–1953 | N.D. |

**Supreme Court of Dakota (Dakota):** Cite to N.W..

| | | |
|---|---|---|
| North Western Reporter | 1879–1889 | N.W. |
| Dakota Reports | 1867–1889 | Dakota |

| Category | Dates | Abbreviation |
|---|---|---|
| **Court of Appeals of North Dakota (N.D. Ct. App.): Cite to N.W.2d.** | | |
| North Western Reporter | 1987–date | N.W.2d |
| **Statutory compilations: Cite to N.D. Cent. Code.** | | |
| North Dakota Century Code (LexisNexis) | | N.D. Cent. Code § x-x-x (<year>) |
| West's North Dakota Century Code Annotated | | N.D. Cent. Code Ann. § x-x-x (West <year>) |
| **Session laws: Cite to N.D. Laws.** | | |
| Laws of North Dakota | | <year> N.D. Laws <page no.> |
| North Dakota Century Code <year> Advance Legislative Service (LexisNexis) | | <year>-<pamph. no.> N.D. Cent. Code Adv. Legis. Serv. <page no.> (LexisNexis) |
| West's North Dakota Legislative Service | | <year> N.D. Legis. Serv. <page no.> (West) |
| **Administrative compilation** | | |
| North Dakota Administrative Code | | N.D. Admin. Code <rule no.> (<year>) |

## Ohio

**Public Domain Citation Format:** Ohio has adopted a public domain citation format for cases decided after April 30, 2002. *See* Supreme Court of Ohio Writing Manual (2d ed. 2013). The format is:

- *Bonacorsi v. Wheeling & Lake Erie Ry. Co.*, 95 Ohio St.3d 314, 2002-Ohio-2220, 767 N.E.2d 707, ¶ 15
- *Bowling Green v. Godwin*, 110 Ohio St.3d 58, 2006-Ohio-3563, 850 N.E.2d 698, ¶ 13, fn. 1
- *Byer v. Wright*, 160 Ohio App.3d 472, 2005-Ohio-1797, 827 N.E.2d 835 (11th Dist.)

**Supreme Court (Ohio): Cite to N.E., N.E.2d, or N.E.3d.**

| Category | Dates | Abbreviation |
|---|---|---|
| North Eastern Reporter | 1885–date | N.E., N.E.2d, N.E.3d |
| Ohio State Reports | 1852–date | Ohio St., Ohio St. 2d, Ohio St. 3d |
| Ohio Reports | 1821–1851 | Ohio |
| Wilcox's Condensed Reports | 1821–1831 | Wilc. Cond. Rep. |
| Wright | 1831–1834 | Wright |

| Category | Dates | Abbreviation |
|---|---|---|
| Ohio Unreported Cases | 1809–1899 | Ohio Unrep. Cas. |

**Court of Appeals (Ohio Ct. App.):** Cite to N.E., N.E.2d, or N.E.3d.

| Category | Dates | Abbreviation |
|---|---|---|
| North Eastern Reporter | 1926–date | N.E., N.E.2d, N.E.3d |
| Ohio Appellate Reports | 1913–date | Ohio App., Ohio App. 2d, Ohio App. 3d |
| Ohio Circuit Court Reports | 1914–1917 | Ohio C.C. |
| Ohio Courts of Appeals Reports | 1916–1922 | Ohio Ct. App. |

**Other law courts:** Cite to N.E., N.E.2d, or N.E.3d, if found there; else, cite to another reporter in the following order of preference.

| Category | Dates | Abbreviation |
|---|---|---|
| North Eastern Reporter | 1926–date | N.E., N.E.2d, N.E.3d |
| Ohio Miscellaneous Reports | 1962–2012 | Ohio Misc., Ohio Misc. 2d |
| Ohio Bar Reports | 1982–1987 | Ohio B. |
| Ohio Opinions | 1934–1982 | Ohio Op., Ohio Op. 2d, Ohio Op. 3d |
| Ohio Law Abstract | 1922–1964 | Ohio Law Abs. |
| Ohio Nisi Prius Reports | 1903–1934 | Ohio N.P., Ohio N.P. (n.s.) |
| Ohio Decisions | 1894–1921 | Ohio Dec. |
| Ohio Decisions, Reprint | 1840–1893 | Ohio Dec. Reprint |
| Ohio Circuit Decisions | 1885–1923 | Ohio Cir. Dec. |
| Ohio Circuit Court Decisions | 1901–1923 | e.g., 13-23 Ohio C.C. Dec. |
| Ohio Circuit Court Reports | 1885–1901 | Ohio C.C. |
| Ohio Law Bulletin | 1876–1921 | Ohio L. Bull. |
| Ohio Circuit Court Reports, New Series | 1903–1917 | Ohio C.C. (n.s.) |
| Ohio Law Reporter | 1903–1934 | Ohio L.R. |
| Tappen's Reports | 1816–1819 | Tapp. Rep. |
| Anderson's Unreported Ohio Appellate Cases | 1990 | Ohio App. Unrep. |

**Statutory compilations:** Cite to one of the following codes.

| Category | Dates | Abbreviation |
|---|---|---|
| Page's Ohio Revised Code Annotated (LexisNexis) | | Ohio Rev. Code Ann. § x.x (LexisNexis \<year\>) |
| Baldwin's Ohio Revised Code Annotated (West) | | Ohio Rev. Code Ann. § x.x (West \<year\>) |

**Session laws:** Cite to Ohio Laws.

**State of Ohio:** Legislative Acts Passed and Joint Resolutions Adopted \<year\> Ohio Laws \<page no.\>

| | | |
|---|---|---|
| Page's Ohio Legislative Bulletin (LexisNexis) | | \<year\> Ohio Legis. Bull. \<page no.\> (LexisNexis) |
| Baldwin's Ohio Legislative Service Annotated (West) | | \<year\> Ohio Legis. Serv. Ann. \<page no.\> (West) |

**Administrative compilation**

| | | |
|---|---|---|
| Baldwin's Ohio Administrative Code (West) | | Ohio Admin. Code \<rule no.\> (\<year\>) |

**Administrative and executive registers:** Cite to one of the following registers.

| | | |
|---|---|---|
| Baldwin's Ohio Monthly Record | 1977–date | Ohio Monthly Rec. \<page no.\> (\<month year\>) |
| Ohio Government Reports | 1965–1976 | Ohio Gov't \<page no.\> (\<month day, year\>) |
| Ohio Department Reports | 1914–1964 | Ohio Dep't \<page no.\> (\<month day, year\>) |

## Oklahoma

**Public domain citation format:** Oklahoma has adopted a public domain citation format for cases after May 1, 1997. *See* Oklahoma Supreme Court Rule 1.200(f) and Oklahoma Criminal Appeals Rule 3.5(c). The format is:

- *Skinner v. Braum's Ice Cream Store*, 1995 OK 11, 890 P.2d 922
- *Skinner v. Braum's Ice Cream Store*, 1995 OK 11, ¶9, 890 P.2d 922
- *Hunter v. State*, 1953 OK CR 155, 97 Okl.Cr. 402, 264 P.2d 997
- *Robinson v. State*, 1997 OK CR 24, ¶ 3, 68 OBJ 1379, 1381

**Supreme Court (Okla.):** Cite to P., P.2d, or P.3d.

| | | |
|---|---|---|
| Pacific Reporter | 1890–date | P., P.2d, P.3d |
| Oklahoma Reports | 1890–1953 | Okla. |

**Court of Appeals of Indian Territory (Indian Terr.):** Cite to S.W..

| | | |
|---|---|---|
| South Western Reporter | 1896–1907 | S.W. |

| Category | Dates | Abbreviation |
|---|---|---|
| Indian Territory Reports | 1896–1907 | Indian Terr. |

**Court of Criminal Appeals (Okla. Crim. App.), before 1959 Criminal Court of Appeals (Okla. Crim. App.): Cite to P., P.2d, or P.3d.**

| Pacific Reporter | 1908–date | P., P.2d, P.3d |
| Oklahoma Criminal Reports | 1908–1953 | Okla. Crim. |

**Court of Civil Appeals (Okla. Civ. App.): Cite to P.2d or P.3d.**

| Pacific Reporter | 1971–date | P.2d, P.3d |

**Statutory compilations: Cite to Okla. Stat..**

| Oklahoma Statutes (West) | | Okla. Stat. tit. x, § x (<year>) |
| Oklahoma Statutes Annotated (West) | | Okla. Stat. Ann. tit. x, § x (West <year>) |

**Session laws: Cite to Okla. Sess. Laws.**

| Oklahoma Session Laws (West) | | <year> Okla. Sess. Laws <page no.> |
| Oklahoma Session Law Service (West) | | <year> Okla. Sess. Law Serv. <page no.> (West) |

**Administrative compilation**

| Oklahoma Administrative Code | | Okla. Admin. Code § x:x-x-x (<year>) |

**Administrative registers: Cite to one of the following sources.**

| Oklahoma Register 1983–date | | <vol. no.> Okla. Reg. <page no.> (<month day, year>) |
| Oklahoma Gazette 1962–1983 | | <vol. no.> Okla. Gaz. <page no.> (<month day, year>) |

## Oregon

**Supreme Court (Or.): Cite to P., P.2d, or P.3d.**

| Pacific Reporter | 1883–date | P., P.2d, P.3d |
| Oregon Reports | 1853–date | Or. |

**Court of Appeals (Or. Ct. App.): Cite to P.2d or P.3d.**

| Pacific Reporter | 1969–date | P.2d, P.3d |
| Oregon Reports, Court of Appeals | 1969–date | Or. App. |

**Tax Court (Or. T.C.): Cite to Or. Tax.**

| Oregon Tax Reports | 1962–date | Or. Tax |

**Statutory compilations: Cite to Or. Rev. Stat..**

| Category | Dates | Abbreviation |
|---|---|---|
| Oregon Revised Statutes | | Or. Rev. Stat. § x.x (\<year\>) |
| West's Oregon Revised Statutes Annotated | | Or. Rev. Stat. Ann. § x.x (West \<year\>) |

**Session laws:** Cite to Or. Laws. When citing statutes repealed during or after 1953, indicate parenthetically the former Or. Rev. Stat. sections.

| Category | Dates | Abbreviation |
|---|---|---|
| Oregon Laws and Resolutions | | \<year\> Or. Laws \<page no.\> |
| | | \<year\> Or. Laws Spec. Sess. \<page no.\> |
| | | \<year\> Or. Laws Adv. Sh. No. x, \<page no.\> |
| West's Oregon Legislative Service | | \<year\> Or. Legis. Serv. \<page no.\> (West) |

**Administrative compilation**

| Category | Dates | Abbreviation |
|---|---|---|
| Oregon Administrative Rules | | Or. Admin. R. \<rule no.\> (\<year\>) |

**Administrative register**

| Category | Dates | Abbreviation |
|---|---|---|
| Oregon Bulletin | | \<vol. no.\> Or. Bull. \<page no.\> (\<month day, year\>) |

Pennsylvania

**Supreme Court (Pa.):** Cite to A., A.2d, or A.3d.

| Category | Dates | Abbreviation |
|---|---|---|
| Atlantic Reporter | 1885–date | A., A.2d, A.3d |
| Pennsylvania State Reports | 1845–date | Pa. |
| Monaghan | 1888–1890 | Monag. |
| Sadler | 1885–1889 | Sadler |
| Walker | 1855–1885 | Walk. |
| Pennypacker | 1881–1884 | Pennyp. |
| Grant | 1814–1863 | Grant |
| Watts and Sergeant | 1841–1845 | Watts & Serg. |
| Wharton | 1835–1841 | Whart. |
| Watts | 1832–1840 | Watts |
| Rawle | 1828–1835 | Rawle |
| Penrose and Watts | 1829–1832 | Pen. & W. |
| Sergeant and Rawle | 1814–1828 | Serg. & Rawle |
| Binney | 1799–1814 | Binn. |
| Yeates | 1791–1808 | Yeates |

| Category | Dates | Abbreviation |
|---|---|---|
| Addison | 1791–1799 | Add. |
| Dallas | 1754–1806 | Dall. |
| Alden | 1754–1814 | Ald. |

**Superior Court (Pa. Super. Ct.):** Cite to A., A.2d, or A.3d. For cases decided after December 31, 1998, use the following public domain citation format:

- *Jones v. Smith*, 1999 PA Super 1

| | | |
|---|---|---|
| Atlantic Reporter | 1931–date | A., A.2d, A.3d |
| Pennsylvania Superior Court Reports | 1895–1997 | Pa. Super. |

**Commonwealth Court (Pa. Commw. Ct.):** Cite to A.2d or A.3d.

| | | |
|---|---|---|
| Atlantic Reporter | 1970–date | A.2d, A.3d |
| Pennsylvania Commonwealth Court Reports | 1970–1994 | Pa. Commw. |

**Other lower courts:** Cite to Pa. D. & C., Pa. D. & C.2d, Pa. D. & C.3d, Pa. D. & C.4th, or Pa. D. & C.5th. Not all lower court decisions are reproduced in the reporters listed below, and it may be necessary, on occasion, to cite to the legal reporter for an individual county, if available. For a comprehensive list of Pennsylvania county court reports, consult chapter seven, appendix four, Frank Y. Liu et al., Pennsylvania Legal Research Handbook (2008).

| | | |
|---|---|---|
| Pennsylvania District and County Reports | 1918–date | Pa. D. & C., Pa. D. & C.2d, Pa. D. & C.3d, Pa. D. & C.4th, Pa. D. & C.5th |
| Pennsylvania District Reports | 1892–1921 | Pa. D. |
| Pennsylvania County Court Reports | 1870–1921 | Pa. C. |

**Statutory compilations:** Cite to Pa. Cons. Stat. (79 titles). These publications should not be confused with Pa. Code, which is a code of regulations, not of legislation.

| | | |
|---|---|---|
| Pennsylvania Consolidated Statutes | | <tit. no.> Pa. Cons. Stat. § x (<year>) |
| Purdon's Pennsylvania Statutes and Consolidated Statutes Annotated (West) | | <tit. no.> Pa. Stat. and Cons. Stat. Ann. § x (West <year>) |

**Session laws:** Cite to Pa. Laws.

| | | |
|---|---|---|
| Laws of Pennsylvania | | <year> Pa. Laws <page no.> |

| Category | Dates | Abbreviation |
|---|---|---|
| Purdon's Pennsylvania Legislative Service (West) | | `<year>` Pa. Legis. Serv. `<page no.>` (West) |

**Administrative compilation**

| | | |
|---|---|---|
| Pennsylvania Code (Fry Communications) | | `<tit. no.>` Pa. Code § x.x (`<year>`) |

**Administrative register**

| | | |
|---|---|---|
| Pennsylvania Bulletin (Fry Communications) | | `<vol. no.>` Pa. Bull. `<page no.>` (`<month day, year>`) |

Rhode Island

**Supreme Court (R.I.):** Cite to A., A.2d or A.3d.

| | | |
|---|---|---|
| Atlantic Reporter | 1885–date | A., A.2d, A.3d |
| Rhode Island Reports | 1828–1980 | R.I. |

**Statutory compilations:** Cite to R.I. Gen. Laws.

| | | |
|---|---|---|
| General Laws of Rhode Island (LexisNexis) | | `<tit. no.>` R.I. Gen. Laws § x-x-x (`<year>`) |
| West's General Laws of Rhode Island Annotated | | `<tit. no.>` R.I. Gen. Laws Ann. § x-x-x (West `<year>`) |

**Session laws:** Cite to R.I. Pub. Laws.

| | | |
|---|---|---|
| Public Laws of Rhode Island and Providence Plantations | | `<year>` R.I. Pub. Laws `<page no.>` |
| Acts and Resolves of Rhode Island and Providence Plantations | | `<year>` R.I. Acts & Resolves `<page no.>` |
| Rhode Island Advance Legislative Service (LexisNexis) | | `<year>`-`<pamph. no.>` R.I. Adv. Legis. Serv. `<page no.>` (LexisNexis) |
| West's Rhode Island Advance Legislative Service | | `<year>` R.I. Adv. Legis. Serv. `<page no.>` (West) |

**Administrative compilation**

| | | |
|---|---|---|
| Code of Rhode Island Rules (LexisNexis) | | `<tit. no.>`-`<ch. no.>` R.I. Code R. § x (LexisNexis `<year>`) |

**Administrative register**

| Category | Dates | Abbreviation |
|---|---|---|
| Rhode Island Government Register (LexisNexis) | | `<iss. no.>` R.I. Gov't Reg. `<page no.>` (LexisNexis `<month year>`) |

South Carolina

**Supreme Court after 1868 (S.C.):** Cite to S.E. or S.E.2d.

| | | |
|---|---|---|
| South Eastern Reporter | 1887–date | S.E., S.E.2d |
| South Carolina Reports | 1868–date | S.C. |

**Court of Appeals (S.C. Ct. App.):** Cite to S.E.2d.

| | | |
|---|---|---|
| South Eastern Reporter | 1983–date | S.E.2d |
| South Carolina Reports | 1983–date | S.C. |

**Courts of law before 1868:** Cite to South Carolina Law Reports (S.C.L.)

| | | |
|---|---|---|
| Richardson (37–49) | 1850–1868 | e.g., 37 S.C.L. (3 Rich.) |
| Strobhart (32–36) | 1846–1850 | e.g., 32 S.C.L. (1 Strob.) |
| Richardson (30–31) | 1844–1846 | e.g., 30 S.C.L. (1 Rich.) |
| Speers (28–29) | 1842–1844 | e.g., 28 S.C.L. (1 Speers) |
| McMullan (26–27) | 1840–1842 | e.g., 26 S.C.L. (1 McMul.) |
| Cheves | 1839–1840 | 25 S.C.L. (Chev.) |
| Rice | 1838–1839 | 24 S.C.L. (Rice) |
| Dudley | 1837–1838 | 23 S.C.L. (Dud.) |
| Riley | 1836–1837 | 22 S.C.L. (Ril.) |
| Hill (19–21) | 1833–1837 | e.g., 19 S.C.L. (1 Hill) |
| Bailey (17–18) | 1828–1832 | e.g., 17 S.C.L. (1 Bail.) |
| Harper | 1823–1824 | 16 S.C.L. (Harp.) |
| McCord (12–15) | 1821–1828 | e.g., 12 S.C.L. (1 McCord) |
| Nott and McCord (10–11) | 1817–1820 | e.g., 10 S.C.L. (1 Nott & McC.) |
| Mill (Constitutional) (8–9) | 1817–1818 | e.g., 8 S.C.L. (1 Mill) |
| Treadway (6–7) | 1812–1816 | e.g., 6 S.C.L. (1 Tread.) |
| Brevard (3–5) | 1793–1816 | e.g., 3 S.C.L. (1 Brev.) |
| Bay (1–2) | 1783–1804 | e.g., 1 S.C.L. (1 Bay) |

**Courts of equity before 1868:** Cite to South Carolina Equity Reports (S.C. Eq.)

| Category | Dates | Abbreviation |
|---|---|---|
| Richardson's Equity (24–35) | 1850–1868 | e.g., 24 S.C. Eq. (3 Rich. Eq.) |
| Strobhart's Equity (20–23) | 1846–1850 | e.g., 20 S.C. Eq. (1 Strob. Eq.) |
| Richardson's Equity (18–19) | 1844–1846 | e.g., 18 S.C. Eq. (1 Rich. Eq.) |
| Speers' Equity | 1842–1844 | 17 S.C. Eq. (Speers Eq.) |
| McMullan's Equity | 1840–1842 | 16 S.C. Eq. (McMul. Eq.) |
| Cheves' Equity | 1839–1840 | 15 S.C. Eq. (Chev. Eq.) |
| Rice's Equity | 1838–1839 | 14 S.C. Eq. (Rice Eq.) |
| Dudley's Equity | 1837–1838 | 13 S.C. Eq. (Dud. Eq.) |
| Riley's Chancery | 1836–1837 | 12 S.C. Eq. (Ril. Eq.) |
| Hill's Chancery (10–11) | 1833–1837 | e.g., 10 S.C. Eq. (1 Hill Eq.) |
| Richardson's Cases | 1831–1832 | 9 S.C. Eq. (Rich. Cas.) |
| Bailey's Equity | 1830–1831 | 8 S.C. Eq. (Bail. Eq.) |
| McCord's Chancery (6–7) | 1825–1827 | e.g., 6 S.C. Eq. (1 McCord Eq.) |
| Harper's Equity | 1824 | 5 S.C. Eq. (Harp. Eq.) |
| Desaussure's Equity (1–4) | 1784–1817 | e.g., 1 S.C. Eq. (1 Des. Eq.) |
| Statutory compilation | | |
| Code of Laws of South Carolina 1976 Annotated | | S.C. Code Ann. § x-x-x (<year>) |
| Session laws | | |
| Acts and Joint Resolutions, South Carolina | | <year> S.C. Acts <page no.> |

**Administrative compilation:** Administrative regulations appear in volumes 1–10 of S.C. Code Ann. This publication should not be confused with the statutory compilation of the same name, which also contains volumes 1–10.

| | | |
|---|---|---|
| Code of Laws of South Carolina 1976 Annotated:Code of Regulations (West) | | S.C. Code Ann. Regs. <reg no.> (<year>) |

**Administrative register**

| | | |
|---|---|---|
| South Carolina State Register | | <vol. no.> S.C. Reg. <page no.> (<month day, year>) |

| Category | Dates | Abbreviation |
|---|---|---|
| South Dakota | | |

**Public domain citation format:** South Dakota has adopted a public domain citation format for cases after December 31, 1996. *See* South Dakota Rules of Civil Procedure § 15-26A-69.1 and Supreme Court Rule 10-05. The format is:

- *Smith v. Jones*, 1996 S.D. 15, 600 N.W. 2d 900
- *Smith v. Jones*, 1996 S.D. 15, ¶ 21, 500 N.W.2d 900, 901

| Category | Dates | Abbreviation |
|---|---|---|
| **Supreme Court (S.D.):** Cite to N.W. or N.W.2d. | | |
| North Western Reporter | 1890–date | N.W., N.W.2d |
| South Dakota Reports | 1890–1976 | S.D. |
| **Supreme Court of Dakota (Dakota):** Cite to N.W.. | | |
| North Western Reporter | 1879–1889 | N.W. |
| Dakota Reports | 1867–1889 | Dakota |
| Statutory compilation | | |
| South Dakota Codified Laws (West) | | S.D. Codified Laws § x-x-x (<year>) |
| **Session laws:** Cite to S.D. Sess. Laws. | | |
| Session Laws of South Dakota | | <year> S.D. Sess. Laws <ch. x § x> <page no.> |
| **Administrative compilation** | | |
| Administrative Rules of South Dakota | | S.D. Admin. R. <rule no.> (<year>) |
| **Administrative register** | | |
| South Dakota Register | | <vol. no.> S.D. Reg. <page no.> (<month day, year>) |
| Tennessee | | |
| **Supreme Court (Tenn.):** Cite to S.W., S.W.2d, or S.W.3d. | | |
| South Western Reporter | 1886–date | S.W., S.W.2d, S.W.3d |
| Tennessee Reports | | |
| 60 Tenn. to 225 Tenn. | 1872–1972 | Tenn. |
| Heiskell | 1870–1874 | e.g., 48 Tenn. (1 Heisk.) |
| Coldwell | 1860–1870 | e.g., 41 Tenn. (1 Cold.) |
| Head | 1858–1860 | e.g., 38 Tenn. (1 Head) |

| Category | Dates | Abbreviation |
|---|---|---|
| Sneed | 1853–1858 | e.g., 33 Tenn. (1 Sneed) |
| Swan | 1851–1853 | e.g., 31 Tenn. (1 Swan) |
| Humphreys | 1839–1851 | e.g., 20 Tenn. (1 Hum.) |
| Meigs | 1838–1839 | 19 Tenn. (Meigs) |
| Yerger | 1818–1837 | e.g., 9 Tenn. (1 Yer.) |
| Martin & Yerger | 1825–1828 | 8 Tenn. (Mart. & Yer.) |
| Peck | 1821–1824 | 7 Tenn. (Peck) |
| Haywood | 1816–1818 | e.g., 4 Tenn. (1 Hayw.) |
| Cooke | 1811–1814 | 3 Tenn. (Cooke) |
| Overton | 1791–1815 | e.g., 1 Tenn. (1 Overt.) |

**Court of Appeals (Tenn. Ct. App.):** Cite to S.W.2d or S.W.3d.

| | | |
|---|---|---|
| South Western Reporter | 1932–date | S.W.2d, S.W.3d |
| Tennessee Appeals Reports | 1925–1971 | Tenn. App. |

**Court of Criminal Appeals (Tenn. Crim. App.):** Cite to S.W.2d or S.W.3d.

| | | |
|---|---|---|
| South Western Reporter | 1967–date | S.W.2d, S.W.3d |
| Tennessee Criminal Appeals Reports | 1967–1971 | Tenn. Crim. App. |

**Statutory compilations:** Cite to Tenn. Code Ann. (published by LexisNexis).

| | |
|---|---|
| Tennessee Code Annotated (LexisNexis) | Tenn. Code Ann. § x-x-x (<year>) |
| West's Tennessee Code Annotated | Tenn. Code Ann. § x-x-x (West <year>) |

**Session laws:** Cite to Tenn. Pub. Acts or Tenn. Priv. Acts.

| | |
|---|---|
| Public Acts of the State of Tennessee | <year> Tenn. Pub. Acts <page no.> |
| Private Acts of the State of Tennessee | <year> Tenn. Priv. Acts <page no.> |
| Tennessee Code Annotated Advance Legislative Service (LexisNexis) | <year>-<pamph. no.> Tenn. Code Ann. Adv. Legis. Serv. <page no.> (LexisNexis) |
| West's Tennessee Legislative Service | <year> Tenn. Legis. Serv. <page no.> (West) |

**Administrative compilation**

| Category | Dates | Abbreviation |
|---|---|---|
| Official Compilation Rules & Regulations of the State of Tennessee | | Tenn. Comp. R. & Regs. `<rule no.>` (`<year>`) |
| **Administrative register** | | |
| Tennessee Administrative Register | | `<vol. no.>` Tenn. Admin. Reg. `<page no.>` (`<month year>`) |

**Texas**

**Supreme Court (Tex.):** Cite to S.W., S.W.2d, or S.W.3d.

| | | |
|---|---|---|
| South Western Reporter | 1886–date | S.W., S.W.2d, S.W.3d |
| Texas Reports | 1846–1962 | Tex. |
| Synopses of the Decisions of the Supreme Court of Texas Arising from Restraints by Conscript and Other Military Authorities (Robards) | 1862–1865 | Robards (no vol. number) |
| Texas Law Review (containing previously unpublished cases from the 1845 term) | 1845–1846 | 65 Tex. L. Rev. |
| Digest of the Laws of Texas (Dallam's Opinions) | 1840–1844 | Dallam (no vol. number) |
| Texas Supreme Court Journal | 1957–date | Tex. Sup. Ct. J. |

**Court of Criminal Appeals (Tex. Crim. App.), previously Court of Appeals (Tex. Ct. App.):** Cite to S.W., S.W.2d, or S.W.3d.

| | | |
|---|---|---|
| South Western Reporter | 1892–date | S.W., S.W.2d, S.W.3d |
| Texas Criminal Reports | 1892–1962 | Tex. Crim. |
| Texas Court of Appeals Reports | 1876–1892 | Tex. Ct. App. |
| Condensed Reports of Decisions in Civil Causes in the Court of Appeals (White & Willson | 1876–1883 1883–1892 | White & W. Willson |

| Category | Dates | Abbreviation |
|---|---|---|
| vol. 1) (Willson vols. 2–4) | | |

**Commission of Appeals (Tex. Comm'n App.):** Cite to S.W. or S.W.2d.

| Category | Dates | Abbreviation |
|---|---|---|
| South Western Reporter | 1886–1892 | S.W. |
| | 1918–1945 | S.W.2d |
| Texas Reports | 1879–1892 1918–1945 | Tex. |
| Texas Unreported Cases (Posey) | 1879–1884 | Posey |
| Condensed Reports of Decisions in Civil Causes in the Court of Appeals (White & Willson) | 1879–1883 | White & W. |

Officially published opinions of the Commission of Appeals from 1879 to 1892 were adopted by the Supreme Court and should be cited as opinions of the Supreme Court. Opinions of the Commission of Appeals from 1918 to 1945 have a notation from the Supreme Court that usually appears in the final paragraph of the opinion, e.g., "opinion adopted," "holding approved," or "judgment adopted." Commission opinions that were adopted by the Supreme Court should be cited as opinions of the Supreme Court. "Holding approved" and "judgment adopted" opinions are cited by using "holding approved" or "judgm't adopted."

**Courts of Appeals (Tex. App.), previously Courts of Civil Appeals (Tex. Civ. App.):** Cite to S.W., S.W.2d, or S.W.3d.

| Category | Dates | Abbreviation |
|---|---|---|
| South Western Reporter | 1892–date | S.W., S.W.2d, S.W.3d |
| Texas Civil Appeals Reports | 1892–1911 | Tex. Civ. App. |

**For additional information on the history and structure of Texas courts and on local citation rules, the following sources are suggested: Texas Law Review Ass'n, The Greenbook:** Texas Rules of Form (12th ed. 2010); Lydia M.V. Brandt, Texas Legal Research (1995); and A Reference Guide to Texas Law and Legal History (Karl T. Gruben & James E. Hambleton eds., 2d ed. 1987).

**Statutory compilations:** Texas is nearing the completion of a recodification of its laws. Cite to the new subject-matter Tex. Code Ann., if found there; else, cite to Tex. Rev. Civ. Stat. Ann. or to one of the independent codes contained in the series Vernon's Texas Civil Statutes or Vernon's Texas Statutes Annotated. Note that the independent codes are not part of the new subject-matter Tex. Code Ann.

| Category | | Abbreviation |
|---|---|---|
| Vernon's Texas Codes Annotated (West) | | Tex. <Subject> Code Ann. § x (West <year>) |
| Vernon's Texas Revised Civil Statutes Annotated (West) | | Tex. Rev. Civ. Stat. Ann. art. x, § x (West <year>) |
| Vernon's Texas Business Corporation Act Annotated (West) | | Tex. Bus. Corp. Act Ann. art. x (West <year>) |

| Category | Dates | Abbreviation |
|---|---|---|
| Vernon's Texas Code of Criminal Procedure Annotated (West) | | Tex. Code Crim. Proc. Ann. art. x (West \<year\>) |
| Vernon's Texas Insurance Code Annotated (West) | | Tex. Ins. Code Ann. art. x (West \<year\>) |
| Vernon's Texas Probate Code Annotated (West) | | Tex. Prob. Code Ann. § x (West \<year\>) |
|     Agriculture | | Agric. |
|     Alcoholic Beverage | | Alco. Bev. |
|     Business and Commerce | | Bus. & Com. |
|     Business Organizations (effective Jan. 1, 2006) | | Bus. Orgs. |
|     Civil Practice and Remedies | | Civ. Prac. & Rem. |
|     Education | | Educ. |
|     Election | | Elec. |
|     Estates | | Est. |
|     Family | | Fam. |
|     Finance | | Fin. |
|     Government | | Gov't |
|     Health and Safety | | Health & Safety |
|     Human Resources | | Hum. Res. |
|     Insurance | | Ins. |
|     Labor | | Lab. |
|     Local Government | | Loc. Gov't |
|     Natural Resources | | Nat. Res. |
|     Occupations | | Occ. |
|     Parks and Wildlife | | Parks & Wild. |
|     Penal | | Penal |
|     Property | | Prop. |
|     Special District Local Laws | | Spec. Dists. |
|     Tax | | Tax |
|     Transportation | | Transp. |
|     Utilities | | Util. |
|     Water | | Water |

| Category | Dates | Abbreviation |
|---|---|---|

**Session laws:** Cite to Tex. Gen. Laws.

| | | |
|---|---|---|
| General and Special Laws of the State of Texas | | `<year>` Tex. Gen. Laws `<page no.>` |
| Vernon's Texas Session Law Service (West) | | `<year>` Tex. Sess. Law Serv. `<page no.>` (West) |
| Laws of the Republic of Texas | | `<year>` Repub. Tex. Laws `<page no.>` |

Session laws passed before 1941 must be cited according to the exact title, e.g., Tex. Loc. & Spec. Laws, Tex. Gen. & Spec. Laws, and Tex. Gen. Laws. The Revised Statutes were enacted and published separately in 1879, 1895, 1911, and 1925 and should be cited as `<year>` Tex. Rev. Civ. Stat. xxx. The Code of Criminal Procedure and Penal Code were enacted and published separately in 1856, 1879, 1895, 1911, and 1925 and should be cited as `<year>` Tex. Crim. Stat. xxx.

**Administrative compilation**

| | | |
|---|---|---|
| Texas Administrative Code (West) | | `<tit. no.>` Tex. Admin. Code § x.x (`<year>`) |

**Administrative register**

| | | |
|---|---|---|
| Texas Register (LexisNexis) | | `<vol. no.>` Tex. Reg. `<page no.>` (`<month day, year>`) |

Utah

**Public domain citation format:** Utah has adopted a public domain citation format for cases after December 31, 1998. *See* Utah Supreme Court Standing Order No. 4 (effective Jan. 18, 2000). The format is:

- *Smith v. Jones*, 1999 UT 16. (Before publication in Utah Advanced Reports)
- *Smith v. Jones*, 1999 UT App 16.
- *Smith v. Jones*, 1999 UT 16, 380 Utah Adv. Rep. 24. (Before publication in Pacific Reporter but after publication in Utah Advance Reports)
- *Smith v. Jones*, 1999 UT App 16, 380 Utah Adv. Rep. 24.
- *Smith v. Jones*, 1999 UT 16, 998 P.2d 250. (After publication in Pacific Reporter)
- *Smith v. Jones*, 1999 UT App 16, 998 P.2d 250.

**Supreme Court (Utah):** Cite to P., P.2d, or P.3d.

| | | |
|---|---|---|
| Pacific Reporter | 1881–date | P., P.2d, P.3d |
| Utah Reports | 1873–1974 | Utah, Utah 2d |

**Court of Appeals (Utah Ct. App.):** Cite to P.2d or P.3d.

| | | |
|---|---|---|
| Pacific Reporter | 1987–date | P.2d, P.3d |

**Statutory compilations:** Cite to one of the following codes.

| Category | Dates | Abbreviation |
|---|---|---|
| Utah Code Annotated (LexisNexis) | | Utah Code Ann. § x-x-x (LexisNexis <year>) |
| West's Utah Code Annotated | | Utah Code Ann. § x-x-x (West <year>) |

**Session laws:** Cite to Utah Laws.

| | | |
|---|---|---|
| Laws of Utah | | <year> Utah Laws <page no.> |
| Utah Code <year> Advance Legislative Service (LexisNexis) | | <year>-<pamph. no.> Utah Adv. Legis. Serv. <page no.> (LexisNexis) |
| Utah Legislative Service (West) | | <year> Utah. Legis. Serv. <page no.> (West) |

**Administrative compilation**

| | | |
|---|---|---|
| Utah Administrative Code | | Utah Admin. Code r. x-x-x (<year>) |

**Administrative register**

| | | |
|---|---|---|
| Utah State Bulletin | | <iss. no.> Utah Bull. <page no.> (<month day, year>) |

Vermont

**Public domain citation format:** Vermont has adopted a public domain citation format for cases after December 31, 2002. *See* Vt. R. App. P. 28.2. The format is:

- *Smith v. Jones*, 2001 VT 1, ¶ 12, 169 Vt. 203, 850 A.2d 421

**Supreme Court (Vt.):** Cite to A., A.2d or A.3d.

| Category | Dates | Abbreviation |
|---|---|---|
| Atlantic Reporter | 1885–date | A., A.2d, A.3d |
| Vermont Reports | 1826–date | Vt. |
| Aikens | 1825–1828 | Aik. |
| Chipman, D. | 1789–1824 | D. Chip. |
| Brayton | 1815–1819 | Brayt. |
| Tyler | 1800–1803 | Tyl. |
| Chipman, N. | 1789–1791 | N. Chip. |

**Statutory compilations:** Cite to Vt. Stat. Ann. (published by LexisNexis), if found there

| | | |
|---|---|---|
| Vermont Statutes Annotated (LexisNexis) | | Vt. Stat. Ann. tit. x, § x (<year>) |
| West's Vermont Statutes Annotated | | Vt. Stat. Ann. tit. x, § x (West <year>) |

**Session laws:** Cite to Vt. Acts & Resolves.

| Category | Dates | Abbreviation |
|---|---|---|
| Acts and Resolves of Vermont | | `<year>` Vt. Acts & Resolves `<page no.>` |
| Vermont `<year>` Advance Legislative Service(LexisNexis) | | `<year>`-`<pamph. no.>` Vt. Adv. Legis. Serv. `<page no.>` (LexisNexis) |
| West's Vermont Legislative Service | | `<year>` Vt. Legis. Serv. `<page no.>` (West) |

**Administrative compilation**

| | | |
|---|---|---|
| Code of Vermont Rules (LexisNexis) | | `<tit. no.>`-`<ch. no.>` Vt. Code R. § x (`<year>`) |

**Administrative register**

| | | |
|---|---|---|
| Vermont Government Register (LexisNexis) | | `<iss. no.>` Vt. Gov't Reg. `<page no.>` (LexisNexis `<month year>`) |

Virginia

**Supreme Court (Va.), previously Supreme Court of Appeals (Va.):** Cite to S.E. or S.E.2d.

| | | |
|---|---|---|
| South Eastern Reporter | 1887–date | S.E., S.E.2d |

Virginia Reports

| | | |
|---|---|---|
| 75 Va. to date | 1880–date | Va. |
| Grattan | 1844–1880 | e.g., 42 Va. (1 Gratt.) |
| Robinson | 1842–1844 | e.g., 40 Va. (1 Rob.) |
| Leigh | 1829–1842 | e.g., 28 Va. (1 Leigh) |
| Randolph | 1821–1828 | e.g., 22 Va. (1 Rand.) |
| Gilmer | 1820–1821 | 21 Va. (Gilmer) |
| Munford | 1810–1820 | e.g., 15 Va. (1 Munf.) |
| Hening & Munford | 1806–1810 | e.g., 11 Va. (1 Hen. & M.) |
| Call | 1779–1825 | e.g., 5 Va. (1 Call) |
| Virginia Cases, Criminal | 1789–1826 | e.g., 3 Va. (1 Va. Cas.) |
| Washington | 1790–1796 | e.g., 1 Va. (1 Wash.) |

**Court of Appeals (Va. Ct. App.):** Cite to S.E.2d.

| | | |
|---|---|---|
| South Eastern Reporter | 1985–date | S.E.2d |
| Virginia Court of Appeals Reports | 1985–date | Va. App. |

**Circuit Court (Va. Cir. Ct.):** Cite to Va. Cir.

| Category | Dates | Abbreviation |
|---|---|---|
| Virginia Circuit Court Opinions | 1957–date | Va. Cir. |

**Statutory compilations:** Cite to Va. Code Ann. (published by LexisNexis).

| | | |
|---|---|---|
| Code of Virginia 1950 Annotated (LexisNexis) | | Va. Code Ann. § x-x (<year>) |
| West's Annotated Code of Virginia | | Va. Code Ann. § x-x (West <year>) |

**Session laws:** Cite to Va. Acts.

| | | |
|---|---|---|
| Acts of the General Assembly of the Commonwealth of Virginia | | <year> Va. Acts <page no.> |
| Virginia <year> Advance Legislative Service (LexisNexis) | | <year>-<pamph. no.> Va. Adv. Legis. Serv. <page no.> (LexisNexis) |
| West's Virginia Legislative Service | | <year> Va. Legis. Serv. <page no.> (West) |

**Administrative compilation**

| | | |
|---|---|---|
| Virginia Administrative Code (West) | | <tit. no.> Va. Admin. Code § x-x-x (<year>) |

**Administrative register**

| | | |
|---|---|---|
| Virginia Register of Regulations (LexisNexis) | | <vol. no.> Va. Reg. Regs. <page no.> (<month day, year>) |

## Washington

**Supreme Court (Wash.):** Cite to P., P.2d, or P.3d.

| | | |
|---|---|---|
| Pacific Reporter | 1880–date | P., P.2d, P.3d |
| Washington Reports | 1889–date | Wash., Wash. 2d |
| Washington Territory Reports | 1854–1888 | Wash. Terr. |

**Court of Appeals (Wash. Ct. App.):** Cite to P.2d or P.3d.

| | | |
|---|---|---|
| Pacific Reporter | 1969–date | P.2d, P.3d |
| Washington Appellate Reports | 1969–date | Wash. App. |

**Statutory compilations:** Cite to Wash. Rev. Code.

| | | |
|---|---|---|
| Revised Code of Washington | | Wash. Rev. Code § x.x.x (<year>) |

| Category | Dates | Abbreviation |
|---|---|---|
| West's Revised Code of Washington Annotated | | Wash. Rev. Code Ann. § x.x.x (West <year>) |
| Annotated Revised Code of Washington (LexisNexis) | | Wash. Rev. Code Ann. § x.x.x (LexisNexis <year>) |

**Session laws:** Cite to Wash. Sess. Laws.

| | | |
|---|---|---|
| Session Laws of Washington | | <year> Wash. Sess. Laws <page no.> |
| West's Washington Legislative Service | | <year> Wash. Legis. Serv. <page no.> (West) |

**Administrative compilation**

| | | |
|---|---|---|
| Washington Administrative Code | | Wash. Admin. Code § x-x-x (<year>) |

**Administrative register**

| | | |
|---|---|---|
| Washington State Register | | <iss. no.> Wash. Reg. <page no.> (<month day, year>) |

West Virginia

**Supreme Court of Appeals (W. Va.):** Cite to S.E. or S.E.2d.

| | | |
|---|---|---|
| South Eastern Reporter | 1886–date | S.E., S.E.2d |
| West Virginia Reports | 1864–date | W. Va. |

**Statutory compilations:** Cite to W. Va. Code.

| | | |
|---|---|---|
| West Virginia Code | | W. Va. Code § x-x-x (<year>) |
| Michie's West Virginia Code Annotated (LexisNexis) | | W. Va. Code Ann. § x-x-x (LexisNexis <year>) |
| West's Annotated Code of West Virginia | | W. Va. Code Ann. § x-x-x (West <year>) |

**Session laws:** Cite to W. Va. Acts.

| | | |
|---|---|---|
| Acts of the Legislature of West Virginia | | <year> W. Va. Acts <page no.> |
| West Virginia <year> Advance Legislative Service (LexisNexis) | | <year>-<pamph. no.> W. Va. Adv. Legis. Serv. <page no.> (LexisNexis) |

| Category | Dates | Abbreviation |
|---|---|---|
| West's West Virginia Legislative Service | | \<year\> W. Va. Legis. Serv. \<page no.\> |
| **Administrative compilation** | | |
| West Virginia Code of State Rules | | W. Va. Code R. § x-x-x (\<year\>) |
| **Administrative register** | | |
| West Virginia Register | | \<vol. no.\> W. Va. Reg. \<page no.\> (\<month day, year\>) |

Wisconsin

**Public domain citation format:** Wisconsin has adopted a public domain citation format for cases decided after December 31, 1999. *See* Wisconsin Supreme Court Rule 80. The format is:

- *Smith v. Jones*, 2000 WI 14, ¶6
- *Smith v. Jones*, 214 Wis. 2d 408, ¶12
- *Doe v. Roe*, 2001 WI App 9, ¶17
- *Doe v. Roe*, 595 N.W.2d 346, ¶27

**Supreme Court (Wis.):** Cite to N.W. or N.W.2d.

| | | |
|---|---|---|
| North Western Reporter | 1879–date | N.W., N.W.2d |
| Wisconsin Reports | 1853–date | Wis., Wis. 2d |
| Pinney | 1839–1852 | Pin. |
| Chandler | 1849–1852 | Chand. |
| Burnett | 1842–1843 | Bur. |
| Burnett (bound with session laws for Dec. 1841) | 1841 | Bur. |

**Court of Appeals (Wis. Ct. App.):** Cite to N.W.2d.

| | | |
|---|---|---|
| North Western Reporter | 1978–date | N.W.2d |
| Wisconsin Reports | 1978–date | Wis. 2d |

**Statutory compilations:** Cite to Wis. Stat..

| | |
|---|---|
| Wisconsin Statutes | Wis. Stat. § x.x (\<year\>) |
| West's Wisconsin Statutes Annotated | Wis. Stat. Ann. § x.x (West \<year\>) |

**Session laws:** Cite to Wis. Sess. Laws.

| | |
|---|---|
| Wisconsin Session Laws | \<year\> Wis. Sess. Laws \<page no.\> |

| Category | Dates | Abbreviation |
|---|---|---|
| West's Wisconsin Legislative Service | | \<year\> Wis. Legis. Serv. \<page no.\> (West) |
| **Administrative compilation** | | |
| Wisconsin Administrative Code | | Wis. Admin. Code \<agency abbreviation\> § x-x (\<year\>) |
| **Administrative register** | | |
| Wisconsin Administrative Register | | \<iss. no.\> Wis. Admin. Reg. \<page no.\> (\<month day, year\>) |

## Wyoming

**Public domain citation format:** Wyoming has adopted a public domain citation format for cases decided after December 31, 2003. *See* Order Amending Citation Format (Aug. 19, 2005). The format is:

- *Doe v. Roe*, 2001 WY 12
- *Doe v. Roe*, 2001 WY 12, 989 P.2d 1312 (Wyo. 2001)

**Supreme Court (Wyo.):** Cite to P., P.2d, or P.3d.

| | | |
|---|---|---|
| Pacific Reporter | 1883–date | P., P.2d, P.3d |
| Wyoming Reports | 1870–1959 | Wyo. |

**Statutory compilations:** Cite to Wyo. Stat. Ann. (published by LexisNexis).

| | |
|---|---|
| Wyoming Statutes Annotated (LexisNexis) | Wyo. Stat. Ann. § x-x-x (\<year\>) |
| West's Wyoming Statutes Annotated | Wyo. Stat. Ann. § x-x-x (West \<year\>) |

**Session laws:** Cite to Wyo. Sess. Laws.

| | |
|---|---|
| Session Laws of Wyoming | \<year\> Wyo. Sess. Laws \<page no.\> |
| West's Wyoming Legislative Service | \<year\> Wyo. Legis. Serv. \<page no.\> (West) |
| **Administrative compilation** | |
| Code of Wyoming Rules (LexisNexis) | \<tit. no.\>-\<ch. no.\> Wyo. Code R. § x (LexisNexis \<year\>) |
| **Administrative register** | |
| Wyoming Government Register (LexisNexis) | \<iss. no.\> Wyo. Gov't Reg. \<page no.\> (LexisNexis \<month year\>) |

## American Samoa

**High Court of American Samoa (Am. Samoa):** Cite to Am. Samoa, Am. Samoa 2d, or Am. Samoa 3d.

| Category | Dates | Abbreviation |
|---|---|---|
| American Samoa Reports | 1900–date | Am. Samoa, Am. Samoa 2d, Am. Samoa 3d |
| **Statutory compilation** | | |
| American Samoa Code Annotated | | Am. Samoa Code Ann. § x (<year>) |
| **Administrative compilation** | | |
| American Samoa Administrative Code | | Am. Samoa Admin. Code § x (<year>) |

## Canal Zone

**United States District Court for the Eastern District of Louisiana (E.D. La.):** This court has jurisdiction over litigation pending as of Apr. 1, 1982, in the United States District Court for the District of the Canal Zone. Cite to F. Supp.

| | | |
|---|---|---|
| Federal Supplement | 1982–1983 | F. Supp. |

**United States District Court for the District of the Canal Zone (D.C.Z.):** This court ceased to exist on Mar. 31, 1982. Cite to F. Supp.

| | | |
|---|---|---|
| Federal Supplement | 1946–1982 | F. Supp. |
| **Statutory compilation** | | |
| Panama Canal Code | | C.Z. Code tit. x, § x (<year>) |

## Guam

**Supreme Court of Guam (Guam):** *See* Sandra E. Cruze, How To Cite Guam Law, Third Edition, September 2002. For example:

- *Santos v. Carney et. al.*, 1997 Guam 4; 1997 WL 460435 (Sup. Ct. Guam 1997)

**District Court of Guam (D. Guam):** Cite to F. Supp., F. Supp. 2d, or F. Supp. 3d.

| | | |
|---|---|---|
| Federal Supplement | 1951–date | F. Supp., F. Supp. 2d, F. Supp. 3d |
| Guam Reports | 1955–1980 | Guam |
| **Statutory compilation** | | |
| Guam Code Annotated | | <tit. no.> Guam Code Ann. § x (<year>) |
| **Session laws** | | |
| Guam Session Laws | | Guam Pub. L. <law no.> (<year>) |
| **Administrative compilation** | | |
| Administrative Rules & Regulations of the | | <tit. no.> Guam Admin. R. & Regs. § x (<year>) |

| Category | Dates | Abbreviation |
|---|---|---|
| Government of Guam | | |

**Navajo Nation**

**Supreme Court (Navajo), previously Court of Appeals (Navajo):** Cite to Navajo Rptr.

| Navajo Reporter | 1969–date | Navajo Rptr. |
|---|---|---|

**District Court (Navajo D. Ct.):** Cite to Navajo Rptr.

| Navajo Reporter | 1969–date | Navajo Rptr. |
|---|---|---|
| Statutory compilation | | |
| Navajo Nation Code Annotated (West) | | Navajo Nation Code Ann. tit. x, § x (<year>) |

**Northern Mariana Islands**

**Public domain citation format:** The Commonwealth of the Northern Mariana Islands has adopted a public domain citation format. *See* General Order 01-100 (March 13, 2001). The format is:

- *ABC Company vs. XYZ Company*, 2001 MP 1 ¶10

**Supreme Court (N. Mar. I.):** Cite to N. Mar. I.

| Northern Mariana Islands Reporter | 1989–date | N. Mar. I. |
|---|---|---|

**District Court for the Northern Mariana Islands, Trial and Appellate Divisions (D. N. Mar. I. and D. N. Mar. I. App. Div.), and Commonwealth Superior Court (N. Mar. I. Commw. Super. Ct.), previously Commonwealth Trial Court (N. Mar. I. Commw. Trial Ct.):** Cite to F. Supp., F. Supp. 2d, or F. Supp. 3d.

| Federal Supplement | 1979–date | F. Supp., F. Supp. 2d, F. Supp. 3d |
|---|---|---|
| Northern Mariana Islands Commonwealth Reporter | 1979–date | N. Mar. I. Commw. |
| Statutory compilation | | |
| Northern Mariana Islands Commonwealth Code (LexisNexis) | | <tit. no.> N. Mar. I. Code § x (<year>) |
| Session laws | | |
| Northern Mariana Islands Session Laws | | <year> N. Mar. I. Pub. L. <law no.> |
| **Administrative compilation** | | |
| Northern Mariana Islands Administrative Code | | <tit. no.> N. Mar. I. Admin. Code § x (<year>) |

| Category | Dates | Abbreviation |
|---|---|---|
| **Administrative register** | | |
| Northern Mariana Islands Commonwealth Register | | `<vol. no.>` N. Mar. I. Reg. `<page no.>` (`<month day, year>`) |

Oklahoma Native Americans

**Tribal Courts, Courts of Indian Offenses (Appellate Division), Courts of Indian Appeals, and Courts of Indian Offenses:** Cite to Okla. Trib.

| | | |
|---|---|---|
| Oklahoma Tribal Court Reports | 1979–date | Okla. Trib. |

Puerto Rico

**Public domain citation format:** Puerto Rico has adopted a public domain citation format for cases decided after December 31, 1997. The format is:

- *Yumac Home Furniture v. Caguas Lumber Yard*, 2015 TSPR 148

**Supreme Court (P.R.):** Cite to P.R. or P.R. Offic. Trans., if found there; else, cite to P.R. Dec. or P.R. Sent., in that order of preference.

| | | |
|---|---|---|
| Puerto Rico Reports | 1899–1978 | P.R. |
| Official Translations of the Opinions of the Supreme Court of Puerto Rico | 1978–date | P.R. Offic. Trans. |
| Decisiones de Puerto Rico | 1899–date | P.R. Dec. |
| Sentencias del Tribunal Supremo de Puerto Rico | 1899–1902 | P.R. Sent. |

**Circuit Court of Appeals (P.R. Cir.):** Cite to T.C.A

| | | |
|---|---|---|
| Decisiones del Tribunal de Circuito de Apelaciones de Puerto Rico | 1995–date | T.C.A. |

Statutory compilation

| | | |
|---|---|---|
| Laws of Puerto Rico Annotated (LexisNexis) | | P.R. Laws Ann. tit. x, § x (`<year>`) |
| Leyes de Puerto Rico Anotadas (LexisNexis) | | P.R. Leyes An.tit. x, § x (`<year>`) |

Session laws

| Category | Dates | Abbreviation |
|---|---|---|
| Laws of Puerto Rico | | \<year\> P.R. Laws \<page no.\> |
| Leyes de Puerto Rico (LexisNexis) | | \<year\> P.R. Leyes \<page no.\> |

Virgin Islands

**All courts:** Cite to V.I.

| Virgin Islands Reports | 1917–date | V.I. |
|---|---|---|

Statutory compilation

| Virgin Islands Code Annotated (LexisNexis) | 1962–date | V.I. Code Ann. tit. x, § x-x \<year\> |
|---|---|---|

**Session laws:** Cite to V.I. Sess. Laws.

| Session Laws of the Virgin Islands | | \<year\> V.I. Sess. Laws \<page no.\> |
|---|---|---|
| Virgin Islands Code Annotated Advance | | \<year\>-\<pamph. no.\> V.I. Code Ann. Adv. |
| Legislative Service (LexisNexis) | | Legis. Serv. \<page no.\> (LexisNexis) |

**Administrative compilation**

| Code of U.S. Virgin Islands Rules (LexisNexis) | | \<tit. no.\>-\<ch. no.\> V.I. Code R. § x-x (LexisNexis \<year\>) |
|---|---|---|

**Administrative register**

| Virgin Islands Government Register (LexisNexis) | | \<iss. no.\> V.I. Gov't Reg. \<page no.\> (LexisNexis \<month year\>) |
|---|---|---|

# T4. Required Abbreviations for Services

## T4.1. Service Publisher Names

| Service Publisher Name | Abbreviation |
|---|---|
| Bureau of National Affairs | BNA |
| Commerce Clearing House | CCH |
| Matthew Bender | MB |
| Pike & Fischer | P & F |
| Research Institute of America | RIA |

# T4.2. Service Abbreviations

For each looseleaf service title, the appropriate abbreviation is followed by the name of the publisher.

| Service Name | Abbreviation |
|---|---|
| Administrative Law Third Series | Admin. L.3d (BNA) |
| Affirmative Action Compliance Manual for Federal Contractors | Aff. Action Compl. Man. (BNA) |
| AIDS Law & Litigation Reporter | AIDS L. & Litig. Rep. (Univ. Pub. Group) |
| All States Tax Guide | All St. Tax Guide (RIA) |
| American Federal Tax Reports, Second Series | A.F.T.R.2d (RIA) |
| American Stock Exchange Guide | Am. Stock Ex. Guide (CCH) |
| Antitrust & Trade Regulation Report | Antitrust & Trade Reg. Rep. (BNA) |
| Aviation Law Reporter | Av. L. Rep. (CCH) |
| ⇒ *bound as* Aviation Cases | Av. Cas. (CCH) |
| BNA's Banking Report | Banking Rep. (BNA) |
| Bankruptcy Court Decisions | Bankr. Ct. Dec. (LRP) |
| Bankruptcy Law Reports | Bankr. L. Rep. (CCH) |
| Benefits Review Board Service | Ben. Rev. Bd. Serv. (MB) |
| BioLaw | BioLaw (LexisNexis) |
| Blue Sky Law Reporter | Blue Sky L. Rep. (CCH) |
| *Board of Contract Appeals Decisions—see Contract Appeals Decisions* | |
| Business Franchise Guide | Bus. Franchise Guide (CCH) |
| Canadian Commercial Law Guide | Can. Com. L. Guide (CCH) |
| Canadian Tax Reporter | Can. Tax Rep. (CCH) |
| Chemical Regulation Reporter | Chem. Reg. Rep. (BNA) |
| Chicago Board Options Exchange Guide | Chicago Bd. Options Ex. Guide (CCH) |
| Collective Bargaining Negotiations & Contracts | Collective Bargaining Negot. & Cont. (BNA) |
| Collier Bankruptcy Cases, Second Series | Collier Bankr. Cas. 2d (MB) |
| Commodity Futures Law Reporter | Comm. Fut. L. Rep. (CCH) |
| Communications Regulation | Commc'ns Reg. (BNA) |
| Congressional Index | Cong. Index (CCH) |
| Consumer Credit Guide | Consumer Cred. Guide (CCH) |

| Service Name | Abbreviation |
| --- | --- |
| Consumer Product Safety Guide | Consumer Prod. Safety Guide (CCH) |
| Contract Appeals Decisions | Cont. App. Dec. (CCH) |
| ⇒ *bound as* Board of Contract Appeals Decisions | B.C.A. (CCH) |
| *Contracts Cases, Federal—see Government Contracts Reporter* | |
| Copyright Law Decisions | Copyright L. Dec. (CCH) |
| Copyright Law Reporter | Copyright L. Rep. (CCH) |
| Cost Accounting Standards Guide | Cost Accounting Stand. Guide (CCH) |
| The Criminal Law Reporter | Crim. L. Rep. (BNA) |
| Daily Labor Report | Daily Lab. Rep. (BNA) |
| Dominion Tax Cases | Dominion Tax Cas. (CCH) |
| EEOC Compliance Manual | EEOC Compl. Man. (BNA) |
| EEOC Compliance Manual | EEOC Compl. Man. (CCH) |
| Employee Benefits Cases | Empl. Benefits Cas. (BNA) |
| Employee Benefits Compliance Coordinator | Empl. Coordinator (RIA) |
| Employment Practices Guide<br>⇒ *bound as* Employment Practices Decisions<br>⇒ *bound assee also Labor Law Reporter* | Empl. Prac. Dec. (CCH) |
| Employment Safety and Health Guide | Empl. Safety & Health Guide (CCH) |
| ⇒ *bound as* Occupational Safety and Health Decisions | O.S.H. Dec. (CCH) |
| Employment Testing: Law & Policy Reporter | Empl. Testing (Univ. Pub. Am.) |
| Energy Management & Federal Energy Guidelines | Energy Mgmt. (CCH) |
| Environment Reporter | Env't Rep. (BNA) |
| ⇒ *bound as* Environment Reporter Cases | Env't Rep. Cas. (BNA) |
| Environmental Law Reporter | Envtl. L. Rep. (Envtl. Law Inst.) |
| Exempt Organizations Reports | Exempt Org. Rep. (CCH) |
| *Fair Employment Practice Cases—see Labor Relations Reporter* | |
| The Family Law Reporter | Fam. L. Rep. (BNA) |
| Family Law Tax Guide | Fam. L. Tax Guide (CCH) |
| Federal Audit Guides | Fed. Audit Guide (CCH) |
| Federal Banking Law Reporter | Fed. Banking L. Rep. (CCH) |
| Federal Carriers Reports | Fed. Carr. Rep. (CCH) |
| ⇒ *bound as* Federal Carriers Cases | Fed. Carr. Cas. (CCH) |
| Federal Contracts Report | Fed. Cont. Rep. (BNA) |

| Service Name | Abbreviation |
|---|---|
| Federal Election Campaign Financing Guide | Fed. Election Camp. Fin. Guide (CCH) |
| Federal Energy Regulatory Commission Reporter | Fed. Energy Reg. Comm'n Rep. (CCH) |
| Federal Estate and Gift Tax Reporter | Fed. Est. & Gift Tax Rep. (CCH) |
| ⇒ *bound as* Standard Federal Tax Reporter | Stand. Fed. Tax Rep. (CCH) |
| Federal Excise Tax Reporter | Fed. Ex. Tax Rep. (CCH) |
| Federal Income, Gift and Estate Taxation | Fed. Inc. Gift & Est. Tax'n (MB) |
| Federal Rules Service, Second Series | Fed. R. Serv. 2d (West) |
| Federal Securities Law Reporter | Fed. Sec. L. Rep. (CCH) |
| Federal Tax Coordinator Second | Fed. Tax Coordinator 2d (RIA) |
| Federal Tax Guide Reports | Fed. Tax Guide Rep. (CCH) |
| *Fire & Casualty Cases—see Insurance Law Reports* | |
| Food Drug Cosmetic Law Reporter | Food Drug Cosm. L. Rep. (CCH) |
| Government Contracts Reporter | Gov't Cont. Rep. (CCH) |
| ⇒ *bound as* Contracts Cases, Federal | Cont. Cas. Fed. (CCH) |
| Government Employee Relations Report | Gov't Empl. Rel. Rep. (BNA) |
| Housing & Development Reporter | Hous. & Dev. Rep. (RIA) |
| Human Resources Management OSHA Compliance Guide | OSHA Comp. Guide (CCH) |
| Immigration Law Service | Immigr. L. Serv. (West) |
| Insurance Law Reports | Ins. L. Rep. (CCH) |
| ⇒ *bound as* Personal and Commercial Liability | Personal and Comm. Liab. (CCH) |
| ⇒ *bound as* Life, Health & Accident Insurance Cases 2d | Life Health & Accid. Ins. Cas. 2d (CCH) |
| International Environment Reporter | Int'l Env't Rep. (BNA) |
| International Trade Reporter | Int'l Trade Rep. (BNA) |
| IRS Positions | IRS Pos. (CCH) |
| Labor Arbitration Awards | Lab. Arb. Awards (CCH) |
| Labor Law Reporter | Lab. L. Rep. (CCH) |
| ⇒ *bound as* Labor Cases | Lab. Cas. (CCH) |
| ⇒ *bound as* NLRB Decisions | NLRB Dec. (CCH) |
| *see also Employment Practices Guid* | |
| Labor Relations Reporter: | Lab. Rel. Rep. (BNA) |
| ⇒ *bound as* Fair Employment Practice Cases | Fair Empl. Prac. Cas. (BNA) |
| ⇒ *bound as* Labor Arbitration Reports | Lab. Arb. Rep. (BNA) |

| Service Name | Abbreviation |
|---|---|
| ⇒ *bound as* Labor Relations Reference Manual | L.R.R.M. (BNA) |
| ⇒ *bound as* Wage and Hour Cases | Wage & Hour Cas. (BNA) |
| ABA/BNA Lawyers' Manual on Professional Conduct | Laws. Man. on Prof. Conduct (ABA/BNA) |
| *Life, Health & Accident Insurance Cases—see Insurance Law Reports* | |
| Liquor Control Law Reporter | Liquor Cont. L. Rep. (CCH) |
| Media Law Reporter | Media L. Rep. (BNA) |
| Medical Devices Reporter | Med. Devices Rep. (CCH) |
| Medicare and Medicaid Guide | Medicare & Medicaid Guide (CCH) |
| Mutual Funds Guide | Mut. Funds Guide (CCH) |
| National Reporter on Legal Ethics & Professional Responsibility | Nat'l Rep. Legal Ethics (Univ. Pub. Am.) |
| New York Stock Exchange Guide | N.Y.S.E. Guide (CCH) |
| *NLRB Decisions—see Labor Law Reporter* | |
| Nuclear Regulation Reporter | Nuclear Reg. Rep. (CCH) |
| Occupational Safety & Health Reporter | O.S.H. Rep. (BNA) |
| ⇒ *bound as* Occupational Safety & Health Cases | O.S.H. Cas. (BNA) |
| OFCCP Federal Contract Compliance Manual | OFCCP Fed. Cont. Compl. Man. (CCH) |
| Patent, Trademark & Copyright Journal | Pat. Trademark & Copyright J. (BNA) |
| Pension & Benefits Reporter | Pens. & Ben. Rep. (BNA) |
| Pension Plan Guide | Pens. Plan Guide (CCH) |
| Pension & Profit Sharing Second | Pens. & Profit Sharing 2d (RIA) |
| Product Safety & Liability Reporter | Prod. Safety & Liab. Rep. (BNA) |
| Products Liability Reporter | Prod. Liab. Rep. (CCH) |
| Public Utilities Reports | Pub. Util. Rep. (PUR) |
| School Law Reporter | School L. Rep. (Educ. Law Ass'n.) |
| Search & Seizure Bulletin | Search & Seizure Bull. (Quinlan) |
| SEC Accounting Rules | SEC Accounting R. (CCH) |
| Secured Transactions Guide | Secured Transactions Guide (CCH) |
| Securities and Federal Corporate Law Report | Sec. & Fed. Corp. L. Rep. (West) |
| Securities Regulation & Law Report | Sec. Reg. & L. Rep. (BNA) |
| Shipping Regulation | Shipping Reg. (BNA) |

| Service Name | Abbreviation |
|---|---|
| Social Security Reporter | Soc. Sec. Rep. (CCH) |
| Standard Federal Tax Reporter | Stand. Fed. Tax Rep. (CCH) |
| ⇒ *bound as* U.S. Tax Cases | U.S. Tax Cas. (CCH) |
| State and Local Tax Service | St. & Loc. Tax Serv. (RIA) |
| *State and Local Taxes—see All States Tax Guide* | |
| State Inheritance, Estate, and Gift Tax Reporter | St. Inher., Est. & Gift Tax Rep. (CCH) |
| State Tax Guide | St. Tax Guide (CCH) |
| State Tax Reporter | St. Tax Rep. (CCH) |
| Tax Court Memorandum Decisions | T.C.M. (RIA) |
| ⇒ *bound as* Tax Court Reporter | T.C.M. (CCH) [or (RIA)] |
| Tax Court Reported Decisions | Tax Ct. Rep. Dec. (RIA) |
| Tax Court Reports | Tax Ct. Rep. (CCH) |
| Trade Regulation Reporter | Trade Reg. Rep. (CCH) |
| ⇒ *bound as* Trade Cases | Trade Cas. (CCH) |
| Unemployment Insurance Reporter | Unempl. Ins. Rep. (CCH) |
| Uniform Commercial Code Reporting Service Second | UCC Rep. Serv. (West) |
| Union Labor Report Newsletter | Union Lab. Rep. Newsl. (BNA) |
| The United States Law Week | U.S.L.W. (BNA—publisher need not be indicated) |
| The United States Patents Quarterly bound in same name | U.S.P.Q. (BNA) |
| *U.S. Tax Cases—see Federal Estate and Gift Tax Reporter and Standard Federal Tax Reporter* | |
| U.S. Tax Reporter | U.S. Tax Rep. (RIA) |
| U.S. Tax Treaties Reporter | U.S. Tax Treaties Rep. (CCH) |
| Utilities Law Reports | Util. L. Rep. (CCH) |
| *Wage and Hour Cases—see Labor Relations Reporter* | |

## T5. Required Abbreviations for Legislative Documents

Words not on this list that are more than six letters should not abbreviated if the abbreviation would be ambiguous. All articles and prepositions should be removed from the abbreviated title if the document can be unambiguously identified without the articles and prepositions.

| Legislative Document | Abbreviation |
|---|---|
| Annals | Annals |

| Legislative Document | Abbreviation |
|---|---|
| Annual | Ann. |
| Assembly[man, woman, member] | Assemb. |
| Bill | B. |
| Committee | Comm. |
| Concurrent | Con. |
| Conference | Conf. |
| Congress[ional] | Cong. |
| Debate | Deb. |
| Delegate | Del. |
| Document[s] | Doc. |
| Executive | Exec. |
| Federal | Fed. |
| House | H. |
| House of Delegates | H.D. |
| House of Representatives | H.R. |
| Joint | J. |
| Legislat[ion, ive] | Legis. |
| Legislature | Leg. |
| Miscellaneous | Misc. |
| Number | No. |
| Order | Order |
| Record | Rec. |
| Register | Reg. |
| Regular | Reg. |
| Report | Rep. |
| Representative | Rep. |
| Resolution | Res. |
| Senate | S. |
| Senator | Sen. |
| Service | Serv. |
| Session | Sess. |
| Special | Spec. |
| Subcommittee | Subcomm. |

## T6. Required Abbreviations for Treaty Sources

The dates to the year of the treaties contained in the source, not the years in which the source was published.

| Court Name | Date | Abbreviation |
| --- | --- | --- |
| **Official U.S. Sources** | | |
| United States Treaties and Other International Agreements | 1950–date | <volume> U.S.T. xxx |
| Statutes at Large (indexed at 64 Stat. B1107) | 1778–1949 | <volume> Stat. xxx |
| Treaties and Other International Acts Series | 1945–date | T.I.A.S. No. x |
| Treaty Series | 1778–1945 | T.S. No. x |
| Executive Agreement Series | 1922–1945 | E.A.S. No. x |
| Senate Treaty Document | 1981–date | S. Treaty Doc. No. x |
| Senate Executive Documents | 1778–1980 | S. Exec. Doc. No. x |
| **Intergovernmental Treaty sources** | | |
| United Nations Treaty Series | 1946–date | <volume> U.N.T.S. xxx |
| League of Nations Treaty Series | 1920–1945 | <volume> L.N.T.S. xxx |
| Pan-American Treaty Series | 1949–date | <volume> Pan-Am. T.S. xxx |
| European Treaty Series | 1948–2003 | E.T.S. No. xxx |
| Organization of American States Treaty Series | 1970–date | O.A.S.T.S. No. xxx |
| Council of Europe Treaty Series | 2004–date | C.E.T.S. No. xxx |
| **Unofficial Treaty Sources** | | |
| U.S. Treaties on LEXIS | 1776–date | LEXIS xxx |
| International Legal Materials | 1962–date | <volume> I.L.M. xxx |
| Parry's Consolidated Treaty Series | 1648–1919 | <volume> Consol. T.S. xxx |
| Hein's United States Treaties and Other International Agreements | 1984–date | Hein's No. KAV xxxx |
| Bevans | 1776–1949 | <volume> Bevans xxx |

## T7. Required Abbreviations for Arbitral Reporters

| Court Name | Abbreviation |
| --- | --- |
| Arbitration Materials | Arb. Mat' l |
| Hague Court Reports, First Series | Hague Ct. Rep. (Scott) |
| Hague Court Reports, Second Series | Hague Ct. Rep. 2d (Scott) |

| Court Name | Abbreviation |
|---|---|
| International Centre for Settlement of Investment Disputes (ICSID) Reports | ICSID Rep. |
| International Centre for Settlement of Investment Disputes (ICSID) Review | ICSID Rev. |
| International Chamber of Commerce Arbitration | Int' l Comm. Arb. |
| International Tribunal for the Law of the Sea Reports of Judgments, Advisory Opinions and Orders | ITLOS Rep. |
| Investment Treaty Arbitration Investment Treaty Cases | ITA Inv. Treaty Cases |
| Permanent Court of Arbitration Case Repository | PCA Case Repository |
| United Nations Reports of International Arbitral Awards | R.I.A.A. |
| World Arbitration Reporter | World Arb. Rep. (`<issue number>`) |

# T8. Required Abbreviations for Intergovernmental Organizations

## T8.1. United Nations and League of Nations

| Category | Dates | Abbreviation |
|---|---|---|
| **United Nations Documents** | | |
| United Nations Documents | | U.N. Docs. |
| **United Nations Principal Organs** | | |
| General Assembly | | GAOR |
| Security Council | | SCOR |
| Economic and Social Council | | ESCOR |
| Trusteeship Council | | TCOR |
| **International Court of Justice (I.C.J.)** | | |
| Judgments, Advisory Opinions, and Orders | 1946–date | `<year>` I.C.J. xx |
| Pleadings, Oral Arguments, and Documents | 1946–date | `<year>` I.C.J. Pleadings xx |
| Acts and Documents | 1946–date | `<year>` I.C.J. Acts & Docs xx |
| **Treaties and international agreements** | | |
| United Nations Treaty Series | 1946–date | `<year>` U.N.T.S. xxx |
| **League of Nations** | | |
| Permanent Court of International Justice | 1920–1945 | `<year>` P.C.I.J. xxx |
| League of Nations Treaty Series | 1920–1945 | `<year>` L.N.T.S. xxx |

# T8.2. Europe

| Category | Dates | Abbreviation |
|---|---|---|
| **European Union** | | |

**Courts:** Cite cases before the Court of Justice of the European Union (E.C.J.) and the General Court (Ct. of First Instance) to E.C.R.. If not, cite to C.M.L.R., Common Mkt. Rep. (CCH), or CEC (CCH), if found there, in that order. If not, cite to official online sources.

| Category | Dates | Abbreviation |
|---|---|---|
| Reports of cases before the Court of Justice | 1973–date | <year> E.C.R. xxx |
| Common Market Law Reports | 1962–date | <year> C.M.L.R. xxx |
| Common Market Reports | 1962–1988 | <year> Common Mkt. Rep. (CCH) xxx |
| European Community Cases | 1989–2007 | <year> CEC (CCH) xxx |

**Legislative acts:** Cite acts of the European Council and the European Commission to O.J. (the Official Journal of the European Union, formerly the Official Journal of the European Communities). If not, cite to O.J. Spec. Ed.. If not, cite to J.O.. For issues of J.O. before 1967, indicate the issue number. For issues of O.J. and J.O. dating from 1967 and later, indicate the series and issue number.>

| Category | Dates | Abbreviation |
|---|---|---|
| Official Journal of the European Union | 1973–date | <year> O.J. (L <act number>) xxx |
| Official Journal of the European Community, Special Edition 1952–1972 | | <year> O.J. Spec. Ed. xxx |
| Journal Officiel des Communautés Européennes | 1958–date | <year> J.O. (L <act number>) xxx |

**Parliamentary documents**

| Category | Dates | Abbreviation |
|---|---|---|
| European Parliamentary Debates | | Eur. Parl. Deb. (<debate number>) x |
| European Parliament Working Session or Session Documents | | Eur. Parl. Doc. (COM <document number>) x |
| Parlement Européen Documents de Séance | | Parl. Eur. Doc. (SEC <document number>) x |

**European Commission of Human Rights:** Cite to Eur. Comm'n H.R. Dec. & Rep., Y.B. Eur. Conv. on H.R., or Eur. H.R. Rep., in that order.>

| Category | Dates | Abbreviation |
|---|---|---|
| European Commission of Human Rights Collections of Decisions | | <volume> Eur. Comm'n H.R. Dec. & Rep. xxx |
| European Human Rights Reports | | <volume> Eur. H.R. Rep. xxx |
| Yearbook of the European Convention on Human Rights | | Y.B. Eur. Conv. on H.R. |

**European Court of Human Rights:** >

| Category | Dates | Abbreviation |
|---|---|---|
| European Court of Human Rights Reports of Judgments and Decisions | | xx Eur. Ct. H.R. (<year>) |
| Yearbook of the European Convention on Human Rights | | Y.B. Eur. Conv. on H.R. |

## T8.3. Inter-American and International Tribunal

| Category | Abbreviation |
| --- | --- |
| **Inter-American Commission on Human Rights** | |
| Inter-American Commission on Human Rights Annual Reports | Inter-Am. Comm'n H.R. |
| **Inter-American Court of Human Rights:** Cite to Series, to Rep. Inter-Am. Ct. H.R., or to official online sources.> | |
| A - Judgments and Opinions | Inter-Am. Ct. H.R. (ser. A) No. xx |
| B - Pleadings, Oral Arguments and Documents (Relative to Series A) | Inter-Am. Ct. H.R. (ser. B) No. xx, xxx |
| C - Decisions and Judgments | Inter-Am. Ct. H.R. (ser. C) No. xx |
| D - Pleadings, Oral Arguments and Documents (Relative to Series C) | Inter-Am. Ct. H.R. (ser. D) No. xx, xxx |
| E - Provisional Measures | Inter-Am. Ct. H.R. (ser. E) No. xx, xxx |
| F - Procedural Decisions | Inter-Am. Ct. H.R. (ser. F) No. xx, xxx |
| Annual Reports of the Inter-American Court of Human Rights:> | |
| Complete Opinions: 1970-date | Rep. Inter-Am. Ct. H.R. xxx |
| **International Tribunal for the Law of the Sea** | |
| International Tribunal for the Law of the Sea Reports of Judgments, Advisory Opinions and Orders: 1956–date | ITLOS Rep. |

## T8.4. Other Intergovernmental Organizations

| Category | Abbreviation |
| --- | --- |
| Comprehensive Nuclear-Test-Ban Treaty Organization | CTBTO |
| Food and Agriculture Organization | FAO |
| Global Environment Facility | GEF |
| Intergovernmental Panel on Climate Change | IPCC |
| International Atomic Energy Agency | IAEA |
| International Bank for Reconstruction and Development | IBRD |
| International Centre for Settlement of Investment Disputes | ICSID |
| International Civil Aviation Organization | ICAO |
| International Criminal Police Organization | INTERPOL |
| International Development Association | IDA |
| International Finance Corporation | IFC |

| Category | Abbreviation |
|---|---|
| International Fund for Agricultural Development | IFAD |
| International Labour Organization | ILO |
| International Maritime Organization | IMO |
| International Monetary Fund | IMF |
| International Refugee Organization | IRO |
| International Telecommunication Union | ITU |
| International Union for Conservation of Nature | IUCN |
| Multilateral Investment Guarantee Agency | MIGA |
| Organisation for Economic Co-operation and Development | OECD |
| Organisation for the Prohibition of Chemical Weapons | OPCW |
| United Nations | U.N. |
| United Nations Children's Fund | UNICEF |
| United Nations Development Programme | UNDP |
| United Nations Educational, Scientific and Cultural Organization | UNESCO |
| United Nations Environment Programme | UNEP |
| United Nations Industrial Development Organization | UNIDO |
| Universal Postal Union | UPU |
| World Bank Group | WBG |
| World Customs Organization | WCO |
| World Health Organization | WHO |
| World Intellectual Property Organization | WIPO |
| World Meteorological Organization | WMO |
| World Tourism Organization | UNWTO |
| World Trade Organization | WTO |

# T9. Required Abbreviations for Court Names

| Court Name | Abbreviation |
|---|---|
| Administrative Court | Admin. Ct. |
| Admiralty [Court, Division] | Adm. |
| Aldermen's Court | Alder. Ct. |
| Appeals Court | App. Ct. |
| Appellate Court | App. Ct. |
| Appellate Department | App. Dep't |
| Appellate Division | App. Div. |

| Court Name | Abbreviation |
| --- | --- |
| Armed Services Board of Contract Appeals | ASBCA |
| Bankruptcy Appellate Panel | B.A.P. |
| Bankruptcy [Court, Judge] | Bankr. |
| Board of Contract Appeals | B.C.A. |
| Board of Immigration Appeals | B.I.A. |
| Board of Patent Appeals and Interferences | B.P.A.I. |
| Board of Tax Appeals | B.T.A. |
| Borough Court | \<Name> Bor. Ct. |
| Central District | C.D. |
| Chancery [Court, Division] | Ch. |
| Children's Court | Child. Ct. |
| Circuit Court (old federal) | C.C. |
| Circuit Court (state) | Cir. Ct. |
| Circuit Court of Appeals (federal) | Cir. |
| Circuit Court of Appeals (state) | Cir. Ct. App. |
| City Court | \<Name> City Ct. |
| Civil Appeals | Civ. App. |
| Civil Court of Record | Civ. Ct. Rec. |
| Civil District Court | Civ. Dist. Ct. |
| Claims Court | Cl. Ct. |
| Commerce Court | Comm. Ct. |
| Commission | Comm'n |
| Common Pleas | C.P. \<when appropriate, name county or similar subdivision> |
| Commonwealth Court | Commw. Ct. |
| Conciliation Court | Concil. Ct. |
| County Court | \<Name> Cty. Ct. |
| County Judge's Court | Cty. J. Ct. |
| Court | Ct. |
| Court of Appeal (English) | C.A. |
| Court of Appeals (federal) | Cir. |
| Court of Appeal[s] (state) | Ct. App. |
| Court of Appeals for the Armed Forces | C.A.A.F. |

| Court Name | Abbreviation |
|---|---|
| Court of Civil Appeals | Civ. App. |
| Court of Claims | Ct. Cl. |
| Court of Common Pleas | Ct. Com. Pl. |
| Court of Criminal Appeals | Crim. App. |
| Court of Customs and Patent Appeals | C.C.P.A. |
| Court of Customs Appeals | Ct. Cust. App. |
| Court of Errors | Ct. Err. |
| Court of Errors and Appeals | Ct. Err. & App. |
| Court of Federal Claims | Fed. Cl. |
| Court of [General, Special] Sessions | Ct. <Gen. or Spec.> Sess. |
| Court of International Trade | Ct. Int'l Trade |
| Court of Military Appeals | C.M.A. |
| Court of Military Review | C.M.R. |
| Court of Special Appeals | Ct. Spec. App. |
| Court of Veterans Appeals | Ct. Vet. App. |
| Criminal Appeals | Crim. App. |
| Criminal District Court | Crim. Dist. Ct. |
| Customs Court | Cust. Ct. |
| District Court (federal) | D. |
| District Court (state) | Dist. Ct. |
| District Court of Appeal[s] | Dist. Ct. App. |
| Division | Div. |
| Domestic Relations Court | Dom. Rel. Ct. |
| Eastern District | E.D. |
| Emergency Court of Appeals | Emer. Ct. App. |
| Equity [Court, Division] | Eq. |
| Family Court | Fam. Ct. |
| High Court | High Ct. |
| Judicial District | Jud. Dist. |
| Judicial Division | Jud. Div. |
| Judicial Panel on Multidistrict Litigation | J.P.M.L. |
| Justice of the Peace's Court | J.P. Ct. |
| Juvenile Court | Juv. Ct. |

| Court Name | Abbreviation |
|---|---|
| Land Court | Land Ct. |
| Law Court | Law Ct. |
| Law Division | Law Div. |
| Magistrate Division | Magis. Div. |
| Magistrate's Court | Magis. Ct. |
| Middle District | M.D. |
| Municipal Court | <Name> Mun. Ct. |
| Northern District | N.D. |
| Orphans' Court | Orphans' Ct. |
| Parish Court | <Name> Parish Ct. |
| Police Justice's Court | Police J. Ct. |
| Prerogative Court | Prerog. Ct. |
| Probate Court | Prob. Ct. |
| Public Utilities Commission | P.U.C. |
| Real Estate Commission | Real Est. Comm'n |
| Recorder's Court | Rec's Ct. |
| Southern District | S.D. |
| Special Court Regional Rail Reorganization Act | Reg'l Rail Reorg. Ct. |
| Superior Court | Super. Ct. |
| Supreme Court (federal) | U.S. |
| Supreme Court (other) | Sup. Ct. |
| Supreme Court, Appellate Division | App. Div. |
| Supreme Court, Appellate Term | App. Term |
| Supreme Court of Errors | Sup. Ct. Err. |
| Supreme Judicial Court | Sup. Jud. Ct. |
| Surrogate's Court | Sur. Ct. |
| Tax Appeal Court | Tax App. Ct. |
| Tax Court | T.C. |
| Teen Court | Teen Ct. |
| Temporary Emergency Court of Appeals | Temp. Emer. Ct. App. |
| Territor[ial, y] | Terr. |
| Trademark Trial and Appeal Board | T.T.A.B. |
| Traffic Court | Traffic Ct. |

| Court Name | Abbreviation |
|---|---|
| Tribal Court | <Name> Tribal Ct. |
| Tribunal | Trib. |
| Water Court | Water Ct. |
| Western District | W.D. |
| Workmen's Compensation Division | Workmen's Comp. Div. |
| Youth Court | Youth Ct. |

# T10. Required Abbreviations for Titles of Judges and Officials

| Title | Abbreviation |
|---|---|
| Administrative Law Judge | A.L.J. |
| Arbitrator | Arb. |
| Assembly[man, woman, member] | Assemb. |
| Attorney General | Att'y Gen. |
| Baron | B. |
| Chancellor | C. |
| Chief Baron | C.B. |
| Chief Judge, Chief Justice | C.J. |
| Commissioner | Comm'r |
| Delegate | Del. |
| Honorable | Hon. |
| Judge, Justice | J. |
| Judges, Justices | JJ. |
| Lord Justice | L.J. |
| Magistrate | Mag. |
| Master of the Rolls | M.R. |
| Mediator | Med. |
| Referee | Ref. |
| Representative | Rep. |
| Senator | Sen. |
| Vice Chancellor | V.C. |

# T11. Required Abbreviations for Case Names In Citations

| Case Name | Abbreviation |
| --- | --- |
| Academ[ic, y] | Acad. |
| Administrat[ive, ion] | Admin. |
| Administrat[or, rix] | Adm' [r, x] |
| Advertising | Advert. or Adver. |
| Agricultur[e, al] | Agric. |
| Alliance | All. |
| Alternative | Alt. |
| America[n] | Am. |
| and | & |
| Associate | Assoc. |
| Association | Ass'n |
| Atlantic | Atl. |
| Authority | Auth. |
| Automo[bile, tive] | Auto. |
| Avenue | Ave. |
| Bankruptcy | Bankr. |
| Board | Bd. |
| Broadcast[er, ing] | Broad. |
| Brotherhood | Bhd. |
| Brothers | Bros. |
| Building | Bldg. |
| Business | Bus. |
| Casualty | Cas. |
| Cent[er, re] | Ctr. |
| Central | Cent. |
| Chemical | Chem. |
| Coalition | Coal. |
| College | Coll. |
| Commission | Comm'n |
| Commissioner | Comm'r |
| Committee | Comm. |
| Communication | Commc'n |
| Community | Cmty. |

| Case Name | Abbreviation |
|---|---|
| Company | Co. |
| Compensation | Comp. |
| Computer | Comput. |
| Condominium | Condo. |
| Congress[ional] | Cong. |
| Consolidated | Consol. |
| Construction | Constr. |
| Continental | Cont'l |
| Cooperative | Coop. |
| Corporat[e, ion] | Corp. |
| Correction[s, al] | Corr. |
| County | Cty. or Cnty. |
| Defen[der, se] | Def. |
| Department | Dep't |
| Detention | Det. |
| Development | Dev. |
| Digital | Dig. |
| Director | Dir. |
| Discount | Disc. |
| Distribut[or, ing] | Distrib. |
| District | Dist. |
| Division | Div. |
| East[ern] | E. |
| Econom[ic, ical, ics, y] | Econ. |
| Education[al] | Educ. |
| Electr[ic, ical, icity, onic] | Elec. |
| Employee | Emp. |
| Employ[er, ment] | Emp'[r, t] |
| Enforcement | Enf't |
| Engineer | Eng'r |
| Engineering | Eng'g |
| Enterprise | Enter. |
| Entertainment | Entm't |
| Environment | Env't |

| Case Name | Abbreviation |
|---|---|
| Environmental | Envtl. |
| Equality | Equal. |
| Equipment | Equip. |
| Examiner | Exam'r |
| Exchange | Exch. |
| Executive | Exec. |
| Execut[or, rix] | Ex'[r, x] |
| Explorat[ion, ory] | Expl. |
| Export[er, ation] | Exp. |
| Federal | Fed. |
| Federation | Fed'n |
| Fidelity | Fid. |
| Financ[e, ial, ing] | Fin. |
| Foundation | Found. |
| General | Gen. |
| Global | Glob. |
| Government | Gov't |
| Group | Grp. |
| Guaranty | Guar. |
| Hospital[ity] | Hosp. |
| Housing | Hous. |
| Import[er, ation] | Imp. |
| Incorporated | Inc. |
| Indemnity | Indem. |
| Independen[ce, t] | Indep. |
| Industr[y, ies, ial] | Indus. |
| Information | Info. |
| Institut[e, ion] | Inst. |
| Insurance | Ins. |
| International | Int'l |
| Investment | Inv. |
| Investor | Inv'r |
| Laboratory | Lab. |
| Liability | Liab. |

| Case Name | Abbreviation |
|---|---|
| Limited | Ltd. |
| Litigation | Litig. |
| Machine[ry] | Mach. |
| Maintenance | Maint. |
| Management | Mgmt. |
| Manufacturer | Mfr. |
| Manufacturing | Mfg. |
| Maritime | Mar. |
| Market | Mkt. |
| Marketing | Mktg. |
| Mechanic[al] | Mech. |
| Medic[al, ine] | Med. |
| Memorial | Mem'l |
| Merchan[t, dise, dising] | Merch. |
| Metropolitan | Metro. |
| Mortgage | Mortg. |
| Municipal | Mun. |
| Mutual | Mut. |
| National | Nat'l |
| Natural | Nat. |
| North[ern] | N. |
| Northeast[ern] | Ne. |
| Northwest[ern] | Nw. |
| Number | No. |
| Opinion | Op. |
| Organiz[ation, ing] | Org. |
| Pacific | Pac. |
| Parish | Par. |
| Partnership | P'ship |
| Person[al, nel] | Pers. |
| Pharmaceutic[s, al, als] | Pharm. |
| Preserv[e, ation] | Pres. |
| Probat[e, ion] | Prob. |
| Product[ion] | Prod. |

| Case Name | Abbreviation |
| --- | --- |
| Professional | Prof'l |
| Property | Prop. |
| Protection | Prot. |
| Public | Pub. |
| Publication | Publ'n |
| Publishing | Publ'g |
| Railroad | R.R. |
| Railway | Ry. |
| Refining | Ref. |
| Regional | Reg'l |
| Rehabilitat[ion, ive] | Rehab. |
| Reproduct[ion, ive] | Reprod. |
| Resource[s] | Res. |
| Restaurant | Rest. |
| Retirement | Ret. |
| Road | Rd. |
| Savings | Sav. |
| School[s] | Sch. |
| Scien[ce, tific] | Sci. |
| Secretary | Sec'y |
| Securit[y, ies] | Sec. |
| Service | Serv. |
| Shareholder | S'holder |
| Social | Soc. |
| Society | Soc'y |
| Solution | Sol. |
| South[ern] | S. |
| Southeast[ern] | Se. |
| Southwest[ern] | Sw. |
| Steamship[s] | S.S. |
| Street | St. |
| Subcommittee | Subcomm. |
| Surety | Sur. |
| System[s] | Sys. |

| Case Name | Abbreviation |
|---|---|
| Techn[ical, ological, ology] | Tech. |
| Telecommunication | Telecomm. |
| Tele[phone, graph] | Tel. |
| Temporary | Temp. |
| Township | Twp. |
| Transcontinental | Transcon. |
| Transport[ation] | Transp. |
| Trust[ee] | Tr. |
| Turnpike | Tpk. |
| Uniform | Unif. |
| University | Univ. |
| Utility | Util. |
| Village | Vill. |
| West[ern] | W. |

## T12. Required Abbreviations for Geographical Terms

### T12.1. U.S. States, Cities and Territories

| Place | Abbreviation |
|---|---|
| **States** | |
| Alabama | Ala. |
| Alaska | Alaska |
| Arizona | Ariz. |
| Arkansas | Ark. |
| California | Cal. |
| Colorado | Colo. |
| Connecticut | Conn. |
| Delaware | Del. |
| Florida | Fla. |
| Georgia | Ga. |
| Hawaii | Haw. |
| Idaho | Idaho |
| Illinois | Ill. |
| Indiana | Ind. |

| Place | Abbreviation |
| --- | --- |
| Iowa | Iowa |
| Kansas | Kan. |
| Kentucky | Ky. |
| Louisiana | La. |
| Maine | Me. |
| Maryland | Md. |
| Massachusetts | Mass. |
| Michigan | Mich. |
| Minnesota | Minn. |
| Mississippi | Miss. |
| Missouri | Mo. |
| Montana | Mont. |
| Nebraska | Neb. |
| Nevada | Nev. |
| New Hampshire | N.H. |
| New Jersey | N.J. |
| New Mexico | N.M. |
| New York | N.Y. |
| North Carolina | N.C. |
| North Dakota | N.D. |
| Ohio | Ohio |
| Oklahoma | Okla. |
| Oregon | Or. |
| Pennsylvania | Pa. |
| Rhode Island | R.I. |
| South Carolina | S.C. |
| South Dakota | S.D. |
| Tennessee | Tenn. |
| Texas | Tex. |
| Utah | Utah |
| Vermont | Vt. |
| Virginia | Va. |
| Washington | Wash. |
| West Virginia | W. Va. |

| Place | Abbreviation |
|---|---|
| Wisconsin | Wis. |
| Wyoming | Wyo. |
| **Cities**[1] | |
| Baltimore | Balt. |
| Boston | Bos. |
| Chicago | Chi. |
| Dallas | Dall. |
| District of Columbia | D.C. |
| Houston | Hous. |
| Los Angeles | L.A. |
| New York | N.Y.C. |
| Philadelphia | Phila. |
| Phoenix | Phx. |
| San Francisco | S.F. |
| **Territories** | |
| American Samoa | Am. Sam. |
| Guam | Guam |
| Northern Mariana Islands | N. Mar. I. |
| Puerto Rico | P.R. |
| Virgin Islands | V.I. |

Note

1. Abbreviations for city names may also be composed from state name abbreviations above. For example, "Kansas City" should be shortened to "Kan. City."

## T12.2 Australian States and Canadian Provinces and Territories

| Place | Abbreviation |
|---|---|
| **Australia** | |
| Australian Capital Territory | Austl. Cap. Terr. |
| New South Wales | N.S.W. |
| Northern Territory | N. Terr. |
| Queensland | Queensl. |
| South Australia | S. Austl. |

| Place | Abbreviation |
|---|---|
| Tasmania | Tas. |
| Victoria | Vict. |
| Western Australia | W. Austl. |
| **Canada** | |
| Alberta | Alta. |
| British Columbia | B.C. |
| Manitoba | Man. |
| New Brunswick | N.B. |
| Newfoundland & Labrador | Nfld. |
| Northwest Territories | N.W.T. |
| Nova Scotia | N.S. |
| Nunavut | Nun. |
| Ontario | Ont. |
| Prince Edward Island | P.E.I. |
| Quebec | Que. |
| Saskatchewan | Sask. |
| Yukon | Yukon |

# T12.3 Countries and Regions

| Place | Abbreviation |
|---|---|
| Afghanistan | Afg. |
| Africa | Afr. |
| Albania | Alb. |
| Algeria | Alg. |
| Andorra | Andorra |
| Angola | Angl. |
| Anguilla | Anguilla |
| Antarctica | Antarctica |
| Antigua & Barbuda | Ant. & Barb. |
| Argentina | Arg. |
| Armenia | Arm. |
| Asia | Asia |
| Australia | Austl. |
| Austria | Austria |

| Place | Abbreviation |
|---|---|
| Azerbaijan | Azer. |
| Bahamas | Bah. |
| Bahrain | Bahr. |
| Bangladesh | Bangl. |
| Barbados | Barb. |
| Belarus | Belr. |
| Belgium | Belg. |
| Belize | Belize |
| Benin | Benin |
| Bermuda | Berm. |
| Bhutan | Bhutan |
| Bolivia | Bol. |
| Bosnia & Herzegovina | Bosn. & Herz. |
| Botswana | Bots. |
| Brazil | Braz. |
| Brunei | Brunei |
| Bulgaria | Bulg. |
| Burkina Faso | Burk. Faso |
| Burundi | Burundi |
| Cambodia | Cambodia |
| Cameroon | Cameroon |
| Canada | Can. |
| Cape Verde | Cape Verde |
| Cayman Islands | Cayman Is. |
| Central African Republic | Cent. Afr. Rep. |
| Chad | Chad |
| Chile | Chile |
| China, People's Republic of | China |
| Colombia | Colom. |
| Comoros | Comoros |
| Congo, Democratic Republic of the | Dem. Rep. Congo |
| Congo, Republic of the | Congo |
| Costa Rica | Costa Rica |
| Côte d'Ivoire | Côte d'Ivoire |

| Place | Abbreviation |
| --- | --- |
| Croatia | Croat. |
| Cuba | Cuba |
| Cyprus | Cyprus |
| Czech Republic | Czech |
| Denmark | Den. |
| Djibouti | Djib. |
| Dominica | Dominica |
| Dominican Republic | Dom. Rep. |
| Ecuador | Ecuador |
| Egypt | Egypt |
| El Salvador | El Sal. |
| England | Eng. |
| Equatorial Guinea | Eq. Guinea |
| Eritrea | Eri. |
| Estonia | Est. |
| Ethiopia | Eth. |
| Europe | Eur. |
| Falkland Islands | Falkland Is. |
| Fiji | Fiji |
| Finland | Fin. |
| France | Fr. |
| Gabon | Gabon |
| Gambia | Gam. |
| Georgia | Geor. |
| Germany | Ger. |
| Ghana | Ghana |
| Gibraltar | Gib. |
| Great Britain | Gr. Brit. |
| Greece | Greece |
| Greenland | Green. |
| Grenada | Gren. |
| Guadeloupe | Guad. |
| Guatemala | Guat. |
| Guinea | Guinea |

| Place | Abbreviation |
|---|---|
| Guinea-Bissau | Guinea-Bissau |
| Guyana | Guy. |
| Haiti | Haiti |
| Honduras | Hond. |
| Hong Kong | H.K. |
| Hungary | Hung. |
| Iceland | Ice. |
| India | India |
| Indonesia | Indon. |
| Iran | Iran |
| Iraq | Iraq |
| Ireland | Ir. |
| Israel | Isr. |
| Italy | It. |
| Jamaica | Jam. |
| Japan | Japan |
| Jordan | Jordan |
| Kazakhstan | Kaz. |
| Kenya | Kenya |
| Kiribati | Kiribati |
| Korea, North | N. Kor. |
| Korea, South | S. Kor. |
| Kosovo | Kos. |
| Kuwait | Kuwait |
| Kyrgyzstan | Kyrg. |
| Laos | Laos |
| Latvia | Lat. |
| Lebanon | Leb. |
| Lesotho | Lesotho |
| Liberia | Liber. |
| Libya | Libya |
| Liechtenstein | Liech. |
| Lithuania | Lith. |
| Luxembourg | Lux. |

| Place | Abbreviation |
|---|---|
| Macau | Mac. |
| Macedonia | Maced. |
| Madagascar | Madag. |
| Malawi | Malawi |
| Malaysia | Malay. |
| Maldives | Maldives |
| Mali | Mali |
| Malta | Malta |
| Marshall Islands | Marsh. Is. |
| Martinique | Mart. |
| Mauritania | Mauritania |
| Mauritius | Mauritius |
| Mexico | Mex. |
| Micronesia | Micr. |
| Moldova | Mold. |
| Monaco | Monaco |
| Mongolia | Mong. |
| Montenegro | Montenegro |
| Montserrat | Montserrat |
| Morocco | Morocco |
| Mozambique | Mozam. |
| Myanmar | Myan. |
| Namibia | Namib. |
| Nauru | Nauru |
| Nepal | Nepal |
| Netherlands | Neth. |
| New Zealand | N.Z. |
| Nicaragua | Nicar. |
| Niger | Niger |
| Nigeria | Nigeria |
| North America | N. Am. |
| Northern Ireland | N. Ir. |
| Norway | Nor. |
| Oman | Oman |

| Place | Abbreviation |
|---|---|
| Pakistan | Pak. |
| Palau | Palau |
| Panama | Pan. |
| Papua New Guinea | Papua N.G. |
| Paraguay | Para. |
| Peru | Peru |
| Philippines | Phil. |
| Pitcairn Island | Pitcairn Is. |
| Poland | Pol. |
| Portugal | Port. |
| Qatar | Qatar |
| Réunion | Réunion |
| Romania | Rom. |
| Russia | Russ. |
| Rwanda | Rwanda |
| Saint Helena | St. Helena |
| Saint Kitts & Nevis | St. Kitts & Nevis |
| Saint Lucia | St. Lucia |
| Saint Vincent & the Grenadines | St. Vincent |
| Samoa | Samoa |
| San Marino | San Marino |
| São Tomé & Príncipe | São Tomé & Príncipe |
| Saudi Arabia | Saudi Arabia |
| Scotland | Scot. |
| Senegal | Sen. |
| Serbia | Serb. |
| Seychelles | Sey. |
| Sierra Leone | Sierra Leone |
| Singapore | Sing. |
| Slovakia | Slovk. |
| Slovenia | Slovn. |
| Solomon Islands | Solom. Is. |
| Somalia | Som. |
| South Africa | S. Afr. |

| Place | Abbreviation |
|---|---|
| South America | S. Am. |
| Spain | Spain |
| Sri Lanka | Sri Lanka |
| Sudan | Sudan |
| Suriname | Surin. |
| Swaziland | Swaz. |
| Sweden | Swed. |
| Switzerland | Switz. |
| Syria | Syria |
| Taiwan | Taiwan |
| Tajikistan | Taj. |
| Tanzania | Tanz. |
| Thailand | Thai. |
| Timor-Leste (East Timor) | Timor-Leste |
| Togo | Togo |
| Tonga | Tonga |
| Trinidad & Tobago | Trin. & Tobago |
| Tunisia | Tunis. |
| Turkey | Turk. |
| Turkmenistan | Turkm. |
| Turks & Caicos Islands | Turks & Caicos Is. |
| Tuvalu | Tuvalu |
| Uganda | Uganda |
| Ukraine | Ukr. |
| United Arab Emirates | U.A.E. |
| United Kingdom | U.K. |
| United States of America | U.S. |
| Uruguay | Uru. |
| Uzbekistan | Uzb. |
| Vanuatu | Vanuatu |
| Vatican City | Vatican |
| Venezuela | Venez. |
| Vietnam | Viet. |
| Virgin Islands, British | Virgin Is. |

| Place | Abbreviation |
|---|---|
| Wales | Wales |
| Yemen | Yemen |
| Zambia | Zam. |
| Zimbabwe | Zim. |

## T13. Required Abbreviations for Document Subdivisions

| Document Subdivision | Abbreviation |
|---|---|
| addendum | add. |
| amendment | amend. |
| annotation | annot. |
| appendi[x, ces] | app., apps. |
| article | art. |
| bibliography | bibliog. |
| book | bk. |
| chapter | ch. |
| clause | cl. |
| column | col. |
| comment[ary] | cmt. |
| decision | dec. |
| department | dept. |
| division | div. |
| example | ex. |
| figure[1] | fig. |
| folio | fol. |
| footnote[s] in cross-references | note, notes |
| footnote[s] in other references[2] | n., nn. |
| historical note[s][3] | hist. n., hist. nn. |
| hypothetical | hypo. |
| illustration[s] | illus. |
| introduction | intro. |
| line[s] | l., ll. |
| number | no. |
| page[s] in cross-references | p., pp. |

| Document Subdivision | Abbreviation |
|---|---|
| page[s] in other references | [at] |
| paragraph[s] | ¶, ¶¶ |
| paragraph[s] if symbol appears in source | para., paras. |
| part | pt. |
| preamble | pmbl. |
| principle | princ. |
| publication | pub. |
| rule | r. |
| schedule | sched. |
| section[s] in amending act | sec., secs. |
| section[s] in all other contexts | §, §§ |
| series, serial | ser. |
| subdivision | subdiv. |
| subsection | subsec. |
| supplement | supp. |
| table[4] | tbl. |
| title | tit. |
| volume | vol. |

Notes for Table T13:

1. For figures, do not add a space between the abbreviation and the number of letter. For example, "fig.4"

2. For footnotes, do not add a space between the abbreviation and the number of letter. For example, "n.4"

3. For historical notes, do not add a space between the abbreviation and the number or letter. For example, "hist. n.4"

4. For tables, do not add a space between the abbreviation and the number of letter. For example, "tbl.4"

## T14. Required Abbreviations for Explanatory Phrases

If a phrase is followed a case name as the direct object, the comma should be omitted.

**Abbreviated Phrase**

*acq.*

*acq. in result*

*aff'd,*

*aff'd by an equally divided court,*

*aff'd mem.,*

*aff'd on other grounds,*

*aff'd on reh'g,*

*aff'g*

*amended by*

*appeal denied,*

*appeal dismissed,*

*appeal docketed,*

*appeal filed,*

*argued,*

*cert, denied,*

*cert, dismissed,*

*cert, granted,*

*certifying questions to*

*denying cert, to*

*dismissing appeal from*

*enforced,*

*enforcing*

*invalidated by*

*mandamus denied,*

*modified,*

*modifying*

*nonacq.*

*overruled by*

*perm. app. denied,*

*perm. app. granted,*

*petition for cert, filed,*

*prob. juris, noted,*

*reh'g granted [denied],*

*rev'd,*

**Abbreviated Phrase**

*rev'd on other grounds,*

*rev'd per curiam,*

*rev'g*

*vacated,*

*vacating as moot*

*withdrawn,*

# T15. Required Abbreviations for Institutions

| Institution Name | Abbreviation |
| --- | --- |
| Adelaide | Adel. |
| Air Force | A.F. |
| Albany | Alb. |
| American Bar Association (ABA) | A.B.A. |
| American Intellectual Property Law Association | AIPLA |
| American Law Institute | A.L.I. |
| [Journal of the] American Medical Association | [J]AMA |
| American Society of Composers, Authors, & Publishers | ASCAP |
| American University | Am. U. |
| Boston College | B.C. |
| Boston University | B.U. |
| Brigham Young University | BYU |
| Brooklyn | Brook. |
| Buffalo | Buff. |
| California (California Law Review only) | Calif. |
| Capital | Cap. |
| Chapman | Chap. |
| Chartered Life Underwriters | C.L.U. |
| Cincinnati | Cin. |
| City University of New York | CUNY |
| Cleveland | Clev. |
| Columbia | Colum. |
| Cumberland | Cumb. |
| Denver | Denv. |
| Detroit | Det. |

| Institution Name | Abbreviation |
| --- | --- |
| Dickinson | Dick. |
| Duquesne | Duq. |
| East[ern] | E. |
| Foreign Broadcast Information Service | F.B.I.S. |
| George Mason | Geo. Mason |
| George Washington | Geo. Wash. |
| Georgetown | Geo. |
| Gonzaga | Gonz. |
| Harvard | Harv. |
| Howard | How. |
| John Marshall | J. Marshall |
| Judge Advocate General['s] | JAG |
| Las Vegas | L.V. |
| Lawyer's Reports Annotated | L.R.A. |
| Loyola | Loy. |
| Marquette | Marq. |
| Melbourne | Melb. |
| Memphis | Mem. |
| New England | New Eng. |
| New York University [School of Law] | N.Y.U. |
| North[ern] | N. |
| Northeast[ern] | Ne. |
| Northwest[ern] | Nw. |
| Pepperdine | Pepp. |
| Pittsburgh | Pitt. |
| Richmond | Rich. |
| Rocky Mountain Mineral Law Institute | Rocky Mtn. Min. L. Inst. |
| Saint Louis | St. Louis |
| San Fernando Valley | San Fern. V. |
| Southeast[ern] | Se. |
| South[ern] | S. |
| Southern Methodist University | SMU |
| Southwest[ern] | Sw. |
| Stanford | Stan. |

| Institution Name | Abbreviation |
|---|---|
| Temple | Temp. |
| Thomas Jefferson | T. Jefferson |
| Thomas M. Cooley | T.M. Cooley |
| Thurgood Marshall | T. Marshall |
| Toledo | Tol. |
| Tulane | Tul. |
| Universidad de Puerto Rico | U. P.R. |
| University of California | U.C. |
| University of California - Los Angeles | UCLA |
| University of Missouri Kansas City | UMKC |
| University of the District of Columbia, David A. Clarke School of Law | UDC/DCSL |
| University of West Los Angeles | UWLA |
| Valparaiso | Val. |
| Vanderbilt | Vand. |
| Villanova | Vill. |
| Washington & Lee | Wash. & Lee |
| West[ern] | W. |
| William & Mary | Wm. & Mary |
| William Mitchell | Wm. Mitchell |

## T16. Required Abbreviations for Publishing Terms

| Publishing Term | Abbreviation |
|---|---|
| abridge[d, ment] | abr. |
| annotated | ann. |
| anonymous | anon. |
| circa | c. |
| compil[ation, ed] | comp. |
| copyright | copy. |
| draft | drft. |
| edit[ion, or] | ed. |
| manuscript | ms. |
| mimeograph | mimeo. |
| new series | n.s. |
| no date | n.d. |

| Publishing Term | Abbreviation |
|---|---|
| no place | n.p. |
| no publisher | n. pub. |
| offprint | offprt. |
| old series | o.s. |
| permanent | perm. |
| photoduplicated reprint | photo. reprint |
| printing | prtg. |
| replacement | repl. |
| reprint | reprt. |
| revis[ed, ion] | rev. |
| special | spec. |
| temporary | temp. |
| tentative | tent. |
| translat[ion, or] | trans. |
| unabridged | unabr. |
| volume | vol. |

## T17. Required Abbreviations for Month Names

| Month Name | Abbreviation |
|---|---|
| January | Jan. |
| February | Feb. |
| March | Mar. |
| April | Apr. |
| May | May |
| June | June |
| July | July |
| August | Aug. |
| September | Sept. |
| October | Oct. |
| November | Nov. |
| December | Dec. |

## T18. Required Abbreviations for Common Words Used In Periodical Names

The following guidelines are used for abbreviating periodical names:

1. Use the title of the periodical on the issue you are citing, even if the name of the periodical has changed.

2. Use the abbreviations for common institutional names as listed in Table T15 if the name is listed.

3. If the institutional name is not listed in Table T15, use abbreviations as listed in Table T18 and Table T12.

4. If the word is not found in Table T18 or Table T12, do not abbreviate the word in the abbreviated title.

5. Do not use the words "a," "at," "in," "of," and "the" in the abbreviated title, but do use the word "on."

6. If the title consists of "a," "at," "in," "of," or "the" followed by a single word, do not abbreviate the remaining word.

7. If the periodical title has an abbreviation in it, use the abbreviation.

8. Omit all commas in abbreviated titles, but retain other punctuation.

9. If a periodical title has a colon followed by words, omit all that from the abbreviated title.

10. If a periodical has been renumbered into a new series, indicate that by prefacing the series number with "(n.s.)".

11. If there is an online supplement to a print publication, use the proper abbreviation for the print publication, followed by the name of the online supplement.

| Institution Name | Abbreviation |
|---|---|
| Academ[ic, y] | Acad. |
| Account[ant, ants, ing, ancy] | Acct. |
| Administrat[ive, or, ion] | Admin. |
| Advertising | Advert. |
| Advoca[te, cy] | Advoc. |
| Affairs | Aff. |
| Africa[n] | Afr. |
| Agricultur[e, al] | Agric. |

| Institution Name | Abbreviation |
|---|---|
| Amendment | Amend. |
| America[n, s] | Am. |
| Ancestry | Anc. |
| and | & |
| Annual | Ann. |
| Appellate | App. |
| Arbitrat[ion, or, ors] | Arb. |
| Association | Ass'n |
| Attorney | Att'y |
| Bankruptcy | Bankr. |
| Bar | B. |
| Behavior[al] | Behav. |
| British | Brit. |
| Bulletin | Bull. |
| Business | Bus. |
| Capital | Cap. |
| Catholic | Cath. |
| Cent[er, re] | Ctr. |
| Central | Cent. |
| Children['s] | Child. |
| Chronicle | Chron. |
| Circuit | Cir. |
| Civil | Civ. |
| Civil Libert[y, ies] | C.L. |
| Civil Rights | C.R. |
| College | C. |
| Commentary | Comment. |
| Commerc[e, ial] | Com. |
| Communication[s] | Comm. |
| Comparative | Comp. |
| Conference | Conf. |
| Congressional | Cong. |
| Constitution[al] | Const. |
| Contemporary | Contemp. |

| Institution Name | Abbreviation |
| --- | --- |
| Contract[s] | Cont. |
| Conveyancer | Conv. |
| Corporat[e, ion] | Corp. |
| Cosmetic | Cosm. |
| Counsel[or, ors, or's] | Couns. |
| Court | Ct. |
| Courts | Cts. |
| Criminal | Crim. |
| Defense | Def. |
| Delinquency | Delinq. |
| Department | Dep't |
| Derecho | Der. |
| Development[s] | Dev. |
| Digest | Dig. |
| Diplomacy | Dipl. |
| Dispute | Disp. |
| Doctor | Dr. |
| East[ern] | E. |
| Econom[ic, ics, ical, y] | Econ. |
| Education[al] | Educ. |
| Employ[ee, ment] | Emp. |
| English | Eng. |
| Entertainment | Ent. |
| Environment | Env't |
| Environmental | Envtl. |
| Estate[s] | Est. |
| Europe[an] | Eur. |
| Faculty | Fac. |
| Family | Fam. |
| Federal | Fed. |
| Federation | Fed'n |
| Financ[e, ial] | Fin. |
| Fortnightly | Fort. |
| Forum | F. |

| Institution Name | Abbreviation |
| --- | --- |
| Foundation[s] | Found. |
| General | Gen. |
| Government | Gov't |
| Hispanic | Hisp. |
| Histor[ical, y] | Hist. |
| Hospital | Hosp. |
| Human | Hum. |
| Humanit[y, ies] | Human. |
| Immigration | Immigr. |
| Independent | Indep. |
| Industrial | Indus. |
| Inequality | Ineq. |
| Information | Info. |
| Injury | Inj. |
| Institute | Inst. |
| Insurance | Ins. |
| Intellectual | Intell. |
| Interdisciplinary | Interdisc. |
| Interest | Int. |
| International | Int'l |
| Invest[ments, ors] | Inv. |
| Journal | J. |
| Judicial | Jud. |
| Juridical | Jurid. |
| Jurisprudence | Juris. |
| Justice | Just. |
| Juvenile | Juv. |
| Labor | Lab. |
| Law | L. |
| Law (first word) | Law |
| Lawyer[s, s', 's] | Law. |
| Legislat[ion, ive] | Legis. |
| Librar[y, ian, ies] | Libr. |
| Litigation | Litig. |

| Institution Name | Abbreviation |
| --- | --- |
| Local | Loc. |
| Magazine | Mag. |
| Management | Mgmt. |
| Maritime | Mar. |
| Market | Mkt. |
| Matrimonial | Matrim. |
| Medic[al, ine] | Med. |
| Military | Mil. |
| Mineral | Min. |
| Modern | Mod. |
| Municipal | Mun. |
| National | Nat'l |
| Nationality | Nat'lity |
| Natural | Nat. |
| Negligence | Negl. |
| Negotiation | Negot. |
| New Series | n.s. |
| Newsletter | Newsl. |
| Office | Off. |
| Order | Ord. |
| Organization | Org. |
| Pacific | Pac. |
| Patent | Pat. |
| Personal | Pers. |
| Perpsective[s] | Persp. |
| Philosoph[ical, y] | Phil. |
| Planning | Plan. |
| Policy | Pol'y |
| Politic[al, s] | Pol. |
| Practi[cal, ce, tioner(s)] | Prac. |
| Private | Priv. |
| Probat[e, ion] | Prob. |
| Problems | Probs. |
| Proce[edings, dure] | Proc. |

| Institution Name | Abbreviation |
|---|---|
| Products Liability | Prod. Liab. |
| Profession[al] | Prof. |
| Property | Prop. |
| Psycholog[ical, y] | Psychol. |
| Public | Pub. |
| Publishing | Pub. |
| Puertorriqueño | P.R. |
| Quarterly | Q. |
| Record | Rec. |
| Referee[s] | Ref. |
| Register | Reg. |
| Regulat[ion, ory] | Reg. |
| Relations | Rel. |
| Report[s, er] | Rep. |
| Reproduct[ion, ive] | Reprod. |
| Research | Res. |
| Reserve | Res. |
| Resolution | Resol. |
| Responsibility | Resp. |
| Review | Rev. |
| Revista | Rev. |
| Rights | Rts. |
| School | Sch. |
| Scien[ce, ces, tific] | Sci. |
| Scottish | Scot. |
| Section | Sec. |
| Securities | Sec. |
| Sentencing | Sent'g |
| Service | Serv. |
| Social | Soc. |
| Society | Soc'y |
| Sociolog[ical, y] | Soc. |
| Solicitor[s, s', 's] | Solic. |
| State | St. |

| Institution Name | Abbreviation |
|---|---|
| Statistic[s, al] | Stat. |
| Studies | Stud. |
| Supreme Court | Sup. Ct. |
| Survey | Surv. |
| Symposium | Symp. |
| System | Sys. |
| Taxation | Tax'n |
| Teacher | Tchr. |
| Techn[ique, ology] | Tech. |
| Telecommunication[s] | Telecomm. |
| Transnational | Transnat'l |
| Transportation | Transp. |
| Tribune | Trib. |
| Trust[ee, s] | Tr. |
| Uniform Commercial Code | UCC |
| United States | U.S. |
| Universit[ies, y] | U. |
| Urban | Urb. |
| Utilit[ies, y] | Util. |
| Week | Wk. |
| Weekly | Wkly. |
| Yearbook (or Year Book) | Y.B. |

## T19. Table of Citation Guides

The 20th edition of *The Bluebook* is 560 pages. Pages 307–490 are devoted to Table 2, which is named "Foreign Jurisdictions." While *The Bluebook* does an admirable, although some might argue overly specific, job of discussing the citation of U.S. legal materials, Table 2 breezes through 43 foreign jurisdictions at a breathtakingly rapid pace. The authoritativeness and care found in the rest of *The Bluebook* is perhaps not possible when attempting to summarize, for example, the legal system of France in 5 pages. As such, we attempt in this table to direct the reader to a series of other citation guides that are readily available for further guidance.

## T19.1. General Legal Citation Guides

1. New York University School of Law, Guide to Foreign and International Legal Citations, First Edition (2006). (Superseded by Second Edition)

2. Cardiff University, Cardiff Index to Legal Abbreviations, (2011).

3. University of Chicago Law Review, The Maroonbook: The University of Chicago Manual of Legal Citation, (2016).

4. Peter W. Martin, Introduction to Basic Legal Citation, (2015).

5. University of Washington School of Law, Acronyms & Abbreviations, (2015).

6. Washington University in St. Louis Global Studies Law Review, International Citation Manual.

7. American Association of Law Libraries, AALL Universal Citation Guide, Edition 2.1, (2008) (Superseded by Edition 3.0)

## T19.2. Country-Specific Citation Guides

1. New Zealand Law Foundation, New Zealand Law Style Guide, 2nd Edition, (2011).

2. Faulty of Law, University of Oxford, Oxford University Standard for Citation of Legal Authorities, (2006).

3. SILC, Standard Indian Legal Citation, (2014).

4. University of Melbourne, Australian Guide to Legal Citation, Third Edition (2010).

## T19.3. State and Jursisdiction-Specific Legal Citation Guides

1.  Arkansas Reporter of Decisions, House Style Guide, (2010).

2.  Edward W. Jessen, California Style Manual, 4th Edition, (2000).

3.  Office of the Reporter of Judicial Decisions, The Manual of Style for the Connecticut Courts (Third Edition), (2013).

4.  Superior Court of Delaware, Guide to the Delaware Rules of Legal Citation (Second Edition), (2004).

5.  Supreme Court of Illinois, Style Manual for the SUpreme and Appellate Courts of Illinois, Fourth Edition (2012).

6.  Massachusetts Reports, Style Manual Prepared by the Office of the Reporter of Decisions, 2015–2016.

7.  Supreme Court of New Jersey, New Jersey Manual on Style for Judicial Opinions, (2004).

8.  Law Reporting Bureau of the State of New York, New York Official Reports Style Manual, (2015).

9.  U.S. Army Court of Criminal Appeals, Citation Guide, Seventh Edition, (2012).

10. District of Columbia Court of Appeals, Citation and Style Guide, (2009).

11. Department of Justice, United States Department of Justice, Office of the Solicitor General Citation Manual, (2014).

# T20. Tables of Correspondence

The material in this section was originally prepared by Patrick Durusau.

## Forward Lookup

| The Indigo Book | The Bluebook® |
|---|---|
| R1. Two Types of Legal Documents | B1, R1 |
| R2. Typeface Standards | B2, R2 |
| R3. In-Text Citations | B1, R1 |
| R4. Signals | B1.2, R1.2 |
| R5. Capitalization Rules | B8, R8 |
| R6. Signals for Supporting Authority | B1.2, R1.2 |
| R7. Signals for Comparison | B1.2, R1.2(b) |
| R8. Signals for Contradictory Authority | B1.2, R1.2(c) |
| R9. Signals for Background Material | B1.2, R1.2(d) |
| R10. Order of Authorities Within Each Signal / Strength of Authority | B1.2, R1.4 |
| B. CASES | B10, R10 |
| R11. Full citation | B10.1 |
| R12. Court & Year | B10.1.3, R10.4, R10.5 |
| R13. Weight of Authority and Explanatory Parenthetical | B10.1.5, R10.6.1 |
| R14. History of the Case | B10.1.6, R10.7 |
| R15. Short Form Citation for Cases | B10.2, R10.9 |
| C. STATUTES, RULES, REGULATIONS, AND OTHER LEGISLATIVE & ADMINISTRATIVE MATERIALS | R12, R13, R14 |
| R16. Federal Statutes | B12.1.1, R12 |
| R17. State Statutes | B12.1.2, R12 |
| R18. Rules of Procedure and Evidence, Restatements, and Uniform Acts | B12.1.3, R12.9.3, R12.9.4 |
| R19. Administrative Rules and Regulations | B14, R14 |
| R20. Federal Taxation Materials | B12.1.4, R12.9.1 |
| R21. Legislative Materials | B13, R13 |
| R22. Short Form Citation of Legislative and Administrative Materials | R13.8 |
| R23. Sources and Authorities: Constitutions | B11, R11 |
| D. COURT & LITIGATION DOCUMENTS | R10.8.3 |
| R24. Citing Court or Litigation Documents from Your Case | R10.8.3 |

| The Indigo Book | The Bluebook® |
|---|---|
| R25. Citing Court or Litigation Documents from Another Case | R10.8.3 |
| R26. Short Form Citation for Court Documents | B4, R4 |
| R27. Capitalization Within the Text of Court Documents and Legal Memoranda | B8, R8 |
| E. BOOKS & NON-PERIODICALS | B15, R15 |
| R28. Full Citation for Books & Non-Periodicals | B15.1 |
| R29. Short Form Citation for Books & Non-Periodicals | B15.2 |
| F. JOURNALS, MAGAZINES, & NEWSPAPER ARTICLES | R16 |
| R30. Full Citation for Journals, Magazines & Newspaper Articles | B16.1 |
| R31. Short Form Citation for Journals, Magazines & Newspaper Articles | B16.2 |
| G. INTERNET SOURCES | B18, R18 |
| R32. General Principles for Internet Sources | R18.2.1 |
| R33. Basic Formula for Internet Sources | B18.1.1, R18.1 |
| R34. Short Form Citations for Internet Sources | B18.2 |
| H. EXPLANATORY PARENTHETICALS | R12.8 |
| R35. General Principles for Explanatory Parentheticals | B1.3 |
| R36. Order of parentheticals | R1.5(b) |
| I. QUOTATIONS | B5, R5 |
| R37. General Principles for Quotations | B5.1 |
| R38. Alterations of Quotations | R5.2 |
| R39. Omissions in Quotations | R5.3 |
| R40. Special Rules for Block Quotations | B5.2 |
| J. TABLES | |
| T1. Federal Judicial and Legislative Materials | T1.1 |
| T2. Federal Administrative and Executive Materials | T1.2 |
| T3. U.S. States and Other Jurisdictions | T1.3 |
| T4. Required Abbreviations for Services | T15 |
| T4.1. Service Publisher Names | T15 |
| T4.2. Service Abbreviations | T15 |
| T5. Required Abbreviations for Legislative Documents | T9 |
| T6. Required Abbreviations for Treaty Sources | T4 |
| T7. Required Abbreviations for Arbitral Reporters | T5 |
| T8. Required Abbreviations for Intergovernmental Organizations | T3 |
| T8.1. United Nations and League of Nations | T3.1, T3.2 |

| The Indigo Book | The Bluebook® |
|---|---|
| T8.2. Europe | T3.3, T3.4, T3.5 |
| T8.3. Inter-American and International Tribunal | T3.6, T3.7, T3.8 |
| T8.4. Other Intergovernmental Organizations | T3.9 |
| T9. Required Abbreviations for Court Names | T7 |
| T10. Required Abbreviations for Titles of Judges and Officials | T11 |
| T11. Required Abbreviations for Case Names In Citations | T6 |
| T12. Required Abbreviations for Geographical Terms | T10 |
| T12.1 U.S. States, Cities and Territories | T10.1 |
| T12.2 Australian States and Canadian Provinces and Territories | T10.2 |
| T20.3 Countries and Regions | T10.3 |
| T13. Required Abbreviations for Document Subdivisions | T16 |
| T14. Required Abbreviations for Explanatory Phrases | T8 |
| T15. Required Abbreviations for Institutions | T13.1 |
| T16. Required Abbreviations for Publishing Terms | T14 |
| T17. Required Abbreviations for Month Names | T12 |
| T18. Required Abbreviations for Common Words Used In Periodical Names | T13.2 |
| T19. Table of Citation Guides | T2 |

## Reverse Lookup

| The Bluebook® | The Indigo Book |
|---|---|
| B1, R1 | R1. Two Types of Legal Documents |
| B2, R2 | R2. Typeface Standards |
| B1, R1 | R3. In-Text Citations |
| B1.2, R1.2 | R4. Signals |
| B8, R8 | R5. Capitalization Rules |
| B1.2, R1.2 | R6. Signals for Supporting Authority |
| B1.2, R1.2(b) | R7. Signals for Comparison |
| B1.2, R1.2(c) | R8. Signals for Contradictory Authority |
| B1.2, R1.2(d) | R9. Signals for Background Material |
| B1.2, R1.4 | R10. Order of Authorities Within Each Signal / Strength of Authority |
| B10, R10 | B. CASES |
| B10.1 | R11. Full citation |
| B10.1.3, R10.4, R10.5 | R12. Court & Year |

| The Bluebook® | The Indigo Book |
|---|---|
| B10.1.5, R10.6.1 | R13. Weight of Authority and Explanatory Parenthetical |
| B10.1.6, R10.7 | R14. History of the Case |
| B10.2, R10.9 | R15. Short Form Citation for Cases |
| R12, R13, R14 | C. STATUTES, RULES, REGULATIONS, AND OTHER LEGISLATIVE & ADMINISTRATIVE MATERIALS |
| B12.1.1, R12 | R16. Federal Statutes |
| B12.1.2, R12 | R17. State Statutes |
| B12.1.3, R12.9.3, R12.9.4 | R18. Rules of Procedure and Evidence, Restatements, and Uniform Acts |
| B14, R14 | R19. Administrative Rules and Regulations |
| B12.1.4, R12.9.1 | R20. Federal Taxation Materials |
| B13, R13 | R21. Legislative Materials |
| R13.8 | R22. Short Form Citation of Legislative and Administrative Materials |
| B11, R11 | R23. Sources and Authorities: Constitutions |
| R10.8.3 | D. COURT & LITIGATION DOCUMENTS |
| R10.8.3 | R24. Citing Court or Litigation Documents from Your Case |
| R10.8.3 | R25. Citing Court or Litigation Documents from Another Case |
| B4, R4 | R26. Short Form Citation for Court Documents |
| B8, R8 | R27. Capitalization Within the Text of Court Documents and Legal Memoranda |
| B15, R15 | E. BOOKS & NON-PERIODICALS |
| B15.1 | R28. Full Citation for Books & Non-Periodicals |
| B15.2 | R29. Short Form Citation for Books & Non-Periodicals |
| R16 | F. JOURNALS, MAGAZINES, & NEWSPAPER ARTICLES |
| B16.1 | R30. Full Citation for Journals, Magazines & Newspaper Articles |
| B16.2 | R31. Short Form Citation for Journals, Magazines & Newspaper Articles |
| B18, R18 | G. INTERNET SOURCES |
| R18.2.1 | R32. General Principles for Internet Sources |
| B18.1.1, R18.1 | R33. Basic Formula for Internet Sources |
| B18.2 | R34. Short Form Citations for Internet Sources |
| R12.8 | H. EXPLANATORY PARENTHETICALS |
| B1.3 | R35. General Principles for Explanatory Parentheticals |
| R1.5(b) | R36. Order of parentheticals |
| B5, R5 | I. QUOTATIONS |
| B5.1 | R37. General Principles for Quotations |

| The Bluebook® | The Indigo Book |
|---|---|
| R5.2 | R38. Alterations of Quotations |
| R5.3 | R39. Omissions in Quotations |
| B5.2 | R40. Special Rules for Block Quotations |
| | J. TABLES |
| T1 | Federal Jurisdictions |
| T1.1 | T1. Federal Judicial and Legislative Materials |
| T1.2 | T2. Federal Administrative and Executive Materials |
| T1.3 | T3. U.S. States and Other Jurisdictions |
| T2 | T19. Table of Citation Guides |
| T3 | T8. Required Abbreviations for Intergovernmental Organizations |
| T3.1, T3.2 | T8.1. United Nations and League of Nations |
| T3.3, T3.4, T3.5 | T8.2. Europe |
| T3.6, T3.7, T3.8 | T8.3. Inter-American and International Tribunal |
| T3.9 | T8.4. Other Intergovernmental Organizations |
| T4 | T6. Required Abbreviations for Treaty Sources |
| T5 | T7. Required Abbreviations for Arbitral Reporters |
| T6 | T11. Required Abbreviations for Case Names In Citations |
| T7 | T9. Required Abbreviations for Court Names |
| T8 | T14. Required Abbreviations for Explanatory Phrases |
| T9 | T5. Required Abbreviations for Legislative Documents |
| T10 | T12. Required Abbreviations for Geographical Terms |
| T10.1 | T12.1 U.S. States, Cities and Territories |
| T10.2 | T12.2 Australian States and Canadian Provinces and Territories |
| T10.3 | T12.3 Countries and Regions |
| T11 | T10. Required Abbreviations for Titles of Judges and Officials |
| T12 | T17. Required Abbreviations for Month Names |
| T13 | Required Abbreviations for Periodical Names |
| T13.1 | T15. Required Abbreviations for Institutions |
| T13.2 | T18. Required Abbreviations for Common Words Used In Periodical Names |
| T14 | T16. Required Abbreviations for Publishing Terms |
| T15 | T4. Required Abbreviations for Services |
| T15 | T4.1. Service Publisher Names |
| T15 | T4.2. Service Abbreviations |
| T16 | T13. Required Abbreviations for Document Subdivisions |

# K. CODICIL

*The Indigo Book: A Manual of Legal Citation* is distributed as a single document coded with the HTML 5 and Cascading Style Sheet (CSS) standards.

Each rule and section of the file have a unique ID, making them individually addressable. Examples are:

- Each Rule has an ID starting with the letter R and then the rule number. For example, Rule 1.1 can be addressed by adding #R1.1 to the URL.

- Each Section has an ID starting with the letter S and then the rule letter. For example, the Codicil can be addressed by adding #SK to the URL.

- Each Table has an ID starting with the letter T and then the table number. For example, Table T1.1 can be addressed by adding #T1.1 to the URL.

The header of the file calls two open source Google fonts. If those fonts are not available, the CSS style sheet falls back to Georgia, which is present on most computers, and then to the generic serif font. The fonts we use are:

- For the cover, Alice, which was designed by Ksenia Erulevich and inspired by Lewis Carrol's novel.

- For the body of the document, Libre Baskerville, based on the 1941 American Type Founder's Baskerville, but optimized for web use.

To clearly distinguish our work from other citation manuals, we have forgone the use of the color Royal Blue in favor of Indigo, in solidarity with the ryots of Bengal who were oppressed by the insatiable British demand for blue and the profits that flowed from it, leading to the Nilbridroha (Indigo revolt) and the beginning of the road that led to independence.

The CSS has been coded with support for printing on US Letter size paper. We use Prince XML to convert the HTML document to PDF format.

It is also possible to dynamically change the styles to perform tasks such as making *all text in italics* "pop" by turning it crimson or back to normal .

To create a file for use in Microsoft Word, an easy method is to comment out the calls to Google fonts, upload the document to Google Docs, and then downloading it in Word format.

# L. ACKNOWLEDGMENTS

*The Indigo Book: A Manual of Legal Citation* was created under the direction of Professor Christopher Jon Sprigman. Professor Sprigman's research assistant is Daryl Steiger. Students who worked on the document include Manuel Antunes, Tommy Bird, Ty Callahan, Isha Ghodke, Kaitlyn Gosewehr, Nireeti Gupta, Rebecca Laskey, Nicole Lieberman, Junru Liu, Colinford Mattis, Adine Mitrani, Edwin Mok, Christian Scarlett, Alexander Stillman, Alec Webley, Chris Weldon, and Alex Young.

During the pre-review release period, extensive comments were received from Professor Frank Bennett, Dr. Rintze Zelle, Professor Christopher Jon Sprigman, Professor Pamela Samuelson, Professor Peter W. Martin, Point.B Studio, and the anonymous students of Professor Sprigman.

During the public Request for Comments period, comments were received from Deborah Bouchoux, Nate Cardozo, Alvin Y.H. Cheung, Jill Dinneen, Patrick Durusau, John Flatness, Paul Gowder, Leonid Grinberg, Misha Guttentag, Elayne Harmer, Adi Kamdar, Sue Liemer, Mike Lissner, Stephen Mortellaro, Stephen Paskey, Theodore Rostow David Sorkin, Dustin Watkins, David Ziff, and Michael Zuckerman.

Joseph C. Gratz of Durie Tangri LLP represented Public Resource during pre-publication discussions.

www.ingramcontent.com/pod-product-compliance
Lightning Source LLC
Chambersburg PA
CBHW081150270326
41930CB00014B/3101